What's Exactly The Matter With Me?

Memoirs of a life in music

P.F. Sloan and
S.E. Feinberg

What's Exactly The Matter With Me?

Memoirs of a life in music

P.F. Sloan and S.E. Feinberg

WHAT'S EXACTLY THE MATTER WITH ME?
Memoirs of a life in music
P.F. Sloan and S.E. Feinberg

A Jawbone book
First edition 2014
Published in the UK and the USA by
Jawbone Press
2a Union Court,
20–22 Union Road,
London SW4 6JP,
England
www.jawbonepress.com

ISBN 978-1-908279-57-6

EDITOR Tom Seabrook
JACKET DESIGN Mark Case

Printed by Regent Publishing Services Limited, China

1 2 3 4 5 18 17 16 15 14

CONTENTS

ILLUSTRATIONS   6

FOREWORD   17
by Rumer

WRITING WITH P.F. SLOAN   19
by S.E. Feinberg

INTRODUCTION   25
The birth of P.F. Sloan

BOOK ONE (1945–1967)

CHAPTER 1   28
What's exactly the matter with me? • I don't
care if the sun don't shine • the fires of hell ain't
no fun place to be

CHAPTER 2   36
The Garden Of Allah • the most beautiful eyes
I had ever seen • Freddy, Big Jim, and jumping
the moon • the cardboard man

CHAPTER 3   45
The only thirteen-year-old Jewish R&B artist in
town • rock'n'roll high • I don't want anything
to do with him • a mysterious package from
Liverpool • you can have her for a song

CHAPTER 4   62
Summer means fun • cowabunga dreamin'
• you only get interested in your wife when
somebody else is • Baggys postscript

CHAPTER 5   **71**
A kaleidoscopic event • the hitmen • the Dancing Dunhills

CHAPTER 6   **81**
The night that changed my life

CHAPTER 7   **90**
Night of The Iguanas • Mr. Terry, the tambourine man • the session • the Prince of Protest • hanging on a scaffold

CHAPTER 8   **111**
Highway 61 on shag • The Grass Roots (take one) • it's all Dunhill from here

CHAPTER 9   **124**
A tale of three cities • California dreamin' • walking with Turtles • the onion truck

CHAPTER 10   **139**
From Crescent Heights to Laurel Canyon • secret agent • a cry in the wilderness • running with Turtles • missing the beat

CHAPTER 11   **151**
Twelve More Times • four hippies in a bathtub • precious times • *The Black Plague* • little big songs • The Grass Roots (take two)

CHAPTER 12   **164**
The 'Paint It Black' session • the millionaire's club • the infamous Sunset Strip riots

CHAPTER 13   **176**
Jimmy Webb (a prelude) • let's live for today • Grand Funk Knights in Cleveland • the golden key

CHAPTER 14   **192**
If you're going to San Francisco … • secret plans and the Monterey Pop Festival • a gathering of beautiful things • a queen of rags • beware … the Wolf King lurks • your money or your life

BOOK TWO (1968–2014)

CHAPTER 15   **210**
No one will be able to leave once the door is closed • the loft • Sun Studios

CHAPTER 16   **220**
The angels of Greenwich Village • the magic dragon • return from Egypt

CHAPTER 17   **230**
A typical day • my life as a zombie • if the mailman comes with a letter for me, just forward it to Malibu

CHAPTER 18   **242**
Afternoon tea at the Chateau Marmont • Malibu lost • home again, naturally • what is Pat Boone doing in my head?

CHAPTER 19   **251**
Sleep time • E.T.'s in the front yard • Bombay alley

CHAPTER 20   **259**
The bottom line • ER India

CHAPTER 21   **267**
Can you write another one just as good? • the big lie • *Seven Sisters* • Dr. Z and the reluctant rock star • Tokyo Phil

CHAPTER 22   **280**
The review • a picnic at the Greek

AFTERWORD   **290**
by Creed Bratton

THE P.F. SLOAN SONGBOOK   **291**

SELECT DISCOGRAPHY   **313**

ACKNOWLEDGMENTS   **313**

INDEX   **314**

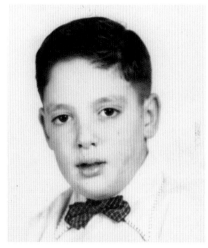

ABOVE Me at eight in Queens, New York.
LEFT My parents, Claritsa and Harry George
Schlein. **BELOW** Third Street School, Los
Angeles—I'm fourth from the right in the
bottom row.

THIRD STREET
SCHOOL
GRADE A-6
RM. 18

MAY   1957

ABOVE LEFT In the choir at John Burroughs Middle School. **ABOVE RIGHT** Song sheet for 'All I Want Is Loving,' my first single for Aladdin Records. Note the credit: F. Sloan. **LEFT** Evy K. and me at my tenth birthday party in New Hyde Park, Long Island, New York.

ABOVE A contact sheet of photos of Steve Barri and me, taking during a demo session at Western Recorders.

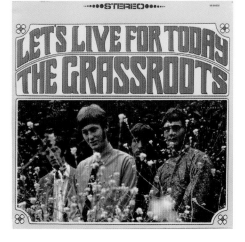

TOP LEFT A publicity photo of Steve and me, circa 1964. *Michael Ochs Archives/ Getty Images*. **TOP RIGHT** The Million Dollar Party: my first live gig. **ABOVE** A pair of LPs by The Fantastic Baggys and The Grass Roots (featuring Creed Bratton, far right).

RIGHT At Dunhill Records in 1965, from *Cashbox* magazine. 'Eve' was about to hit No. 1. Left to right: Bobby Roberts, Lou Adler, me, and Jay Lasker. **BELOW** Barry McGuire peering out of a manhole—the underground coming up to the mainstream. Barry's idea. **BELOW RIGHT** A pensive and contemplative P.F. Sloan on the sheet music for 'The Sins Of A Family.'

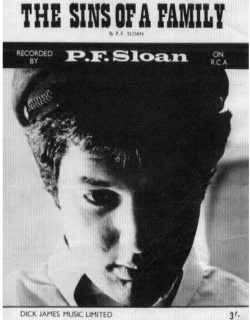

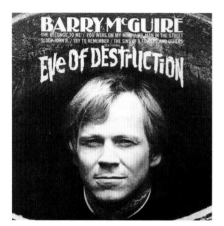

ABOVE Playing my Harmony Soverign at an impromptu concert. *Photo by Guy Webster.*
LEFT Barry McGuire, riding high in the musical *Hair*. *Alan Band/Fox Photos/Getty Images.*

LEFT Performing at the Mount Tamalpais Fantasy Fair in Marin County, California, 1967. **ABOVE** Looking inward, with my eyes wide shut, on the cover of *Measure Of Pleasure*. **BELOW** My first album, *Songs Of Our Times*.

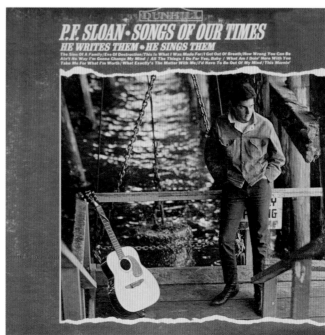

ABOVE Guy Webster's handcrafted high-art concept photo for *Twelve More Times*.
RIGHT Flyer for the Fantasy Fair. **BELOW** Me in my English morning coat at the Fantasy Fair.

ABOVE An Ed Caraeff photo for the 1972
Columbia/Mums LP *Raised On Records*.

LEFT John Phillips in his Cossack hat at the Monterey Pop Festival. *Fotos International/Getty Images.* **BELOW** A rare, candid photo of P.F. Sloan. **BOTTOM LEFT** The Japanese 'Sunflower, Sunflower' single. **BOTTOM RIGHT** Being recognized as a songwriter of influence at the National Academy of Songwriters, 1993.

ABOVE An impromptu appearance with The Surf City Allstars featuring Jan & Dean and The Honeys, circa 1997. **ABOVE RIGHT** Reunited with John Phillips in Santa Monica during his Mamas & Papas Revisited tour (note the fear in my eyes). **BELOW LEFT** Backstage at MacArthur Park, looking up to Jimmy Webb, 2013. *Photograph by Rumer.* **BELOW** The *Sailover* album cover, taken in the back alley behind Hightone Records in Oakland, California, by Lori Eanes.

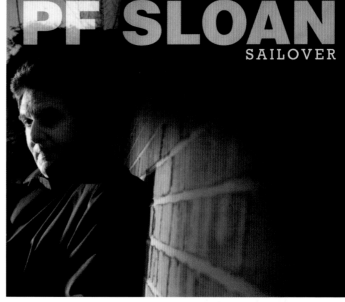

FOREWORD
BY RUMER

I first saw the name P.F. Sloan in 2007, when I was browsing through Paul Zollo's book *Songwriters On Songwriting*. I had never heard of P.F. Sloan or his music. In the book, Jimmy Webb talks about how much he appreciated P.F. Sloan's work. I learned that, by 1965, Sloan was a pioneer singer-songwriter before anyone had branded the term.

In the book, there is also a tale of how, in 1971, no longer with a recording contract, Phil's at a hotdog stand in Hollywood, trying to 'scrape together 50 cents for a hotdog,' when a song comes on the radio. It's 'P.F. Sloan,' sung by The Association and written by Jimmy Webb.

I was a struggling unsigned singer-songwriter at the time, working as a waitress, and the story moved me. A few years later, while researching my covers record *Boys Don't Cry*, a collection of songs written in the 70s by male singer-songwriters of the era, I sat down to study 'P.F. Sloan,' only to find the lyric mysterious. Nixon, a fake London Bridge, a stuffed horse? What did it all mean? In typical Jimmy Webb fashion, it left me scratching my head.

After some exploration and a conversation with a friend, it struck me that each verse was perhaps a portrait of phoniness, crafted by Jimmy to highlight the authenticity of the song's namesake. I'm ashamed to say that I was so deeply involved with trying to figure out who the character in Jimmy's story was—and why he was being compared to a stuffed horse—I barely explored the real Sloan's extraordinary body of work.

Then, after my version of the song was released, I received a mysterious phone call from the man himself.

We arranged to meet in a hotel lobby in Los Angles. As he greeted me, Phil handed me a beautiful tiny music box that played Beethoven. Over dinner, he told incredible story after incredible story. I was so transfixed that I didn't even notice the hours pass and the restaurant closing up around us.

We continued our conversation into the parking lot. I was cold, so he gave me his jacket, and I smoked all of his cigarettes. In his words, and in these small gestures, I felt a warmth from him that was otherworldly.

I left that night knowing that P.F. Sloan was and still is the real deal, just as Jimmy Webb said he was. I have since spent more time talking and playing music with him, and I can honestly say that Phil is beyond being the hero of any popular song, and more incredible than all of his stories. Phil Sloan is a multi-dimensional being, a magical person with the kindest, most loving heart.

If he has ever felt at odds with the world, one should question the sanity of the world, because Phil Sloan is the sanest person I have ever met.

WRITING WITH P.F. SLOAN
BY S.E. FEINBERG

I was sitting in front of the television on September 20 1965, when, on *Hullabaloo*, Jerry Lewis introduced 'Eve Of Destruction,' sung by Barry McGuire, to America. I'll never forget Barry singing on a junkyard set with abstract dancers in the background. I had never heard or seen anything like it. I listened and felt that I was being spoken to by someone with important wisdom to impart—a message from beyond my point of view.

In a little over three minutes, my life had changed. For some reason, the line *this whole crazy world is just too frustratin'* shot through me like adrenaline into an asthmatic. I could breathe again. I wasn't alone.

I bought the record at Central Music in Brockton, Massachusetts, and played that thing hundreds of times. When you play a record that many times, it becomes ingrained into your consciousness. I felt that I had just been given a ticket to the game.

P.F. Sloan did not want to write this book. He had spent years trying to put some very bizarre and painful memories to rest, and here I was asking him to dredge them up again. I knew at the outset that it was going to be sometimes rough but I felt like the story had to be told—this story of a musical prodigy who was an important influence in music during the 60s.

To so many, P.F. Sloan was a mysterious and elusive character—this man behind the red balloon. He was one of the deep ones, all right. There weren't many. Some of them acted deep but weren't. Janis Joplin,

Phil Ochs Bryan MacLean, Bobby Darin, Bob Dylan—they were deep.
And P.F. Sloan was deep.

When Phil got his writing chops, after an apprenticeship in pop music
(and what an apprenticeship it was!), he wrote with such savage honesty
that his music scared people. It scared the record companies and it scared
American society. At nineteen, two of his songs—'Eve Of Destruction'
and 'The Sins Of A Family'—were banned.

Phil Sloan was loved and hated. He was respected and despised.
But all he was ever really about was making music. He kept writing and
singing until it got too much for people and too much for him. He was
cast out, but he kept on singing; and then he was locked away, but he
kept on singing. And then, one day, he shut down and stopped singing.
He stopped everything. He was hurt, and too wounded to make music.

Before we started this narrative, I had written a musical with Phil. We
knew we could work with each other, but we really didn't know what kind
of dangers we were about to face as we navigated up the river in search
of truth and clarity.

We discovered early on that by using humor—laughing at the most
horrible elements of his story—we could get through it. As a matter of
fact, we laughed hardest while writing about some of the most painful
recollections. We discovered that by digging deep into the pain—as
deep as we could go—we were able to tap into the absurd, and therefore
the humor, and in that humor we found it possible to deconstruct and
demystify a very complicated character, thereby enabling us to tell a simple
story about a young man who was in love with music. We really wanted
a book that was like the stories Phil tells between songs at performances:
simple, poignant, and real.

Phil wanted the reader to know the truth as he saw it. Not out of
revenge or spite or anger: he wanted to debunk the mythos that surrounds
his life in music.

We had a difficult time deciding whether or not to include several of
the stories in this narrative. They are the ones that deal with supernatural

events—seeing James Dean two years after his death, for example. Phil was not sure if he should include it, as he knew that it may appear to be contrived for the sake of the abstract. I was concerned that if we included such a memory, it might cloud other stories and create doubt. We talked about it a lot and decided that what Phil saw is what he saw. Was it the ghost of James Dean? Or was it someone who looked like James Dean—a young man who was trying to emulate James Dean, perhaps? It didn't matter. Phil saw James Dean, and that's all there was to it. Phil told me that he trusted the reader and was not afraid to be honest. He encouraged honesty at every story. We spent much time sorting the stories out, chronologically and factually, cross-referencing to the best of our abilities.

I made a deal with Phil. We wouldn't start off to write a book or anything else. I traveled over to his house once or twice a week to tape our conversations, very casually. Over the months we laid down forty or fifty hours of these. Then we took a look at it to see what we had, and we still weren't convinced that a book would be written. Phil was concerned, because it seemed like everyone from back then was writing a book, and he had a shelf full of them—most of them mentioning him in one way or another—some of the authors revising the truth and others doing their best to be accurate. He and I were adamant about not wanting another rock book about being messed over by the record business—we both understood that Phil has no monopoly on that.

We wanted to share with the reader Phil's witness of the events that truly shaped a generation, as well as the events that textured his own life. We also wanted to share the intricacies of the life of an artist-songwriter and hopefully shed a little light on how the foundations of the music business were then. While we were writing *Louis! Louis!*, our musical based on the writings and musings of Ludwig van Beethoven, I would allow myself ten or fifteen minutes after each session to ask Phil questions about his extraordinary musical legacy. He shared his opinions on music, society, spirituality, politics, literature, his ten trips to India—all aspects of life.

I think sociopathic behavior should be taught in every music college—how to deal with the egos of sociopaths. How to deal with people who would kidnap you, dump you onto a highway, find you roaming naked in the desert, clean you up, sit you at a piano and order you to write songs about love, teenage angst, and three-foot swells.

I have enjoyed the music of P.F. Sloan since I was fourteen. His tunes helped me through some very difficult times. When I heard The Turtles' version of 'Let Me Be,' it infused me with an inner strength that came along in my life just at the right moment. To be writing with that person now is a wondrous blessing.

Generally, Phil would sit across from me at a wooden table. I would work on my laptop—sometimes two. We eat bagels and drink coffee. After a couple of hours, we would drink grape juice in frozen glasses. My dog, Rosemary, would lie on the floor. During the writing of a story with a lot of emotional baggage, Phil would pace back and forth, smoking cigarettes.

The first time I saw P.F. Sloan was over at the Rose Cafe in Venice, California. I called him up because I was hoping to get to him a CD by a friend of mine, the legendary guitarist Eric Lilljequist, as Eric had expressed an interest in playing with Phil if possible. When Phil walked into the Rose, I recognized him immediately. Even in a place full of hipsters, you know when you're seeing the real thing. He had the vibe that movie stars have and that commercial jet pilots used to have. I was immediately struck by his face, which had a sense of mischief ingrained into it, as if he understood the grand joke that nobody else in the room quite got.

I watched him for a minute or so, and he seemed to be looking at things as if this was the first time he had ever been in a coffee shop—a look of, *I wonder what's going to happen next.* He sure didn't look summer worn and winter blown, as Jimmy Webb had described him in his remarkable song 'P.F. Sloan.'

I introduced myself and we grabbed a table on the patio. He started rifling around in this Indian bag he carries, pulled out a single cigarette, stuck it in his mouth, and was immediately surrounded by concerned waiters who informed him that smoking was not allowed. We sat at a table and I told Phil how much I enjoyed his music. He acted as if it was the first time anyone had paid him a compliment. I was starting to get the sense that Phil looked at everything as if for the first time.

'Are you working on anything new?' I asked.

'To answer your question, I am working on music for Louie.'

'Louie?'

'I had a dream where Louie came to me and told me to tell people why he wanted to commit suicide.'

'You mean The Kingsmen's Louie?'

'No, no, no, no, no. Beethoven.'

'Beethoven's Louie?'

'No, Beethoven is Ludvig.'

'Oh, right. Ludvig.'

'But translated into French,' Phil said, 'Ludvig is Louis, and it is pronounced "Louie."'

I was caught in one of those weird spaces where you are too embarrassed to say you do know something, and too embarrassed to admit that you don't.

'Did you know that he was an accomplished guitarist and wrote hundreds of folk songs?' Phil asked.

'Beethoven?'

'Did you know that Beethoven was often referred to in the press as "Papa Hayden's Little Genius Mistake" and a "Mozart wannabe"? You know, I can relate to that. I have been called a Bob Dylan wannabe all my life.'

Phil invited me back to a little studio in his house to hear the songs of *Louis! Louis!* that he had been working on for thousands of hours.

As I put the headphones on I could not help feeling a bit nervous. When a person has been working on something for years, you want to like it. And if you don't like it, you better have something more to say than 'This work is obviously a labor of love.'

I listened to each cut while sitting on a stool with Phil watching my every reaction. No one had ever heard these songs before, he told me. I would be the first person, outside of the musicians, to hear it. I said a little prayer, and my prayers were answered when I heard something that was truly wonderful.

I realized that it must be made into a musical.

Phil was not at all open to that idea, but he wanted to know how long something like that would take.

'It will take one year from the time we begin,' I told him.

I don't know why, but he enthusiastically proclaimed, 'Let's make this folly a reality!'

And there began our partnership.

P.F. Sloan made folk themes reachable. Like such brave souls as John Huss, William Tyndale, and John Bunyan, who were persecuted for bringing the Gospel to the common man, Phil was persecuted for bringing folk songs to the common man—to those who, it was believed, were not supposed to comprehend the intricacies of allegory and irony. The famous folksingers were the high priests who kept the music away from the body of young people—albeit, I would like to think, unknowingly. But there were millions of kids across the globe who wanted to be heard—who wanted to be part of the show.

For his act of heresy, Phil was persecuted and torn apart by the music business and a folk world that believed that a writer of popular songs could never be an authentic folksinger. Phil was not burned at the stake like John Huss, but he was burned. The folk world had sanctioned a select few to be their spokesmen. Sloan was not sanctioned. He was a renegade. An outsider.

INTRODUCTION
THE BIRTH OF P.F. SLOAN

I remember the night I wrote 'Eve Of Destruction.' I'll never forget it. It's a night that has stayed in my memory to this very day. It was the night P.F. Sloan was born—the emergence of a higher form of consciousness.

Up until then, my desire was to be like every other teenager. I wanted to be loved. I wanted a normal family life. I watched *American Bandstand* and I watched the normal kids having fun and dancing and being happy and normal. I wanted to be Elvis, I wanted to be Ricky, I wanted to be Bobby and Johnny and Frankie and anyone else but myself. I wanted love and I felt like I wasn't getting it. But P.F. Sloan? He didn't care about any of that. He wanted honesty and truth.

Where did that need come from? Perhaps it was the uneasy feeling that I was being lied to. Our teachers were calmly telling us that we had nothing to worry about. If there was to be a nuclear attack, it would not be like Hiroshima or Nagasaki. There would still be baseball practice after the flash of light. Ice cream would still be served in the cafeteria on Thursdays.

But if that were not the case, why should I go on? Why should I go to school?

What's the matter with you? Of course you're going to school. Of course there is going to be a world tomorrow. Of course you're going to college and make plans for your future.

Everything that I was being told seemed to be just the opposite of what I was feeling.

Don't think thoughts like that, it's not healthy.

But we were all having the same thoughts.

Nobody was saying anything, but we were all thinking it. I felt isolated. A lot of kids did.

When the Cuban Missile Crisis unfolded, all of my unhealthy thoughts and fears were being played out on the television screen, minute by minute and day after day. You could feel the panic. It was like an oppressive weight on your chest. I watched it like a soap opera on the nightly news. And when the crisis ended, it was back to a new normal.

Don't pay any attention to the bomb sitting in the middle of the room. Don't pay attention to the war. Don't pay any attention to anything.

We had a subconscious feeling that we could be the last generation.

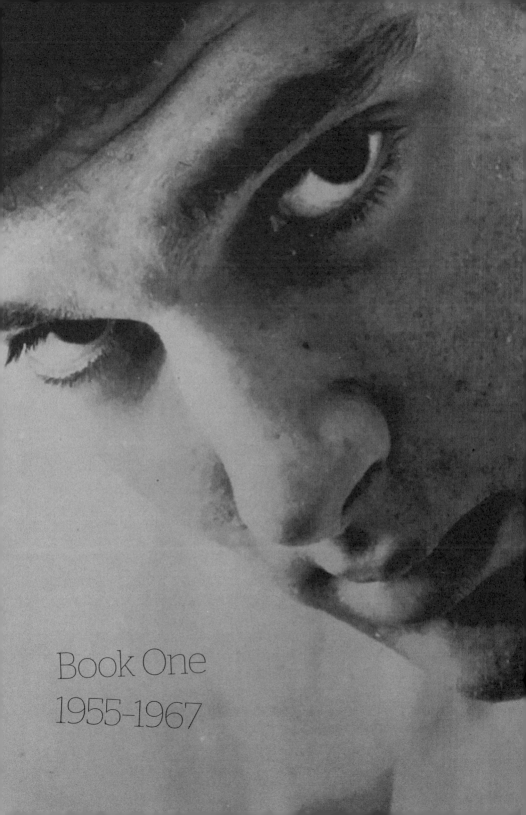

Book One
1955–1967

CHAPTER ONE

WHAT'S EXACTLY THE MATTER WITH ME?

We were living in an apartment on Vyse Avenue in Queens, a street full of massive apartment buildings. The neighborhood was made up of mostly Irish, Jewish, and Italian first- and second-generation immigrants. It was crowded and rough. But the people cared about each other.

At six years old, I lived on the street and ran with a gang that I controlled. We called ourselves The Rooftop Gang. We would steal apples, oranges, or dried fish and run up to the rooftops, where we would jump from building to building and find some hideout to split our booty.

Aside from being beaten continuously by my mother, I had a pretty good childhood. Something in her compelled her to beat me almost every day with a leather strap. I don't know why. She carried a burden I could not see. My father and sister ignored the beatings, which went on for almost a year. I kept the welts on my back hidden.

To expect love and understanding from your mother is not to expect too much. I know that I was precocious, but that behavior did not warrant violent abuse. Beating me would not have slowed me down. My friend Cass Elliot was once asked how best she could describe me.

'Precocious,' she told the interviewer. 'P.F. Sloan is precocious.'

Even when my mother was beating me, I still loved her. But at six years old, I had to let her know that she could not continue with this, because at times I was afraid that she would beat me to death.

It wasn't the physical pain that hurt so much as the pain that she was hurting me because I was somehow a disappointment to her. I remember asking myself over and over again, *what's exactly the matter with me?* I needed to demonstrate to her that I wasn't afraid.

One day, while she was standing in the kitchen, I removed a sharp knife from the drawer.

'What are you doing with that knife?'

Ever so slowly, as she watched, I sliced into my right thumb. I then peeled back the skin to expose the muscle and bone. I displayed my gruesome thumb to her and she stood in front of me, emotionally and physically frozen.

'If you ever beat me again I will lop off my thumb and cut all of my fingers off until I don't have any fingers left,' I told her, blood spouting onto the floor. 'And you'll have to explain to everybody why this is.'

My mother looked at me in shock, suddenly aware that I was just a little six-year-old kid who didn't want to be hurt and couldn't bear her behavior any longer. An awesome sadness came over my mother as if she had just woken from a nightmare. She began to cry and moan as she wrapped up my thumb. I cried with her. She hugged me and I felt her love. She promised never to hit me again. And she kept her promise.

To not receive the love you need is to leave a hole in your soul that only Divine love can heal.

I DON'T CARE IF THE SUN DON'T SHINE

Elvis was getting ready to break wide open in 1955. I was nine years old. My parents had moved us from the city, into a tract house in New Hyde Park, Long Island, and some of the kids from the neighborhood were over at our place, having a little party in the rumpus room, digging the latest records by The Platters, Chuck Berry, and Bill Hailey & The Comets.

I had a crush on one of the girls—a chick named Sandy. Like most girls, Sandy was in love with Elvis. I knew there was only one way to impress a girl like that. I went into my father's closet and got his blue-and-white tweed sports jacket. It went down to my knees but sort of looked like the kind Elvis was fond of wearing. I went into my mother's makeup kit and got some black mascara and drew sideburns onto my face. Then I went and got some of the white powder that my sister used to keep her saddle shoes white. I covered up my black shoes to make white bucks. I grabbed a beat-up, toy plastic Hopalong Cassidy guitar and appeared at the top of the stairs in great dramatic fashion, singing, *Well, I don't care if the sun don't shine, I get my lovin' in the evening time, when I'm with my baby.*

Unbelievably, Sandy and the other girls started to swoon. It was as if it were part of their DNA. I was a buck-toothed kid pretending to be Elvis, but the girls really saw Elvis. They let me believe *I* was Elvis.

There weren't many moments like that. My life was usually a big ball of angst, wrapped in fear and stuffed into a box of nervousness. I was a misfit. I was in constant trouble at school—me and my pals, Howard Gold and the Roth brothers, Joe and Danny. We were pretty much the only Jews in the neighborhood, so we hung together. I don't think I looked that Jewish at nine years old. I couldn't grow a beard and have payos. I didn't hang on the corner reciting the Book of Leviticus. But the fact I was known to be Jewish was enough for kids to throw my baseball glove onto the roof and rip my homework to shreds. I was the object of a tremendous amount of bullying. I was tormented and harassed. And when I started to fight back, to counter the bullying, the teachers pegged me as a troublemaker.

My father was a pestle-and-mortar druggist. He owned a place out in Forest Hills called Serve-All Drugs. He worked hard and long hours and was rarely home. My mother was suffering from arthritis, and the cold weather of New Hyde Park really put the squeeze on her bones. After the thumb incident, I accidentally slammed a closet door on my sister's fingers, severing her middle digit. I felt terrible about it, and she was slow in forgiving me. There just seemed to be a spirit of doom about the house, and it was starting to press on the family. We could all feel it. We weren't happy.

Late in the summer, the parents planned a picnic at Jones Beach. I wouldn't take 'no' about going into the ocean, and I soon found myself in trouble. Caught in an undertow, I was pinned to the sandy bottom, helplessly watching wave after wave come over me. I felt the unbelievable reality racing through my nine-year-old mind—I was out of air and out of luck and that was it, I was going to die. Funny what you think of at that moment—*I wonder if they'll miss me, or will they be angry with me?* An astounding calm embraced me, and all the panic left. Suddenly I was pushed up from the bottom, as if a jet were attached to me. I gulped in the fresh air. Deciding in that moment never to mention it to anyone, I was definitely feeling a newfound gratitude to whom they call God!

We moved to Los Angeles because that was about as far away as we could get from New Hyde Park. Southern California was Boomtown in the 1950s. There was money to be made, and it was a good place to raise a family. The weather was sunny and warm, and everything was perfect—or so it seemed on television. Every scene had palm trees, and nobody ever seemed to be cold.

THE FIRES OF HELL AIN'T NO FUN PLACE TO BE

My sister and mother packed ourselves into our '53 two-tone Buick and headed west. My father stayed back east for a time to settle things with the business. But when he joined us in Los Angeles there was to be a change. We would no longer be the Schleins—a German word meaning seller of birdlime, the sticky substance used to trap small birds. Now we were the Sloans—Gaelic for warrior.

The trip down south and then west was wonderful. One thing I remember was stopping at the little diners that were scattered along the roadside. There was always music playing, the jukeboxes jumping with great country tunes. I recall eating a grilled cheese sandwich and sloshing down a cherry Coke with my sister and mother at the counter of this place called Tom and Lil's and listening to Slim Whitman's 'Cattle Call.' Everyone in the place, including the slop cook at the grill, was yodeling along to the record.

We drove down through Georgia, Alabama, and Mississippi—Elvis country—and I saw real poverty for the first time. Black families sat out in front of shacks. Sometimes they looked at us passing by; other times they turned their heads. These scenes left a big impression on me.

'Those people don't look very happy,' I said.

'They're poor,' my mother said. 'That's how you live when you're poor.'

'How do you get that poor?' I asked.

'They've been pushed down too much,' my mother told me. 'And when you're pushed down that much, it's hard to get right again.'

My mother wanted to go through New Orleans, so we headed into the city. It was hot and humid. We parked down behind Bourbon Street in the parking lot of a little church where a nice old guy assured us our car would be safe. There seemed to be music coming out of every door and window. It was the first time I ever heard Dixieland jazz. And I *looooved* it! We went into a little restaurant and had catfish while listening to a trumpet player named Hawk. He played the trumpet for over an hour and didn't ever take the horn away from his lips. Not once.

In West Texas we saw cowboys riding along the road, and in New Mexico we stayed in a motel where the rooms were made to look like teepees. At the restaurant there, the men's room door had 'Chief' written on it and the ladies' room had 'Squaw.' Along the road, we stopped and bought some fried bread from an old Navajo woman. It was hot and covered in butter and sugar.

Driving through Flagstaff, a truck came over a hill in our lane and headed straight toward us. My mother and sister screamed. At that moment, I felt a calm come over me. I touched my sister on the shoulder.

'Never fear, I am here,' I quietly told her.

The truck whooshed by us with its air horn blaring. My mother pulled over to the side of the road until she could gather her wits.

'That would have been it,' my mother said.

'We can't be killed,' I assured her.

'We could be killed like anybody could be killed,' my sister snarled.

'God would not let us be killed before we saw the Pacific Ocean,' I said, and I believed it.

Many years later, during one of the lowest points of my life, Sai Baba, my Guru, came to me in a dream.

'Never fear,' he assured me. 'I am here.'

We stopped in Las Vegas and stayed at the Sands Hotel. My mother saw Sammy Davis Jr. walking down the street and ran over to him.

'Sammy!'

He joked with her and held her hand and made her feel like the most important person in his life. Our first brush with celebrity was positive.

We drove through the California desert, and I thought I was going to burn up. We drove through an agricultural inspection station, and a guy who looked like a cop asked if we were carrying any fruit or plants. My sister had to give up a bag of figs she bought in Arizona.

Right outside of Barstow, California, we stopped in a little shaded rest stop and pulled in under a tree for a nap. A large family packed into a pickup truck with sort of a house built onto it was parked a few spaces away. I walked over and saw a kid about my age sitting under the shade of a tree.

'We're going to Los Angeles,' I told him.

'Yeah, I've been to Los Angeles.'

'Where are you heading?'

'I don't know. We live in this truck, and all we seem to do is drive from town to town. My father is a preacher and we hold church meetings and people get saved.'

'Saved? Saved from what?'

'Saved from burning in the fires of hell, of course.'

'People can get saved from that?'

'Sure,' the kid said. 'I hope you get saved, cos the fires of hell ain't no fun place to be.'

As I thought about what the preacher's kid was telling me, my mother called me back to the car. I kept on thinking about it during that haul between Bartstow and up into the mountains. I couldn't shake it.

We crossed over those San Bernardino Mountains, and our hearts stilled when we saw the sprawl of Los Angeles. When you see Los Angeles for the first time, after driving across the country, you feel that all the bad is left behind. It's a time to begin anew. Maybe that is what the kid meant by 'saved.' Because when we rolled over that mountain and saw LA, I surely did feel saved. I felt like everything was in front of me and nothing was behind me.

We had secured an apartment on Crescent Heights, a block off Sunset Boulevard. Sunset would play a significant role in my life. We lived in the upstairs apartment; the parents of either Marge or Gower

Champion lived downstairs. I'm not sure which one of the Champions the parents belonged to, but we were certain that, although new in town, we were already near royalty. To get so close to such a famous dance team was getting close to Hollywood. Hollywood was living downstairs. Well, Hollywood's parents were living downstairs.

Every Sunday, we would stare out the window as a limousine pulled up with the actual Marge and Gower Champion. Everybody in the neighborhood seemed to love them and wanted to get close to the heat of their vibe. I was eleven years old and I couldn't help but dream about what it would be like to get so much love and attention, and how show business might be a pathway to it. Nobody was there to tell me I might not have had that quite right.

My parents did not exactly dote on me, so love and attention were pretty scarce. I may be wrong, but it seemed that not too many parents doted on their children in those days.

Greenblatt's Delicatessen was a half block from our apartment—one of the holy trinity of LA Jewish delicatessens, along with Canters on Fairfax and Nate and Al's in Beverly Hills. On any given day, we could see George Burns, Jerry Lewis, or Jan Murray walking in. We were not in the Jewish hood but more in a satellite hood. Orthodox Judaism requires that you be within walking distance of a synagogue. For my family, it was to be within walking distance of a world-class delicatessen.

I was an outsider—a lone stranger. I was enrolled at the Third Street School. Mrs. Savage was my teacher, and she lived up to her name. I remember her being a very old and wicked woman, but she was probably only thirty-two.

Like any other place, schools in LA worked on the clique system. The most difficult clique to penetrate was made up of kids who had grown up together since kindergarten; they clumped like mushrooms on a dead stump. You weren't invited into the clump, no matter what, so you made friends with the other outsiders. For the most part, what I was experiencing in life, I was experiencing alone, as I could not find anyone more on the outside than me.

I wrote my first song during this time. It was called 'The Outsider.'

And this idea of being on the outside was perhaps the same experience that had spawned the early birth of the modern Bohemian scene, encouraging a generation into the arts and social movements. Those on the outside are looking in, and those on the inside are looking out. As a Jew and an outsider, I felt a deep connection with African Americans because I was experiencing a similar prejudice. In my opinion, rock'n'roll was derived from this experience. Elvis Presley was a bullied, abused kid. Kids like Elvis faced the prejudice of poverty. He didn't fit in. Rock, soul, blues, and country are all rooted in poverty, prejudice, and loneliness.

How does an artistic, sensitive kid release the aggression caused by abuse, prejudice, and loneliness? He creates. He connects with the world of outsiders—all of those who think they are alone. And when you find out you are not, it's a life-changer. Even in this time of instant text and social media, many are still cut off and face the world alone. Maybe now more than ever.

After Elvis went into the army in 1959 and Buddy Holly was killed, the music world attempted to create a world of perfect, sinless innocence. Fabian and Frankie types were replacing the outsiders like Eddie Cochran, Gene Vincent, and Jerry Lee Lewis—kids who were perceived as always being popular and fun and wonderful and so well adjusted. We created insiders out of outsiders, but in reality they were all self-conscious about their acne, unsure of their talent, and (for the most part) afraid of women.

One Sunday night, September 9 1956, Elvis Presley appeared on *The Ed Sullivan Show*. Ed was recovering from a serious car accident, so the great actor Charles Laughton hosted the show. We sat in our living room as Elvis Presley appeared on the flickering, black-and-white screen.

We had never seen Elvis on television. His energy and spirt came into the room and enveloped us. My sister dropped to her knees in front of the screen and kissed it.

'That's my boy,' my mother said, in a glow of satisfaction. 'That's my boy … *my* boy.'

At that moment, I felt that I had lost the two most important people in my life. And I felt I had to win them back somehow.

CHAPTER TWO

THE GARDEN OF ALLAH

I found a job after school selling newspapers to the passing cars in front of the famous Schwab's Pharmacy on the corner of Sunset Boulevard and Crescent Heights. It was famous because the stars hung out there—Lana Turner, Angela Lansbury—and if you were real lucky you could see Marilyn Monroe, in sunglasses and a scarf, running in for one thing or another. It was across the street from the Garden Of Allah, a bar and a collection of small bungalows where the stars had their trysts.

The Garden Of Allah was decorated like a Middle Eastern movie set, with low lighting to enhance the anonymity of the status of its cliental, who went to this watering hole to drink, smoke marijuana, and have sex. This is where Hollywood royalty went to unwind—one of the many decadent little corners of tinsel town. F. Scott Fitzgerald lived there for a time.

I generally showed up with my papers at about two o'clock, but inside the bar had no connection with outside. It was always night in The Garden Of Allah. I used to get good tips for bringing papers to the little villas or to the bar. I delivered papers to William Holden and Wallace Beery, and, one time, to Clark Gable. William Holden asked me get him a tuna sandwich on a Kaiser roll at Greenblatt's, which I did, and gave me ten dollars.

'What do you want to be when you grow up?' he asked me at the bar.

'Hopalong Cassidy,' I said.

'Hopalong Cassidy?' he chuckled. 'I know Hoppy. The man is a saint. He once healed a kid of terminal cancer in England just by touching him. If you can grow up to be as good as Hoppy, you'll be all right.'

One morning in 1957, I had just picked up my afternoon edition load of the *Herald Examiner Eight Star Edition* from Crazy Arnie, whose little newspaper shack was on the north side of Sunset. Arnie ran all of the newspaper boys from Crescent Heights to Fairfax from this little shack. I think he did all right as he always had a wad of cash, and I also think he was a bookie. Every day a big black car would pull up. The driver would hand Arnie an envelope, and Arnie would hand him back a magazine.

I was standing in front of Schwab's when a silver Porsche Spider pulled up to the curb. My heart started racing. I felt an overwhelming excitement as I recognized the driver as James Dean. He seemed agitated but friendly—nervous that someone might see him. He was wearing a loose-fitting grey crew-neck sweater. He took off his glasses and called me over to the car.

'How many *Herald*s have you got there, kid?'

'About fifty,' I told him.

'I'll tell you what. Here's twenty bucks. That should cover it.'

'It sure will but I'll have to go across to Crazy Arnie to get some change.'

'Keep the change. Look. I just want to cut out a small piece in the back of these papers. I'm going to go around the block and cut the article out and then give the papers back to you, and you can sell these papers again. I don't think anyone is going to notice. OK?'

Dean took off, and in a few minutes he returned with the papers, gave them to me, and tore off at breakneck speed down Sunset Boulevard. I checked the paper and saw that Dean had cut an article out of the entertainment section. I walked across the street and checked a fresh paper. Sure enough, there was an article about James Dean.

I found out from my sister that evening that James Dean had been killed two years before in a silver Porsche. I can't explain this event. But I did have a $20 bill in my pocket at the end of the day.

Meanwhile, I had gotten a few babysitting jobs in hopes of helping out my family. One woman who had recently visited Hawaii gave me the choice of getting paid with a coconut, carved and painted to look like a native with seashells for teeth, or an authentic ukulele with one remaining string. I thought carefully. The coconut was pretty cool, but I chose the ukulele. I have often thought how different my life would have been if I had chosen the coconut.

I spent hours harmonizing on that one string to Everly Brothers songs on the radio. Sometimes I was Phil Everly and sometimes I was Don. This harmonizing seemed to take me into a world of my own. I found comfort in harmony. I got a sense of belonging from it.

My father soon tired of me plucking away on that one string and bought me an inexpensive Kay guitar from Wallach's Music City. It came in a cardboard triangular box. That cardboard box was holy. You walked around with that box and people knew there was a guitar in it. I've spoken to many musicians over the years about their first experience carrying around their guitars in that cardboard box, and they all agree that it was a transcendent moment in time when everything was right with the world.

THE MOST BEAUTIFUL EYES I HAD EVER SEEN

My parents bought a house off Fairfax Avenue and Del Valle Drive. It was a one-story English Tudor with a thatched roof. A lady named Mrs. Adams, who was a direct decedent of John Quincy Adams, lived a few houses from us. She once showed me a closet full of the sixth president's clothes. A few houses down was Mrs. Griffith, a very elderly woman, whose husband Griffith J. Griffith had donated the land for Griffith Park.

Across Crescent Heights was a bronze statue of a forty-niner, panning for gold. The statue was sculpted by Henry Lion, and was put there to honor the spirit of the California gold rush of 1849. The miner gave me a sense of peace and optimism, and I would always go over there and sit beside him on the grassy patch. I would look up into his eyes and he would look down on me as if telling me that everything was going to be OK as long as I didn't give up. If I panned for gold long enough, I was destined to strike it rich. He's still there if anyone cares to see him. (The statue was stolen a few years ago but was found in a scrapyard down in the East Valley. He had already been cut in two, but he was rescued by the watchful eye of a suspicious employee at the yard and is now back at work.)

Around the corner was the Carthay Circle Theatre. Along with

Grauman's Chinese Theatre, it was *the* venue for big movie premiers in Hollywood. On the premiere night of *Around The World In Eighty Days* I decided it was high time I attended such an event myself and took a look at life on the inside. I got dressed in my best suit, which had recently been purchased for my upcoming Bar Mitzvah, walked out the front door, and headed to the street lined with limos and press and stars, like it was nobody's business.

Naturally, I couldn't get in without an invitation, so at intermission, as people were walking out of the theater, I walked in, backward. I took my seat on the little aisle step next to a beautiful woman in a white dress.

My perch was soon discovered by an usher.

'You can't sit here,' he whispered in my ear.

'That boy is with us,' the beautiful woman in the white dress said. 'Is there a problem?'

'I'm so sorry. I didn't know,' the usher said apologetically, as he backed away, bowing.

'Thanks,' I said to the woman, who turned to me and stared at me with the most beautiful lavender eyes I had ever seen. Those eyes tore right through me like a shot of light. It was Elizabeth Taylor and her husband, Mike Todd.

At the end of the film, as my parents, sister, neighbors, and other star-watchers were crowded outside, I walked out of the theater with Elizabeth Taylor and Mike Todd, right behind the great Mexican comic genius Mario Moreno, the man known as Cantinflas. My parents were flabbergasted when they saw me, and many of the neighbors were as well. They started laughing with delight.

'It's Philip!'

When I walked up to my parents and sister, beaming with pride, they straightaway hit me where it hurt, without missing a beat.

'How could you have done this to us?' my mother asked.

'I ...'

'Why did you bring attention to us?' my father asked.

'What if Elizabeth Taylor had called the police because of you harassing her? You could have been arrested.'

'I wasn't harassing her. She was nice.'

'Don't ever take the risk of embarrassing us again,' my father warned.

'He's always doing this sort of thing,' my sister lamented. 'I think he needs a psychiatrist.'

I walked back toward the house alone. I crossed Crescent Heights Boulevard and sat by the statue of the forty-niner. I felt confident near him. Though made of bronze, for me he had more heart than most other people I knew.

FREDDY, BIG JIM, AND JUMPING THE MOON

My mother hired a cleaning lady named Freddy and a gardener named Big Jim. Freddy was a beautiful African American woman in her late thirties. She was kind and loving to me, and I connected with her immediately. Sometimes I would sit in the kitchen, playing my guitar, and she would stop what she was doing and listen. She encouraged me. She told me about her favorite music: Clyde McPhatter, Fats Domino, and Sam Cooke. She brought records in to work with her, and during her lunch break we'd sit in the living room and listen to Brook Benton, Dinah Washington, and The Clovers.

Freddy loved music. She loved R&B and explained to me with great enthusiasm how it came from gospel and jazz and something she called 'jump blues'—louder and faster blues played by a jazz band with drums, sax, trumpet, guitar, and stand-up bass. Freddy taught me that it was OK to believe in music—that my dreams were worthy. She mixed Bible stories in with her music, telling me how Jesus walked on water, and that giants and dragons were as real as fish and sparrows.

Big Jim was aptly named. He was a bear of a man. His hands were large and calloused, like great leather mitts. His seemed to have the strength of ten men. I once saw him pull a tree out of the ground with hardly any digging. He was kind, too. He spoke to all of the flowers and bushes, explaining to them what he was doing and why he was doing it: 'I'm going to pull you out, little baby, but you're going to be fine.'

I know this sounds crazy, but sometimes I thought the flowers were looking at Jim as he passed by them. He spoke to the birds and the bugs.

He spoke to all living things. And he spoke to me. He would ask me how my day was going, and how I was making out in school—simple questions that I did not hear from my parents. Big Jim exuded kindness, strength, and love.

'What kind of music do you like, Big Jim?' I asked.

'I like the crickets rubbing their legs together on a summer night in Georgia. I like the tree frogs chirping in the pond behind my house. And I like the dogs barking in the distance during an early morning heavy fog.'

Big Jim once asked me a question that I will never forget. We were sitting on the front steps and not saying much, just listening to things. It was in the afternoon, and there was a cool breeze blowing. We were drinking lemonade that Freddy had made for us.

'You ever jump the moon?' he asked.

'What do you mean, Jim?' I wondered.

'Did you ever *try* to jump the moon?'

'No. No, I've never tried to jump the moon.'

'Oh,' Big Jim said.

'Have you?' I asked. 'Have you ever tried to jump the moon?'

'No son, but I tried. And you know what? Sometimes that ain't enough … but sometimes it is.'

Freddy would occasionally take me to her church down on Crenshaw, where I could listen to Gospel music—music that stirred my soul. The choir sang with such power and beauty that while I was there I felt at peace. How wonderfully natural it seemed for black and white to be together, sharing their love for God and music.

I appreciated how my parents gave me the freedom to tag along with Freddy. They must have trusted her. But when I asked why Freddy and Big Jim weren't ever invited to eat dinner with us, I was told that they were negroes. As nice as they were, our relationship had its limits.

Freddy died when I was fifteen. It was the first time I lost someone I loved. I didn't think anyone could take her place. She was the one in my life who nurtured my dreams. I don't think I would have ever made as much music as I did without Freddy.

THE CARDBOARD MAN

Wallach's Music City was on Sunset and Vine. This gigantic store took up two city blocks and housed tens of thousands of records, musical instruments, and pages of sheet music. Glass phonograph booths faced the street where you could take any record and listen to it. Wallach's was my temple. That is where my gods lived. When Dion & The Belmonts or Fats Domino came out with a new record, I went to Wallach's to hear both sides. I usually didn't have enough money to buy them, but I could listen to my heart's content.

I took my guitar in the holy triangular box, hopped on the bus at 8th Street and Fairfax, and rode to Sunset and Vine. I was twelve years old. As I got off the bus I noticed a happening going on in front of Wallach's. There were hundreds of excited girls. Policemen had barricaded the door. But I, with my guitar under my arm, was able to stroll right up to the front door.

'Is that a guitar you got in the box?' a policeman asked.

'Yep,' I answered.

Perhaps an angel allowed me to enter the store, or maybe it was the magic triangular box, because the policeman opened the door for me.

'He's a musician,' one of the cops said to another, and I entered the palace of music without incident.

The place was empty and the lights were off. It was eerie. My first instinct was to rob the place blind and stick as many records down my pants as I could, but I was thwarted by a six-foot cutout of Pat Boone standing in front of a wall, advertising his newest record.

An inviting light emanated from a room nearby. I moved toward it. There was a man standing behind a counter—a man to me, at least. He was probably nineteen.

I placed the triangular box on the glass case.

'Who let you in here?' the man asked.

'The police,' I said confidently, before opening the box to reveal my Kay acoustic guitar.

'That's one of ours,' the guy said. 'What about it?'

'I don't know what to do with all of these strings.'

'This is a guitar, kid—guitars have six strings,' he said, looking behind his counter. 'What you need is a book on guitar chords. I have one here by Mel Bay. He's the one that everybody uses.'

As we were talking, the guy behind the counter suddenly turned into cardboard. All signs of life drained from his being. He seemed to become flat and indistinguishable from the other cutouts in the store. I didn't know what to make of it.

I heard footsteps coming down the stairs. I turned around, and there was Elvis Presley. I stared at him—this radiant being—as he moved down the stairs toward me. Time and the world seemed to stop. There he was, standing in front of me—this man who, only a short time before, had stolen the hearts of my mother and sister from me. I should have felt anger and envy. But I didn't. Rather, I felt this incredible energy being transferred into me—an infusion of benevolence, love, and compassion.

Elvis stared deeply into my eyes. He took me into a timeless place. I had never experienced the kind of love he was pouring into me, this great kidnapper of hearts. He pulled his gaze away and turned his attention to my guitar. He reached for the neck of my guitar and gently lifted it.

'I bet you'd like to learn how to play this, son,' he said.

'Yes sir, I would,' I replied, never having used the word 'sir' in my life until now.

He placed the guitar in my hands and positioned himself behind me in order to move my fingers into the shape of a D chord. Then he reached into his pocket, removed a guitar pick from it, and placed it between my index finger and thumb. He moved my right hand to strum the guitar and started to sing in my ear.

Love me ten-der ... love me ... true ...
Never ... let me ... go ...

'Your fingers are too small to barre,' he said. 'I'll show you a simplified version of an A chord.'

Love me tender ... love me true
All my dreams fulfilled ...

He took the guitar from my hands and gently placed it on the glass counter.

'I'm having my guitar gold-plated upstairs,' he said. 'I had a leather guitar cover like Hank Williams did, and I was happy with that, but Colonel Tom wasn't. The Colonel wants gold. But a gold guitar is going to be too heavy to play. He doesn't seem to understand that.'

I sensed his sadness as he said this, and that was something I couldn't fathom. The most famous person in the world—a man who, I believed, had it all—was sad. It was if he were saying, *success and glamour is not all that it seems.* And then I felt sympathy for Elvis, and for myself, because there was no way for me to comfort him.

'Don't worry. I'll make sure you get an autograph for that sister of yours.'

Here's the thing, though: I had never mentioned my sister to Elvis. He took out a pen and piece of paper from his shirt pocket and autographed it.

Elvis then patted me on the shoulder, turned, and started back up the stairs. Midway up the stairs, he stopped and spun around to face me. He extended his left arm, crooked his left leg, and seemed to be standing on the ball of his foot—a pose that in the 70s would become iconic.

'I think you're going to do just fine,' he said, as he turned and walked back upstairs.

The guy behind the counter suddenly became conscious and alive.

'Was Elvis here? Did you talk to him? What did he say to you?'

'I think … umm … I think I'll take that guitar chord book after all.'

I told my sister about what had happened as soon as I got home.

'You're crazy,' she told me.

I presented her with the autograph and she looked at it with disdain.

'Anybody can sign Elvis's name,' she said. 'If you carry on making up stories, you're going to wind up in a mental hospital.'

CHAPTER THREE

THE ONLY THIRTEEN-YEAR-OLD JEWISH R&B ARTIST IN TOWN

I learned a whole lot of chords from Mel Bay's book. And, with Elvis's inspiration, I was playing at every moment. Sometimes I'd wake up in the night and play. And I sang—I sang all day long. And when I wasn't singing, I was thinking about singing or playing or notes or harmony. I played for Freddy and she encouraged me.

Aladdin and Specialty Records were all-black labels in LA. In 1959, Freddy told me that Aladdin was holding auditions for new talent, and that some kids from Crenshaw were going down, so maybe I should as well.

'Aladdin is all R&B guys, Freddy,' I said.

'So?'

'So what?'

'So I'm white.'

'What's your color have to do with rhythm & blues?'

'Nothing, I guess. It's just that …'

'You go down there to Aladdin Records. You've got more soul than you know. You go in there and sing. Belt it out loud and true and you'll be OK.'

So I put my guitar in a pillowcase—my holy cardboard box had worn away by now—and caught the bus on Fairfax to Pico.

The company was run by two brothers, Eddie and Leo Mesner. Like Leonard Chess in Chicago, they had tapped into the rich R&B talent in the part of Los Angeles that was segregated from whites after World War II. Aladdin at that time had Amos Milburn, Little Milton, Thurston Harris, Shirley & Lee—all of the greats had recorded there with them.

The Mesners had a small office/studio on Pico Boulevard in Midtown (so named because it was midway between the black and white neighborhoods). I arrived at 10am and waited in line with a couple of hundred young, black musicians and singers. At 4pm they let me in—a pudgy, thirteen-year-old kid with a guitar in a pillowcase.

As I walked into the little studio, they turned on the red light and I began to sing 'I Don't Care If The Sun Don't Shine.' After I finished the song, I started to put my guitar back in the pillowcase and they told me to come into the booth; they wanted to sign me to a record deal.

'Do you write any songs?' Leo asked.

'No, but I can,' I answered honestly. They really liked my stuff and told me that they wanted Bumps Blackwell, who was Little Richard's producer, to work with me on a record.

The Mesners gave me a contract to show my parents and told me to come back as soon as it was signed. That ride home from Pico to Fairfax was one of the most extraordinary bus rides in my life. I don't ever remember being so excited. I was going to be a real R&B singer-songwriter.

When I got home my parents told me that I would not be anything of the sort. They ensured me that this crazy dream would destroy their plans of me graduating from UCLA, going to medical school, or becoming a pharmacist. My family was seeking legitimacy, since my father, even though he was a successful man, considered himself to be third-rate because he had not become a doctor. My uncle Herman, who was the first licensed chiropractor in the state of New York, was considered a quack. The family needed redemption.

Freddy found some time for a little private chat with me.

'Whatever happens with this Aladdin business, I want you to know that I am just so proud of you. I knew you had it in you, and I want you to keep it in you no matter what. You promise?'

'I promise, Freddy.'

'No matter what?'

Eddie and Leo showed up at the house and convinced my parents that money was involved and that they would take good care of me. They sat with my parents at the kitchen table as my mother served them pound cake and coffee. My parents agreed to give me a shot at making a record, figuring that I would do it and that would be the end of it.

I went in and recorded 'All I Want Is Loving' and 'Little Girl In The Cabin.' My voice had not yet broken but I did my best to feel it and sing like Elvis. I was feeling him all around me. I recorded at RCA Studios with Elvis's black female background singers and some of the best studio guys in the business. Earl Palmer, who had worked with Little Richard, Julie London, and The Strollers, and a future inductee into the Rock and Roll Hall of Fame, was on drums. The great Mike Deasy, Elvis's LA session guitarist. Plas Johnson, who played bass on numerous Elvis sessions. I was standing in the spot where Elvis recorded.

Bumps Blackwell—who was already a legend, having worked with Little Richard, Sam Cooke, and Ray Charles—produced the record. He was sweet and supportive, and treated me like I belonged in that studio. He put me at ease and made me understand that I didn't have to prove anything.

Everyone was pleased with the finished work. One can deduce from listening to the record that I was having a great time, but I felt I was bluffing my way through it. It came out and got a *Billboard* 'Best Pick' in 1959, and Flip Sloan took his place at the end of a very long line of great black artists to have recorded for Aladdin Records.

Aladdin went out of business not too long after I cut my record for them, so I was back on track to pharmacy school and legitimacy. My family hoped the experience had gotten the music out of my system. But it just made it stronger.

The kids at school would point me out as I walked down the hall.

'Did you know he made a record?'

'Yeah, but it wasn't a hit.'

Even with the magic lamp of Aladdin, I was still an outsider.

ROCK'N'ROLL HIGH

Fairfax High School was one of the top scholastic schools in the country. Everybody knew it was a very high achieving school because we hadn't won a football game in seventeen years. Fairfax High was basically a

Jewish Yeshiva for science, math, and music geeks. It was 98 percent Jewish. There was one black kid who wandered around in a daze and two Asians who the Jews referred to as 'Buddha heads.'

Phil Spector went to Fairfax, and so did Carol Connors and Marshall Lieb. They started The Teddy Bears together and had a huge hit with 'To Know Him Is To Love Him.' And there was Herb Alpert and Lou Adler—a man who would depend on me for my creativity and punish me for trying to express myself. Then there was Steve Barri, my future writing partner. Russ Titelman, the famous record producer, was in the class behind me.

My best pal Jerry was originally from Canada, which was like being from another world. We knew it existed, but few of us cared about anything Canadian, unless you were into hockey—and nobody was. We thought Canadians lived in the wilderness and ate wolves and took their dates out on dogsleds. I certainly had no way of knowing that in very short order my songs would dominate the Canadian songscape thanks to Terry Black's masterful teen-idol recordings.

Although Jerry had spent most of his life in LA, he was still considered an outsider. He and I listened to a lot of music together. His parents had purchased one of the first stereo players, so we sat on his living room floor and dissected records like we did rats in biology class. What kinds of guitars were being played? How did they get such a crisp sound in the production? We loved the B-sides almost as much as the A-sides at a time when nobody cared about such things. For example, the flipside of a big hit called 'Eddie My Love' by The Teen Queens was a song called 'Just Goofed,' which to this day is still one of the greatest records I ever heard.

We weren't being told what was good; we were deciding for ourselves. That was cool. That empowered our sensibilities.

We couldn't possibly buy enough records to satisfy all of the music we wanted, so Jerry and I formed a partnership to attain more records. We had to feed the music monkey.

We formulated a plan. We walked into Wallach's Music City, stuck records down our pants, and weaseled out the door. On one occasion, we were nabbed in the act and given a scare. It was then that Jerry and

I realized: you don't steal from the temple. Radio stations and record companies, however, were fair game.

Jerry and his brother were partners in a small printing-press business they ran from their parents' garage, so we printed a phony letter from Fairfax High's Assistant Principal, Mr. Hunt, stating that we represented the school's dance committee and would very much appreciate new records. We would go to the major radio stations—KFWB, KRLA, KFI. At first it worked but then they caught on somehow. The record labels, however, felt that this could be some good teenage publicity.

The people at Columbia would never give us their 45 hits but did let us help ourselves to the trash bin, where LPs went to die. That's where I got my first Bob Dylan album. I was able to find old Harry Belafonte albums from RCA. Woody Guthrie, Odetta, Leadbelly, and Brownie & McGee albums were free—thrown into the trash heap because they hadn't sold or were getting old! At the little record companies on Sunset Boulevard, we got Pee Wee Crayton, Clarence 'Frogman' Henry, and Dobie Gray singing 'Delia's Gone.'

In order to make money to buy records, I started a band called The Continentals. Bob Myman was another pal—a great-looking kid and an insider who had grown up in LA. He had a drum set at home, and for him to consent to play with an outsider was unheard of, but he loved playing the drums. We would rehearse at his house, and we'd get gigs at teenage parties. We bought red vests and printed some cards to hand out at school. We played a lot of parties for twenty bucks a pop. I sang lead and played an electric guitar that I was able to buy from a pawnshop with the help from my father. It was a Gibson Custom 1959 ES-175, known as the jazzbox. It was a great guitar then—and a classic today.

Songs were pouring out of me. I was writing them by the dozen. My parents had a fabulous Webcor tape recorder—curiously, the same one Paul McCartney raved about. It had what they called the magic green eye; when you pushed the record button, the green eye would go on. It was a huge, 85lb machine. Jerry and I learned how to overdub our background vocals over my lead. We laid down a lot of songs and sweet harmonies in front of that all-discerning green eye.

In 1960, I set out to audition for every record company in Los Angeles. The closest label to my home was Mart/Arwin Records over on North Canon Drive in Beverly Hills. I decided to strike there first. I was fourteen years old and I feared nothing.

Mart/Arwin was owned by Marty Melcher. Aside from being Doris Day's husband, he was also a successful producer of movies like *Pillow Talk, It Happened To Jane, Please Don't Eat The Daisies*—pretty much anything starring Doris Day. He was a walrus of a man. You went into his office, shook his hand, and you felt like your life had been somehow fulfilled, and that everything had led up to that golden moment.

Also there was the composer and producer Joe Lubin. Joe, who signed his first publishing contract after meeting Noel Gay in the middle of an air raid in London during World War II, was now in his early forties, his hair slicked back with Vaseline. He had arranged and sanitized Little Richard's 'Tutti-Frutti' for Pat Boone, which got him a shared writing credit on the song, along with Little Richard and Dorothy LaBostrie.

Arwin had some big hit records. There was an instrumental called 'Chi-hua-hua' by The Pets, and Jan & Arnie's 'Jenny Lee,' produced by Joe. It was a major national breakout record and it made the label. Eventually, Jan & Arnie evolved into Jan & Dean. Jan Berry, Arnie Ginsburg, and Dean Torrence were pals at University High School in West LA and sang together in the glee club.

Bruce Johnston and Terry Melcher—later to become Bruce & Terry, as well as The Rip Chords—were also at Arwin. Terry was Marty's son, and he and Bruce had recorded a few songs together. And there were Mel Carter and James Griffin, who would cofound the group Bread with David Gates. All in all, Arwin was a pretty neat little record label.

I auditioned for Hylton Shane, a young, very cool, and very sharp Ivy League cat. To my disbelief, Arwin offered me a record contract! But when I tried to share my good news with my family, they were indifferent and suspicious. I couldn't believe it.

'So, who in hell is this Marty Melcher?'

'He's Marty Melcher, Ma. He's married to Doris Day.'

'I don't know. I'm not that crazy about Doris Day. She seems too goy for me.'

'She's the number one star in the country. Everybody loves Doris Day.'

'And does everybody love Doris Day's husband?'

'Ma …'

I went into Harmony Recorders and cut two songs I had recently written: 'She's My Girl,' which was influenced by Richie Valens, and 'If You Believe In Me,' which was in the style of Ricky Nelson. The legendary drummer Sandy Nelson—who with his recording of 'Teen Beat' had one of the top records of 1958—treated me as an equal in the studio, and that gave me a great deal of confidence. Sandy would unfortunately lose a leg in a motorcycle accident in 1963. Bill Pittman was on Dano electric guitar, and Steve Douglas played a very mean sax. Steve later became a superstar sax player with Phil Spector and John Lennon. These were session guys who would be part of what became the Wrecking Crew— some of the greatest, world-renowned studio musicians, alongside the Funk Brothers of Motown. I did my first overdub on electric guitar, and I had a really great time. In the short time between Aladdin and Arwin I had matured as a musician.

We got another 'Pick Hit' in *Billboard*. This time I used the name Phil Sloan; I had outgrown Flip, my sister's pet name for me. I had my second single and my fourth writing credit. Looking back, giving a fourteen-year-old kid a writing credit in those days was pretty rare, if not unheard of. Though the record didn't go anywhere or do anything, I was now smitten by the music bug. Stardom and success lay in front of me now, followed by destruction and ultimately resurrection.

I DON'T WANT ANYTHING TO DO WITH HIM

I was hanging around Harmony Recorders, and just down the street there was a tiny record label called Skylark Records, operated by Ben and Leonard Wiseman. My sister was dating Ben and had mentioned that I had made a couple of records, so they invited me down to see what I had.

Skylark sort of looked like an Amsterdam whorehouse—everything took place looking out onto the street. I brought my Webcor reel-to-reel recorder with me, and Ben and Leonard asked me play them something. I told them it was hard to pick because I had a hundred or so songs on the recorder.

I started at the beginning of the tape and they listened to one song after another. They listened to fifteen or so songs, and by this point they were starting to have a meltdown. They were visualizing yachts and mansions in Monaco. This was like a dream come true for these guys. Nobody walked into a place with a hundred new songs.

The Wisemans had a deal with United Artists Records. United Artists said that if Ben and Lenny came up with an artist, they would release the record—assuming it was any good. The Wisemans already made a recording called 'Wonderful, Wonderful,' and, keen to save money, they decided to take the old vocal off and put mine on. They sent it to United Artists, and United Artists sent Steve Venet, who worked as an A&R man, over to the Wisemans' storefront to investigate further.

Steve's brother Nick—the producer of Bobby Darin, the early Beach Boys and a lot of folk acts coming through Capitol—said he wanted to hear more from this Phil Sloan. I got the Webcor and played him the tape. After a dozen or so songs, Steve told me to lose Lenny and Ben and said he would get me an audition at Screen Gems, Columbia's Music Publishing Company. Ben and Lenny gave me their blessing; they thought they could possibly manage me, but that never materialized. They were beautiful guys. Very decent.

So I headed over to Screen Gems Music. I had been trying to get into Screen Gems for months. I'd go after school with my tape recorder and sit on their couch but I could never get a meeting. I stopped trying after a while. Screen Gems Music was the publishing arm of Columbia Pictures and the West Coast office of the New York publishing company Aldon Music, run by Al Nevins and Don Kirshner—Al being the real genius of the two, in my opinion. Aldon had a stable of the greatest hit songwriters in music: Carole King and Gerry Goffin, Barry Mann and Cynthia Weil, Neil Sedaka and Harold Greenfield, to name but a few. Most of those songs were going out on Dimension Records.

I was sitting on the couch again as Steve played my songs for Lou Adler in his office.

'I don't like any of them,' Adler said. 'I don't want anything to do with this kid.'

Al Nevins was in the next room, however, and when he heard the music through the wall he told Adler to sign me as a songwriter and Steve Venet as an A&R guy for bringing me in. That was the beginning of my tumultuous relationship with Lou Adler.

Aldon signed me for $10 a week. A couple of months later, Venet and Adler had a clash, Adler fired Venet, and of all things gave me his job but with no extra money. At sixteen, I was the head of A&R at Screen Gems Music, as well as a staff songwriter for the publishing company. After school, I would go to work at Screen Gems, writing songs and listening to demos that were sent by artists and writers from all over the country.

It was around this time that I met Steve Barri. His birth name was Stephen Lipkin, and he came into the picture as a Jewish Ricky Nelson wannabe. He waltzed into Adler's office with Carol Connors from The Teddy Bears. That group had already disbanded, and Phil Spector was on the road to becoming an entrepreneur-producer of his own label, Phillies Records. But Carol still had a name as an insider. She had had a relationship with Elvis Presley, who was a huge fan of her beautiful singing voice. She was also a talented songwriter and would go on to write 'Hey Little Cobra' for The Rip Chords, among many other big songs. But I guess none of that mattered to Lou Adler.

Steve Barri was working at Norty's Record store on Fairfax. Norty's was primarily a Jewish record store but it sold popular music as well. It was one of several record shops in LA that radio stations called to find out if any new records were breaking out. Carol and Steve made a record together, along with Carol's sister, and called themselves The Storytellers. They were trying to sell the master recording, having spent their own money for the musicians and the studio time—that's the way Phil Spector got 'To Know Him Is To Love Him' out.

Adler did not particularly like the song, but there was something about Steve Barri with which he connected. Steve was older than me; he was married and had a new baby at home. Adler convinced Steve to work as a staff writer at Screen Gems. He gave him $10 a week and threw him in the room with me.

'You two fight it out and write together,' Adler told us.

Imagine what it was like from Steve Barri's point of view: being thrown into the piano room with a sixteen-year-old kid and told to write songs with him. It really must have been a nightmare. He needed real money to support his wife and child, and this didn't look like it to him. I picked up on that immediately. The first songs I played him were 'Kick That Little Foot Sally Ann,' 'Unless You Care,' and 'Blue Lipstick.' Steve played a few songs on a four-stringed guitar, and they were basically not very interesting. That was our initial meeting. But we were partners now, and we would make the best of it.

Steve and I began writing together—slowly at first, but then after a few months he began to trust my musical ability and ditched his other writing-partner friends. We started doing demos every week. We'd lay down four or five demos at a time—songs that were geared as follow-ups to hit records for acts like The Drifters or Bobby Rydell. We started to work with the great studio musicians like Hal Blaine, Ray Pohlman, Leon Russell, and Tommy Tedesco. The going rate was $15 a song. These songs were usually recorded in the early morning hours before the guys went off to big sessions with names like Sinatra, Martin, and Presley. I would work with the musicians in the studio on the song arrangements, then do the vocal, and Steve and I would do background harmonies when the song called for it. Then we'd go into the booth and fight it out over the mixing.

We were getting a few cuts from Adler's connections, and that was good. We wrote Connie Stevens's 'A Girl Never Knows' and 'You Say Pretty Words' with Ramona King. These lyrics were more up Steve's alley than mine—songs about rings on fingers and what girls want. The records weren't hits, so there were no royalties, but it felt great to see your name on a record as the writer. We were heading in the right direction.

Adler surprised me when he asked if I wanted to write and produce the next Ann-Margret record. Pierre Cossette and Bobby Roberts were managing her career; this would be a Dunhill Production, and Lou would serve as executive producer on the date. I loved Annie's recording of 'I Just Don't Understand,' which was a hit for her, but she hadn't been on the charts since. We wrote two new songs along those lines, 'He's My Man' and 'Someday Soon.' 'He's My Man' was a nice little blues number that stands up today. I like the way she sang *he my man*—that was a woman with a whole lot soul. I did all of the guitar work and arranged it as well.

Ann was so sweet and humble, taking vocal directions from a teenager.

'Phil, do you think I should be doing it this way?'

'Yes, Annie. You make a man want to turn the lights down low and fantasize.'

When a tube cracked in my Gibson amp in the middle of a take, it began to fuzz.

'What the hell was that?' the engineer asked.

I told him a tube cracked and I needed another.

'Forget that, can you control it?'

'I don't know. Let me try.'

I began kicking the amp with my foot to get the cracked tube to distort as I played. Some believe that was the serendipitous first use of a fuzz guitar. Some say it was Keith Richards on the 'Satisfaction' demo, but still others can trace distortion guitars all the way back to 1955 and Chuck Berry's 'Maybellene.' That is the great fuzz-tone debate. All that mattered to me was that Annie liked the song.

We were doing demos every day, and in so doing, without really being aware of it, we were becoming more professional with our writing, arranging, producing, playing, and singing. We did demos for 'Can I Get To Know You' and 'Just Love Me' with the great Darlene Love. Although Darlene was the voice of The Crystals and Bob B. Soxx & The Blue Jeans, she wasn't seeing much royalty money, so she did these sessions on the side for extra cash.

Every week, Adler would listen to all our demos and decide what to do. Betty Everett, a Chicago-based blues singer on Vee-Jay Records, was coming off a mega-hit called 'The Shoop Shoop Song (It's In His Kiss),' so Adler submitted our demos to them. Vee-Jay gave the green light to 'Can I Get To Know You' as the B-side of Goffin & King's 'I Can't Hear You No More.'

Vee-Jay bought the A-side because it was by Goffin & King, and their track record was phenomenal—they were two of the top songwriters in the world. But when 'I Can't Hear You No More' bombed, Vee-Jay started touting the B-side as the A-side. This saved Betty Everett's record. It also brought attention to Steve and me as a viable songwriting team. We were being mentioned in the same sentence as Goffin & King.

Adler was really pleased and excited and started treating me with some respect. However, Screen Gems in New York was miffed that the West Coast office had bested Goffin & King and seemed to make it clear that Adler was not going to get favorable treatment. They were going to punish him for being successful. Maybe this is where that egocentric psychosis started. How dare Adler beat Goffin & King with two kids who, in their opinion, hadn't earned their songwriting chops?

I think this was the beginning of Adler wanting to leave Screen Gems and start Dunhill. He realized his little office overlooking Sunset Boulevard was no longer secure.

A MYSTERIOUS PACKAGE FROM LIVERPOOL

Part of my role as the head of A&R at Screen Gems was to listen to demos sent by writers from all over the country looking to get signed or have their songs published. However, Adler had clearly instructed me not to listen to anything from outside the country. American music was going overseas to Britain and Europe, but it was unthinkable that music from other countries was going to influence American tastes, which was ridiculous thinking, really. The UK had given us Lonnie Donegan's 'Does Your Chewing Gum Lose Its Flavor On The Bed Post Over Night,' which was a hit but was considered a novelty song. And there was some fabulous talent in England. Tommy Steele and Cliff Richard & The Shadows were huge stars there but were unknown in America.

I was aware that Britain had trad music. Kids were dancing to Dixieland. They had skiffle and a dynamic underground blues world. You had underground R&B and jazz. There was so much action underground in Britain that it was inevitable that one day it would blow and blow with such a force that it would nearly knock the earth off of its axis.

One afternoon, I received a package from the UK, exquisitely wrapped in high quality brown paper. It was from a Brian Epstein. As I recall, the package contained four acetates: 'Please, Please Me,' 'Thank You Girl,' 'Love Me Do,' and 'From Me To You.' I put them on the turntable knowing this was a violation of the rules, but I was curious. When I listened to 'Please, Please Me,' the hairs on the back of my neck stood up—I wasn't aware until then that I even had hair on the back of my neck. I played the other three after that and I didn't know what to do. I didn't say anything to Adler or anyone else that afternoon. I went home and thought about what I had just heard and felt. I couldn't get the songs out of my head.

The next morning, I took the demos into Lou Adler and told him, with great enthusiasm, that this group from the UK was going to be bigger than Elvis. Adler was aware that I had met Elvis, and he knew that I was a huge fan of his, so when I declared that this group was going to be bigger, it meant something to him. He put the acetates on the turntable expectantly and listened.

'Two guys doing a bad imitation of The Everly Brothers,' he said.

That is what *he* heard. That is what he was able to process from the experience. He then threw the acetates in the trash. It was only when I offered him a week's salary for them that he began to have second thoughts.

I brought Adler the wrapping in which acetates had arrived and the letter from Epstein, which included a phone number. He called Brian and told him that I believed this group was going to be bigger than Elvis, and Brian, over the phone, exclaimed, 'I just said that today to the press for the first time—that my boys are going to be bigger than Elvis Presley. He must be one of the boys.'

So a connection was made between Adler, Brian Epstein, and The Beatles. Capitol, which owned EMI, wasn't going to spend money on a British group in America, but had said it wouldn't interfere if Brian could secure another record label to release their masters.

Adler worked his new connection with Jay Lasker at Vee-Jay. 'I've got this kid who believes The Beatles are going to bigger than ...' And Lasker agreed to release a Beatles record.

'Love Me Do,' The Beatles' first single, bombed. Their name was even misspelled ('The Beetles') on the label. The record was hardly played on the radio stations. Everyone was deflated. I had told the executives that this group from England was going to be huge, and it was thought that I had been proven very, very wrong.

Soon after that, I got a package in from Andrew Loog Oldham, the producer of a new band called The Rolling Stones, who he wrote to say Brian Epstein had suggested that I listen to their demos. I listened to two songs, 'Not Fade Away' and 'I Wanna Be Your Man,' written by John Lennon and Paul McCartney, and told Adler this group was going to be as big as The Beatles. I was promptly fired!

In hindsight, what was going on here was the great tidal wave of what later would be known as the British Invasion, and there would be no stopping it.

YOU CAN HAVE HER FOR A SONG

I had just graduated from Fairfax High School in June of that year, and I had decided to go to California State University to study piano. I would forget about Adler and Screen Gems and make my parents happy for a change. I had been there for barely a month when the impossible happened and Kennedy was assassinated. Broken hearted and disillusioned, I left school for good. It was Al Nevins—the head of the entire publishing company—who hired me back.

Across the hall from Screen Gems was a little record company called Domain. It was run by three guys: Tony Sepe, Martin Brooks, and Bob Krasnow. They had not yet come out with a record on the Domain label, but Krasnow had released a parody album during the 1960 presidential campaign called *Report To The Nation*. They were bound and determined to get a song from Screen Gems, preferably by Mann & Weil or Goffin & King. They were always in Lou's office asking. Lou told me to stay away from those guys because he considered them to be hustlers and bottom-feeders. (He considered himself to be a class act.)

Adler was a bit over thirty at the time, although he told people he was twenty-nine. He wore jeans and tennis shoes and expensive, colorful, loose-fitting sweaters. He sat in his office with his feet on the desk, staring out the window. He would speak into his intercom and ask his secretary, Judy, to get him something or other, but it was all for show—he was well aware that Screen Gems West was nothing more than a dead letter office. All of the songwriting and publishing action was in New York at Aldon.

Adler was managing Jan & Dean, and that kept him somewhat busy. He took over that chore while he was a still partner with his high school friend, Herb Alpert. They started a small label named Dore, and Jan & Dean made several national hits there, like 'Baby Talk.' When Adler and Alpert split up, Adler took Jan & Dean and Alpert continued on with the label by himself.

Since there wasn't much going on at Screen Gems, I liked to drop in on Sepe, Brooks, and Krasnow. Their office was empty, except for two cheap, bare desks with two phones. When I walked in they would immediately jump onto the phones.

'Yes, I can get you 10,000 copies by next Friday,' Sepe would say.

'Of course it depends on the distributor,' Marty Brooks would say, feigning a deal. 'There shouldn't be a …'

'It's just Phil,' one of them would say, and the other would hang up the phone.

Bob Krasnow, thinking that a real record person had just entered, would burst in from his office.

'Ten thousand? We can give them twenty-five thousand.'

'It's just Phil, Bob.'

'Oh, Phil. How are you, Phil? You got anything for us today?'

'Nothing today.'

'Why not?' Bob asked. 'All we need is one good song.'

'We'll take care of you, Phil,' Sepe said. 'You give us a song … any song … we're not talking about Handel's "Messiah" … just something kids can dance to.'

'I'm not even supposed to be here.'

'What, not supposed to be here? Forget about Adler. Get us a song and we'll all make money.'

One day, I was getting into the elevator to go up to the office and the Domain boys were inside, accompanied by a morbidly obese Mexican woman. She must have weighed at least 350lbs and dressed in a frightening, tiny red dress that she poured out of from top to bottom. The poor, heaving creature seemed to fill the entire elevator. I squeezed in and we started up. Sepe and Brooks smiled as they saw me staring at her; she was breathing so heavily in this claustrophobic, airless space, reeking of cheap perfume, I thought for sure she was going to have a heart attack.

'You can have her for a song,' Brooks said, getting his own joke, and laughing. 'She's yours for a song, my young friend.'

'Let me out of the elevator,' I begged them. 'I'll see what I can do. I'll get you a song.'

'Kick That Little Foot Sally Ann' had already been rejected as a song for Harry Belafonte, so I saw no harm in giving it to Sepe, Brooks, and Krasnow. I showed up later that afternoon with my guitar and I sat down and played it to the Domain boys.

Sepe's jaw dropped and slowly turned into a grin, as if he had just projected into the future and liked what he saw. Marty Brooks opened the window and yelled out to Sunset Boulevard.

'We've got a hit! What did we tell you?'

'Get a hold of yourself,' Bob told Marty.

'You!' Bob exclaimed, pointing his finger at me. 'You know what you are? You're a genius.'

'There is one problem with the song,' Tony said. 'We need to have something about Slauson Avenue. The Slauson is going to be the next big dance craze—bigger than the Twist.'

So I inserted the phrase 'Slauson Avenue' into the song as many times as I could. The genius of Sepe, Brooks, and Krasnow was getting Jack Nitzsche as an arranger and an African American singer from Slauson Avenue they called Round Robin. Jack asked me to play lead acoustic guitar and built the session around my playing, which created waves with the musicians, in particular Tommy Tedesco, a well-known session guitarist, who didn't like following a seventeen-year-old who had little experience in the studio. This was for professionals! Jack told the musicians to follow my lead and Tommy didn't like it.

'Hey kid, do we modulate up for the second part of the song?'

'I don't know,' I said. 'I don't read music.'

Tommy walked into the booth and shouted at Jack. 'You've got to be out of your mind if you think I'm going to follow a kid who can't even read music and is threatening to take the food off of my family's table.'

'You'll play on this date or you'll never work for Phil Spector again,' Jack said. And that was that.

Tommy sat down in his chair and played. Darlene Love sang gospel replies to Robin's vocals, and the Crystals sang backup harmonies. Round Robin performed the song on Dick Clark's *American Bandstand* on May 30 1964, and it spent eight weeks in the Top 100. Domain had their start, Screen Gems-Columbia published the song, and I had my first hit record.

Sepe, Brooks, and Krasnow built on that record and came out with several more Slauson dance hits, including a song called 'Pied Piper Man,' which I wrote for Lloyd Thaxton, who had an afternoon dance show filmed in Los Angeles and syndicated across America. Thaxton signed with Domain because of how much he dug 'Kick That Little Foot Sally Ann.'

Later that same year, Bob Krasnow took over Loma Records. He then started Blue Thumb Records, where he signed Dave Mason, and eventually became the chairman of Warner-Elektra-Atlantic. From humble beginnings, Tony Sepe went on to produce and write many disco records in the 70s. Martin Brooks joined Tony for several of these songs, most notably 'Baby Blues,' which was co-written and performed by Barry White. These two guys, who seemed to be the very antithesis of soul, put Slauson Avenue on the soul map of the world. To this day, when music fans come to LA, they head over to Slauson Avenue to catch a little of the magic created by the boys at Domain Records.

CHAPTER FOUR

SUMMER MEANS FUN

And if that pretty little girl from across the street
Who's been botherin' me for days
To go swimmin' in her pool, well her pool's real cool
But it hasn't got ten foot waves …

Gidget was published in 1959. It was the story of a young girl who hung out on the beach with her cool pals. Her father listened to her stories after she returned from the beach and turned them into the book. Darrilyn Zanuck was the daughter of the Hollywood monarch Daryl Zanuck. As the story goes, Kathy Kohner, who was the real Gidget, was watching Darrylyn surfing and fantasized about being her, as Darrilyn was a bit older. Some attribute the character of Gidget to Darrilyn, others to Kathy. In any case, *Gidget* knocked Jack Kerouac off the No. 1 spot on the *New York Times* Bestsellers List and surf trumped beat. The book was then made into a movie starring James Darren, Sandra Dee, and Cliff Robertson. By 1962, on the strength of the movie, surf music—along with mass-produced surf boards and the energy of the beach—had drawn an entire generation bopping to the shore to ride the wild surf.

'Surf City' is the song that romanticized the surf culture for the world. Written by Brian Wilson and Jan Berry and performed by Jan & Dean, it put all three on the world stage. Everything from then on flowed from the energy of that No. 1 song. Surf Music became bankable.

'I don't know why it's so amazing that people would notice the ocean and begin to write songs about it,' my friend Bob Burchman once told me. Bob and I were pals in junior high, along with a girl named Barbara Charren, who went by the name Babs. Babs later married Dennis Wilson, and Bob wound up writing a song with Dennis that appeared on The Beach Boys' *Sunflower* album.

The action at the center of this vortex of surf music was taking place at Western/United Recorders on Sunset Boulevard, east of Vine, in Studio Three, where the Beach Boys recorded, and Studio A (aka 'the big studio'), where Jan and Dean were, a half-block away. We were all running back and forth from studio to studio, listening to new song ideas, giving each other feedback, and trying out new ideas. Jan, Dean, Bruce Johnston, Terry Melcher, Roger Christian, Don Altfeld, Gary Usher, and Brian Wilson were the genius innovators of this new sound.

When Jan's original backing group The Matadors split up after the release of 'Honolulu Lulu,' Lou told Jan not to worry: Steve and I were doing beautiful harmonies together, he said, and we could fill this melodious void. Jan was already used to not paying much money to his group for long hours of hard work, and Adler assured him that we would do it for less. The carrot on the stick was that we might get a song on a Jan & Dean album.

The first Jan & Dean song we worked on was the 1963 single 'Drag City.' We worked long hours for days on end to get the harmonies Jan required. I was thrilled to be working with these stars, but Steve wasn't so thrilled because he needed to make a living. The kicker came when Jan asked me to sing over Dean's falsetto part. At first it was merely to double it, like Brian had done on 'Surf City,' but then he removed Dean's part completely. As a fan, I really loved Dean's falsettos, so I felt uncomfortable about it.

Adler discovered that he could sell Steve and me in various ways, including as a made-up surf group he called The Rincon Surf Band. We cut a sing-along album, singing all of harmonies to the Jan & Dean and Beach Boys songs without the lead vocals. I played the vocal lines on my guitar. People were amazed at how good we sounded, and that gave Adler the idea to do an album with us as a new surf group that he would market—but this time he would get the publishing rights as well, because it was all in-house.

Adler had connections to Liberty/Imperial through Jan & Dean, and later through Johnny Rivers. I loved Imperial. It was the home of Fats Domino and Ricky Nelson. Adler set up a deal with the Skaff brothers to receive $15,000 in return for an album by a new surf group called The Baggys. He told the Skaff brothers that he had two guys doing backup for Jan & Dean, that everyone liked their voices—and that they also wrote and produced their own material.

Adler had no trouble selling them on the idea. I didn't know that we were just being set up again for a production-money deal—easy money for Adler, and very little for us. I called up my high school friends Jerry Cargman and Bobby Myman, believing that we would be an actual group and might become successful. Jerry was learning bass and Bob was already playing drums. Steve handled the percussion.

Writing the songs and recording them was a big commitment. I got to play all the guitar, piano, and organ parts and arrange the songs and harmonies. Most of the lyrics—cool little colorful phrases—came from *Surf* magazines. I loved to bodysurf and spent as much time as I could around the ocean. Chuck Britz, Brian Wilson's engineer, made the mixing easy. We shot an album cover with the great photographer Guy Webster, and we were off to the races. When the Stones came to LA to do their first gigs, Adler met with their manager, Andrew Oldham—to whom I had been introduced a few months earlier—and played The Baggys' album for him, Mick, and Keith. 'That's fantastic!' Mick said, which is how we became The Fantastic Baggys.

'Tell 'Em I'm Surfin'' was released as a single and went to No. 1 in Hawaii, Indonesia, Australia, and all of the surfing countries around the world. In Los Angeles it was played like an anthem. But this was Lou Adler's worse nightmare. Adler had told us there would be no live or TV appearances. We were in-house staff writers with Screen Gems Music, and that's where he wanted us to stay. It was hard to accept. Steve and I did talk about leaving at that point, but whatever little money we were making at the time was enough motivation for us to stay put.

I felt sorry for Steve—I knew he really wanted The Fantastic Baggys to work because it was a possible fulfillment of his dream of being a recording star. Needless to say, Jerry and Bob Myman were deeply disappointed. But I had the time of my life creating those Baggys songs—being in the studio, creating songs from scratch, and turning them into completed projects of which I could feel proud.

Terry Melcher began recording almost every song from the Baggys album and turning them into Bruce & Terry records. 'Summer Means Fun,' 'Big Gun Board,' 'This Little Woody,' 'Wah Wahini,' and 'One Piece Topless Bathing Suit' all made the charts. Coincidentally, Steve's former partner Carol Connors was just hitting it big with her 'Three Window Coupe' for Terry's Rip Chords. And I was getting the opportunity to play lead guitar on the Bruce & Terry records—while also getting union scale for the gigs.

I started to establish a working relationship with Terry. He had got his start producing for Columbia because of his mother, Doris Day. His stepfather, Marty Melcher, had gotten rid of Mart/Arwin and given Doris to Columbia with a long-term contract that came with one stipulation: you want Doris Day, the biggest star in America, you take Terry as part of the package.

Terry was a cool and sexy-looking guy. He was a wealthy, fun-loving playboy in his twenties, and a part of the in-crowd, but he was deadly earnest about his work. Columbia, strangely enough, was not interested in pop music at all. The label wasn't interested in folk or blues either. They had Billie Holiday, who they didn't want, and Bob Dylan, who they were trying to figure out how to dump. They were just happy with acts like Mitch Miller, Tony Bennett, and Rosemary Clooney. It was known as a very classy label. You didn't put out surf records—even if they were hits—and expect Columbia to be happy. They didn't like Terry much, but they had to lump it, because of Doris.

COWABUNGA DREAMIN'

The Million Dollar Party was to be a concert promoted by K-POI, the No. 1 radio station in Oahu, Hawaii. Jan & Dean were going to headline along with The Beach Boys, and I was asked to play guitar for Jan with Glen Campbell on bass and Hal Blaine on drums. Jimmy Clanton, Ray Peterson, The Kingsmen, The Rivingtons, Jody Miller, Bruce & Terry, Jimmy Griffen, Mary Saenz, and Peter & Gordon all made the trip to Hawaii in early 1964. I told my mother about this event and invited her to join the fun. She had never been to Hawaii, and I thought it might be a real thrill for her.

'Tell 'Em I'm Surfin'' was No. 1 in Hawaii when we arrived and The Fantastic Baggys were all over the radio waves. Not only that but the entire album was being played on air. It truly was a surfer boy's dream come true—although not quite a dream come true because the Baggys were not allowed to play. Adler didn't want to lose us to the road. Terry Melcher got a big kick out of our record being played all over the place, but Jan, who was used to being the center of attention, didn't find it amusing.

I was first and foremost a fan. To me, all of the folks on the tour were authentic recording stars; just a few years earlier, I had been trading their records on the floor with Jerry Cargman. Originally, I was set to play guitar, but since Glen Campbell decided that he wanted to do that lead, I was told that I wouldn't be able to participate. Al 'Papa Oom Mow Mow' Frazier of The Rivingtons suggested I play bass instead. I had never played it before but I figured I could do it.

During one of the breaks at rehearsals, I was accidentally locked out of the arena. I didn't have any way to get back in. I waited at the side door, figuring somebody would miss me and come looking for me, but that didn't happen. Forty-five minutes later, Carl Wilson of The Beach Boys, who I would see at Western Recorders all the time, approached the door.

'Carl!' I called out, relieved.

'Yeah?'

'I'm locked out,' I said. 'I need to get back in.'

'What do you do?' he asked.

Carl had changed. There was anger on his face. He seemed to be different, arrogant and aloof.

'Do I know you?' he asked.

'What are you talking about?'

'I don't know you.'

'I'm Phil Sloan, Carl.'

Carl didn't look drunk but he had to be high on something. He banged on the door, and a Hawaiian security guard opened it. I started to walk in with Carl and the security guard stopped me.

'I'm with the band,' I said.

'He's not with my band,' Carl said.

Carl went in and the door closed behind him, locking me out.

I didn't pound and pound on the door. I suddenly felt really embarrassed. It was a feeling of not being part of the gang—like I wasn't authentic. I wanted to throw myself into one of those Hawaiian volcanoes and disappear forever. I had that feeling of being an outsider again. My song was all over the airwaves, but I was still an outsider.

Finally—and I would like to believe after Carl had come to his senses—Tom Moffitt, the promoter of the show, came out and got me.

'Where have you been, Phil?'

'I've been right here.'

'I was worried about you.'

That was the best thing anyone could have said to me at that moment. I went in and got a little rehearsal time.

I played bass for the entire concert except The Beach Boys' part, and man, did my fingers bleed. Al Frazier, bless his heart, could see that I was in pain—the blood was pouring out of my fingers—so he handed me a handkerchief to soak it up. I kept on playing, having the time of my life. I had to show them—I had to show them I was just as good as they were. Fortunately, I knew every song by heart, so I did the job and I did it well. It was my first time playing in a major venue, and watching the performers perform and seeing the audience react to them from this unique vantage point—even though I was in pain—I felt elated.

The morning after the show, a lot of the performers left for home, but I headed to the Big Island and Black Sand Beach with my mother and Al Frazier. The three of us were lying on the volcanic sand. I hadn't ever seen my mother so happy. If I had been able to sing 'Tell 'Em I'm Surfin'' with my mother in the audience, that would have been it for me. The payoff was that I saw my mother serene for the first time in my life, and I was grateful for that.

YOU ONLY GET INTERESTED IN YOUR WIFE WHEN SOMEBODY ELSE IS

In 1964, Bobby Darin was at the zenith of his career as a superstar and heir apparent to Frank Sinatra. He was smart and a savvy businessman, too. He was going to perform at the Coconut Grove, a famous nightclub on Wilshire Boulevard, and Terry Melcher invited Lou Adler and me as his guests for the opening night. Adler got the impression that Darin wanted to meet with him. Bobby was married to Sandra Dee. Lou Adler was married to Shelley Fabares. It was a natural hookup, since they had each married one of America's sweethearts.

Adler's desire was to sign Bobby Darin to Dunhill Productions and become his record producer. Darin was on Atco, a subsidiary of Atlantic, and was doing very well. From the moment Adler told me about the upcoming show, he was ecstatic. For days he kept going on about how it he was sure he could snag Darin, and what a coup that was going to be.

We drove over to the Coconut Grove in Adler's Jag. I had never really been truly alone with him. The time we spent together was always at the office or the studio, or at his apartment once, but this was the first time I was ever on a social outing.

The thing about Lou was he always gave you the impression that he was larger than life. That's why people felt good and important when around him. After the show, Lou and I were escorted backstage. Terry Melcher greeted us as we walked back and immediately moved us right over to Darin, who was standing in the middle of the room with dozens of people, glowing from just having given a double-encore performance, his tuxedo shirt wet and unbuttoned. Only now there was a bigger personality in the room. Adler was convinced that this was going to be the night that would make his Dunhill Productions legitimate, without question, and so he greeted Bobby warmly.

Darin ushered us into his private dressing room. Terry then

introduced me to Bobby, who gave me a big hug. Adler had no idea that Terry Melcher had set this whole thing up, at Darin's request, for him to meet me, not Lou. From that moment on, Darin did not show any sign of interest whatsoever in Adler, even though I sensed that he was waiting to hear comments like, *Lou, I've followed your career with great interest from your days of writing with Herbie for Sam Cooke. And now you're starting this great new production venture. And here we are, both married to the most sought-after girls in America. How can I make this happen?*

Instead, Bobby talked me up about writing these great new surf songs he said he loved.

'I've been wanting to tell you that I listen to the Fantastic Baggys album all the time,' he said. 'I consider you to be up there with Jan and Terry and Brian Wilson. I would like to talk to you about joining Terry and me in my new publishing company, TM music. You don't have to give me an answer right now, but I do want you to consider it.'

In a normal business situation, the Baggys' pipeline of songs should have gone to Jan & Dean, since we were all under the same roof. Instead, it was feeding Jan's competition, and gave Terry all the bragging rights. This wasn't about business, though. This was about beating Adler at his own game. Terry liked Lou and Lou liked Terry, but there was a sort of sibling rivalry between them. Terry enjoyed the sport of sticking it to Lou, but Adler found no joy in being beaten at anything.

Lou Adler's excitement turned into just wanting to get out of there as soon as possible. Bobby excused himself to be with his guests and invited us to stay for the after-party, but Lou told him we had to leave. The ride home was deathly quiet. Adler dropped me off at my car.

'Lou. I've been offered this opportunity. Don't you think it would be a good move for me to take advantage of it? I know I get under your skin.'

'No, I don't.'

'Why?'

I wanted to believe that he really had my best interest at heart. Surely he would offer me sage advice.

'You only get interested in your wife when someone else is,' he said, and then he took off driving up Palms Avenue.

BAGGYS POSTSCRIPT

Jerry, now known as Jered, became a successful entrepreneur and businessman. He married his high school sweetheart, Donna Loren, a music star in many of the Frankie and Annette beach movies, and the first and only Dr. Pepper Girl. We are close friends to this day.

Bob Myman became a successful entertainment lawyer and formed a TV and movie production company with the great actor John Ritter called Adam Productions. Bob told me that at his lowest point in life, while in Canada, he walked into a record store and saw an enormous poster of The Fantastic Baggys. Somebody recognized him as one of them, and in twenty minutes, after various phone calls had been made, he was surrounded by loving fans. He considers this strange event to have been a turning point in his life.

CHAPTER FIVE

A KALEIDOSCOPIC EVENT

The TAMI Show ('Teen Age Music International') was filmed over two days at the Santa Monica Civic Center and featured performances by The Rolling Stones, Chuck Berry, The Beach Boys, Jan & Dean, The Barbarians, Marvin Gaye, The Supremes, Leslie Gore, Gerry & The Pacemakers, Billy J. Kramer & The Dakotas, and James Brown. This was the show in which James Brown electrified the world with a performance never before seen by a white middle-class audience. According to the producer Rick Rubin, it was the greatest single performance of an artist ever captured on film—eighteen minutes of pure soul dynamite. Mick Jagger, to this day, is adamant about Brown being responsible for influencing his dancing style, while Keith Richards refers to the show as a kaleidoscopic event.

My job was to write a theme song for the show. A competition had been set up, with many other writers participating for the prize. I was handed a sheet of paper with a list of the performers' names and from where they originated. It was a simple song and it didn't take much thought or introspection. It was basically a fact sheet set to music, but the chorus had a kick to it and it excited me. I called it 'Here They Come From All Over The World.' I played it on guitar for Adler and the film's producers, William Sargent and Steve Binder, and the musical director, Jack Nitzsche. They loved it and asked me to demo it. The producers then coerced Adler to convince Jan & Dean that they had to sing the song, as they were slated to be the hosts of the show. Adler really didn't want them to record the song—maybe because he was not ready to hand me a hit with his Jan & Dean.

We recorded the song at United Recorders. Steve, Jan, and I sang the background harmonies as usual, including what should have been Dean's falsetto part. I played lead guitar, which was unusual because I had never played guitar on their records. Everybody in the studio—Hal Blaine, Carol Kaye, Joe Osborne, Ray Pohlman, Bill Pitman, Leon Russell, Tommy Tedesco, and Glen Campbell—seemed happy for me. I was finally getting a shot at some money.

During the filming of *The T.A.M.I. Show*, every performer sang live except for Jan & Dean—the reason being that Jan did not want Dean singing falsetto live. Again, I can't tell you why, as Dean's falsettos were so good. My falsetto parts on 'From All Over The World,' 'Sidewalk Surfin',' and 'Little Old Lady From Pasadena' were pre-recorded; Dean lip-synched to tape. The skateboard bit was probably set up so that Dean did not have to be anywhere near a microphone.

Of course, I was looking forward to the show but Adler refused to let me go to the taping. I suspect he didn't want me rubbing elbows with Jagger and getting the wrong idea that I was somebody.

The film came out and it was a smash hit. Radio stations all over the country were clamoring for the theme song, and Adler was forced by Liberty Records to release it as a single. And that, to Adler's dismay, was how I wrote my first hit song for Jan & Dean, and how I was able to buy a 1965 Corvette Stingray—just like Jan's.

I felt like I was finally beginning to be part of the club. It was then that I heard a voice inside myself. *You are here to witness*, the voice said. *You cannot belong.* The voice had authority, and it frightened me. I couldn't begin to understand the implications of what this meant. So I dismissed it, and I continued trying to belong.

THE HITMEN

The engineers and second engineers are the unsung heroes of the recording world. Their science has become an art form. These are the men and women who knew how to get the best sound from every instrument and the room. The sound that Phil Spector is celebrated for having created—the so-called Wall of Sound—actually came from Larry

Levine, second engineer at Gold Star Studios. Larry set up one mic in the middle of the room so all of the sound could leak into it. It was all allowed to stew together, without separation, and was then put through an echo chamber, creating an enormous sound.

The engineers knew EQ (or equalization). They knew where to add treble or highs, and where to take off or add bass or lows or *chunka chunkas*—musician lingo for a two-four backbeat—which can make all the difference in the world to the ultimate sound of what we hear on a record.

Lanky Linstrot, Bones Howe, Chuck Britz, and Henry Louie were the sound engineers of the Wrecking Crew. Lanky had engineered Frank Sinatra, Ella Fitzgerald, Sammy Davis, Dean Martin, and all of the greats, and was recognized as the number one engineer in the city. Bones was under Lanky. According to union rules, there had to be a second engineer at a recording session. The second engineer was basically responsible for pressing buttons. But Lanky and Bones changed all of that. They became co-engineers and trusted each other's instincts.

Bones was the second engineer for Lanky on all of the Jan & Dean records I worked on. He was more approachable than Lanky. When you asked Lanky to do something unusual, he would generally say that it couldn't, wouldn't, and will never be done. But Bones always liked to say, with a smile, 'Yeah, there's a way we could do that.' And when you heard Bones say that, you knew that you were about to be part of a magic show. Bones would work all day and into the night to help Jan get the sound he was looking for, and when you were dealing with Jan, it was out of love and dedication mostly, because there was very little pay, if any.

In the early 60s, when a song was recorded, one limiter was generally used. A limiter is a sound compressor that makes it possible to limit the impact of a frequency and move one instrument back without losing volume so that another instrument can be heard more evenly. This technique was used primarily for brass instruments, which would dominate the track. Jan had a wall of limiters, thereby making it possible to create a fuller sound that allowed him to keep the track fresh and even without losing the volume or attack of the instruments being added. With so many limiters, there was no restriction to what Jan could add to the track—two sets of drums, four guitars, two pianos, horns, harpsichords, overdubbed background singers. The result was a song like 'Little Old Lady From Pasadena.' Bones Howe was the guy who put all of that together. Lanky wasn't crazy about limiters and thought it was a bit much, but Bones was open to Jan's vision and made it happen. (You can't blame Lanky. He was used to working with live orchestras without overdubs.)

Bones would eventually leave the Dunhill orbit scarred and damaged like nearly everyone else who worked for the company. But when he struck out on his own to become a record producer, he was wildly successful. He went on to produce The Turtles, The Association, The Fifth Dimension, The Monkees, and Tom Waits, as well as racking up many movie credits.

Chuck Britz sported a buzz cut even as the artists continued to allow their hair to grow. He was like a kindly drill sergeant or astronaut. As long as you kept your hands off the board and the dials, he was happy. In later years that would become impossible, and he would sit in his chair like the head of an asylum for the criminally insane while the patients played with his machinery. He was so very likable, and taught so many artists the tricks of the engineering trade. In the end he put himself out of business because of that. He recorded The Beach Boys, The Grass Roots, Barry McGuire, Three Dog Night—hundreds and hundreds of famous recordings.

Henry Louie was a second engineer at many late-night sessions when it was impossible to get anyone to work. Always quiet and invisible, he worked his magic. He became a very successful record producer as well.

Hal Blaine got his start in drumming, working for Tommy Sands in Las Vegas. He eventually found his way into the studios of Los Angeles and became the most celebrated studio drummer in music history. Hal would always tell me, in a very soft, gentle soothing voice, 'Don't be excited, don't get crazy. Take your time … relax … tell me what you're thinking and I will make it happen.'

Hal became great friends with my mother for a time while his second and third marriages were failing. She would visit him at his home in the Hollywood Hills, giving him Jewish motherly advice on relationships. Considering she had no interest in my involvement in the music business, I found it humorous that she started giving professional and romantic advice to Hal, and later to Phil Ochs. Hal used to call me Flip, but then Phil as I became more successful, and finally P.F., which he said with much relish and respect. And respect is what I had for Hal.

Joe Osborne was the superman of the bass disguised as a mild-mannered reporter. He was quiet and slow to laugh or show any emotion. Hal was always trying to make him laugh: 'Hey, Joe, did you hear the one about the optimistic clarinet player who hired a message service?' Nothing.

I once asked Joe how many times he changed his strings. 'Once, nine years ago,' he said. Joe only played a Fender bass, and he played with the treble up, which cut through everything. You would play Joe a song and immediately he would come up with a riff far better than anything you had imagined. And he did that on hundreds of hit records. Joe was most famous for being Ricky Nelson's bass player—he played on all of his hits and became the most successful bass player in pop history. He played with Johnny Rivers at the Whisky A Go-Go and recorded on all of his hits as well.

I was fifteen when I met Leon Russell, and even then his hair was starting to turn white. He had a great Southern drawl, and the word 'Flip' became two syllables—'Hi-ya, Fli-ip.' Leon could turn the most banal song into a concerto masterpiece or a swamp boogie. He had so many different styles at his command. Leon could find a groove to your song that in your wildest dreams you could not have hoped for.

In his early years, Leon became famous for playing octave notes on his left hand, and he would hit key phrases in octaves that emphasized the melodies. He was easygoing, supportive, and 100 percent present. He would stay after a session for free if you needed more. He started his own label, Shelter Records, and became a master songwriter, artist, and arranger. Today, he is in the Hall of Fame where he belongs—thanks in part to the efforts of Sir Elton John.

Glen Campbell didn't read music. He didn't need to. He was a 'feel' player, and he had liquid fingers. They would fly over the neck of the guitar and bring hoots and hollers from all the cats in the studio. When I first met him, he was being groomed as a recording artist, but nobody really took it seriously. He was on most of the Jan & Dean records, and he was an integral part of the Wrecking Crew. He was an easygoing guy and liked to crack jokes, though he was still somewhat shy. He liked people, though, and people liked him.

Larry Knechtel was the utility infielder on the team. If you couldn't get Joe to play bass, you got Larry. If Hal Blaine needed a tambourine on the main track, Larry would play it. If Leon couldn't make it, Larry played piano. Larry is the guy who wrote the complete opening to 'Bridge Over Troubled Water' and made the song what it was. He did that for hundreds of songs. He became the go-to guy on piano and organ after Leon started to strike out on his own. He got that much respect. He was one of the geniuses of the Wrecking Crew, mild-mannered yet always ready to create something remarkable.

Tommy Tedesco played Spanish and electric guitar—mostly a Fender Telecaster. There were very few musicians who played the Tele at that time; James Burton, Ricky Nelson's guitarist, was the most famous of them. If you were going to play an electric guitar and you weren't going to buy a Gibson because they were too expensive, and since Epiphones didn't become available in the United States until The Beatles made them famous, you had two choices: the Stratocaster, which Buddy Holly made famous, or the Telecaster, which was out of the reach of most young musicians. A Telecaster has a unique sound—far different than the Stratocaster, like the difference between a Chevy Malibu and a Corvette. When you hear a Telecaster, your ears hone in on it. It is a much more metallic sound. And man, Tommy Tedesco could play that Telecaster.

Carol Kaye was a brilliant and creative bass and guitar player. She was the only woman in the Wrecking Crew. Keep in mind that the jokes were usually 'blue' but Carol never had a problem with them. She was hard to get hold of because she was so busy working on major sessions— Frank Sinatra, Elvis Presley, Phil Spector—and then became attached to Brian Wilson and worked almost exclusively for him. I last worked with her in 2010. Frank Black, the writer, singer, and knock-down-dead guitarist of the Pixies, was in LA doing an album called *Fast Man-Raider Man* and hired me to play piano. He asked who I thought should play bass on a number of songs. 'Carol,' I told him. She was over seventy years old but had the energy of a woman of thirty. She was as innovative and brilliant as ever.

Don Randi played piano on all of the big Phil Spector sessions along with Leon Russell. But he also appeared on one of my very early Screen Gems sessions—for a song called 'You And Me And The Devil Makes Three'—and he was very encouraging to me.

There was also Bill Pitman on Dano electric bass and Ray Pohlman on bass. These guys were all so busy, but if you couldn't get one you got the other, and believe me these guys were *artists*. They were interchangeable without compromise of talent. Most of these musicians in the Wrecking Crew were of course eight-to-ten years older than me, but they weren't dismissive because of my age. They were embracing. These were beautiful people. And it was a gift to be able to work with them.

The crew would recommend me to producers if they were looking for a fresh new guitar player, and many of them hired me to play on their records. They helped me to get union wages and some much-needed respectability in the community of players.

THE DANCING DUNHILLS

Lou Adler called me into his office and told me he had decided to leave Screen Gems and start his own label and publishing company. He had already been experimenting with his own production company and now he was ready to make his move. Bobby Roberts and Pierre Cossette were partners in a management firm that handled Ann-Margret, Johnny Rivers, and Jan & Dean; they were going to join as partners. Jay Lasker would come in from Vee-Jay shortly thereafter. Adler wanted Steve and me to go along with him.

'Trust me when I tell you that, from now on, you are family. Great things will happen for you if you listen to me and do what I say,' Adler told me, while eating a corned beef sandwich from Greenblatt's. 'You are now part of the Dunhill family, and we are going to take care of you and Steve.'

I looked to these guys as the adults in the room. Steve was hesitant, because he wasn't earning enough to leave Norty's as yet. And though I was younger than Steve, I felt I needed to take care of him. He had a wife and a child. I liked to think of him as the older brother I never had. So I agreed to join Adler's new venture, believing the decision would benefit the both of us.

When anyone tells you that you are part of a family, go in the opposite direction. Bobby Roberts was formerly a tap-dancing hoofer in a trio known as The Flying Dunhills—that's how Dunhill Productions and Dunhill Records got its name. The first record they released was the sound of John Bubbles, a movie tap-dancing legend from the 1940s. Pierre Cossette was mostly invisible, but he was a decent man. He had morals and integrity. We didn't see much of him.

Trousdale, the chosen name for the publishing company, was the neighborhood in Beverly Hills, where Adler dreamed of living. Dunhill opened up shop at 449 South Beverly Drive. Lou had an office, Pierre had an office, Bobby had an office, and I had a cubbyhole in the back of the suites with a little upright piano.

Pierre invited me to breakfast one morning over at a little coffee shop on Beverly Drive.

'Phil, I like you a lot,' he told me. 'You present yourself in a professional manner and I think you have a hell of a lot of talent.'

'Thanks, Pierre.'

'This is a dirty business, Phil. I've been in management for a long time but I can see that the music business is cutthroat and I don't want to see you get hurt.'

'I understand. Can I count on *you?*'

'You can count on me but I don't know how long I'm going to be around.'

Pierre was telling me something that I couldn't quite wrap my head around. In hindsight, I think he was communicating that there was no room for decency and forthrightness at Dunhill—and if that were the case, he wouldn't be sticking around.

The word around town was that we, at Dunhill, were having fun. It wasn't your typical record label. There was a vacant lot across the street where we would play wiffle ball every day in the early afternoon. The players often included Brian Wilson, Jan Berry, Dean Torrance, Lou Adler, myself, and any visitors to Dunhill, like Phil Skaff or Bones Howe or Hal Blaine. Everyone was playing it very loose, waiting for opportunity to knock. The first knock at the door was Terry Black.

Terry Black became the Canadian Elvis, a teenage idol, screamed at and pawed at by teens all over the great country of Canada. Canada was much like England: until Terry happened, it was mostly just American music being played on radio. Terry and his manager Buddy Clyde came to Dunhill on the strength of having a home recording of the Gospel song 'Dry Bones' that had made it onto the charts in Canada. Terry was sixteen, handsome, and shy, with a wispy voice; Dunhill dug him and signed him. Steve and I were told to write for Terry and produce a record for him.

The first record we did with him was a song I wrote when I was sixteen, with Elvis in mind, called 'Unless You Care.'

Don't ever say you'll love me
Because it would be too much to bare …
Unless you care, uh huh-huh
Unless you care …
And don't put me up in heaven
If I don't belong up there
Unless you care …

The session had Glen Campbell playing an electric twelve-string, and for the instrumental, he did a send-up of the theme song from *The Blob*, a hit drive-in classic that starred a young Steve McQueen. I played my Sovereign acoustic six-string. Hal played drums and Joe Osborne was on bass.

Fantastically, the song broke into the Canadian market at No. 1 and stayed there for weeks. And just as had happened with Elvis, the DJs then turned the record over, and the B-side became a No. 1 hit as well—a song I'd co-written with Steve called 'Can't We Go Somewhere.' Canada had its own star!

Vee-Jay got into the act and became the distributor for Arc Records in the US. The company then decided to start an offshoot label called Tollie just for Terry Black. Vee-Jay also had the rights to release various Beatles masters (via the demos I had heard) but since 'Love Me Do' had failed, the label didn't really know what to do with the Fab Four. They were thinking of passing on any future releases by the band.

Lasker, the head of Vee-Jay at the time, figured that since Canadians were part of the British Empire, maybe *they* would understand The Beatles, since the group had been making hit records in the UK since 1962. So Terry and The Beatles became labelmates. I wanted to get Terry away from the Elvis vibe and began writing Beatles-like songs for him, as I had been aware of the group's genius for writing and sound ever since I opened that package from Brian Epstein.

Contrary to popular belief, The Beatles hit accidentally. Capitol Records had no interest in the band but was forced to release the records due to a contractual agreement with EMI, its sister company in Britain. 'I Want To Hold Your Hand' was only being played in the secondary markets in the United States—little radio stations that had no access to the big stars on Capitol like Vic Damone, Nat 'King' Cole, and Frank Sinatra. That excitement caused Capitol Records to sit up and take notice.

After 'I Want To Hold Your Hand' became a hit, every song by The Beatles that Vee-Jay owned became a mega-hit, including 'Love Me Do,' 'Please, Please Me,' and 'From Me To You.' Vee-Jay started to implode with success, going down in flames because everybody was robbing each other blind. None of them had ever seen money roll in like that. With money in his pocket, Lasker left Vee-Jay and bought himself a sweet partnership at Dunhill.

Terry Black's second record, 'Everyone Can Tell' / 'Say It Again,' became his second double-sided No. 1 hit. By the time of his third and fourth hits, 'Little Liar' and 'Kisses For My Baby,' which we wrote and produced, Adler had pushed Steve and me aside and took over as Terry's producer. Adler's production of 'Only Sixteen' (the Sam Cooke hit) and 'Poor Little Fool' didn't do well; in my opinion, the songs were too slickly produced.

Jay Lasker did not have any sense of loyalty or gratitude. I brought him The Beatles, and Terry—because of his hits and through Tollie—helped to usher The Beatles into the world. This made Lasker rich, and he didn't care. He was one coldhearted, greedy son of a bitch.

CHAPTER SIX

THE NIGHT THAT CHANGED MY LIFE

By late 1964, I had already written 'Eve Of Destruction,' 'The Sins Of A Family,' 'This Mornin',' 'Ain't No Way I'm Gonna Change My Mind,' and 'What's Exactly The Matter With Me?' They all arrived on one cataclysmic evening, and nearly at the same time, as I worked on the lyrics almost simultaneously.

'Eve Of Destruction' came about from hearing a voice, perhaps an angel's. The voice instructed me to place five pieces of paper and spread them out on my bed. I obeyed the voice.

The voice told me that the first song would be called 'Eve Of Destruction,' so I wrote the title at the top of the page. For the next few hours, the voice came and went as I was writing the lyric, as if this spirit—or whatever it was—stood over me like a teacher: 'No, no … not *think of all the hate there is in Red Russia … Red China!*'

I didn't understand. I thought the Soviet Union was the mortal threat to America, but the voice went on to reveal to me the future of the world until 2024. I was told the Soviet Union would fall, and that Red China would continue to be communist far into the future, but that communism was not going to be allowed to take over this Divine Planet—therefore, *think of all the hate there is in Red China.*

I argued and wrestled with the voice for hours, until I was exhausted but satisfied inside with my plea to God to either take me out of the world, as I could not live in such a hypocritical society, or to show me a way to make things better. When I was writing 'Eve,' I was on my hands and knees, pleading for an answer—praying my guts out for understanding.

The eastern world, it is explodin'
Violence flarin', bullets loadin'
You're old enough to kill but not for votin'
You don't believe in war but what's that gun you're totin'
And even the Jordan River has bodies floatin'

But you tell me
Over and over again, my friend
You don't believe
We're on the eve
Of destruction

Don't you understand what I'm tryin' to say
Can't you feel the fears I'm feelin' today?
If the button is pushed, there's no runnin' away
There'll be no one to save with the world in a grave
Take a look around ya, boy
It's bound to scare ya, boy

But you tell me
Over and over again, my friend
You don't believe
We're on the eve
Of destruction

My blood get so mad, feels like coagulatin'
I'm sittin' here just contemplatin'
They can't twist the truth, it knows no regulation
Like a handful of senators can't pass legislation
And marches alone can't bring integration
When human respect is disintegratin'
This whole crazy world is just too frustratin'

And you tell me
Over and over again, my friend
You don't believe
We're on the eve
Of destruction

Think of all the hate there is in Red China
Then take a look around to Selma, Alabama
You may leave here for four days in space
But when you return, it's the same old place
The poundin' of the drums, the pride and disgrace
You can bury your dead, but don't leave a trace
Hate your next-door neighbor but don't forget to say grace

And tell me over and over and over again, my friend
You don't believe
We're on the eve
Of destruction
No no, you don't believe
We're on the eve
Of destruction

'The Sins Of A Family' was a song about Barbara, my first cousin—her mother was my father's sister. Her father, Harry, had been an ensign in the navy during World War II and went through some pretty horrific action. His war experiences caused him to suffer from post-traumatic stress disorder, which went undiagnosed in those days, and Harry found refuge from his pain in a bottle. To add to this difficulty, he wasn't earning as much money as the rest of the family, and this made him angry. He felt like less of a man and suffered from envy and resentment. And envy is not a pretty bird. Because of his drinking, money became tight. Barbara, who I dearly loved, resorted to giving sexual favors to men in order to pay for her schooling—books, clothes, and lunch money. For this, Barbara got a reputation as a wicked, immoral girl.

I started the song out with a joke: *She had a bad childhood when she was very young.* I thought that the subject was going to be so dark that I could distract the listener and keep them guessing what that first line meant while I got into the deeper and darker aspects of the song. By the time the listener realizes the depravity of the theme, it is too late—they are already caught in the maelstrom.

I was pleading with Heaven to allow me to make the best possible case to explain why someone I loved was doing what she was doing. I believed it was wrong for people to quickly pass judgment on her without understanding the situation. Throughout the ages, it has been said that the sins of the father are passed to the sons—generational curses. In my world, the daughters were equally vulnerable.

I didn't know or even care that this was the last thing America wanted to hear at this time. I wasn't trying to write a commercial song; I was merely writing from my heart and conscience. I was making a case for somebody I loved.

She had a bad childhood
When she was very young
So don't judge her too badly
She had a schizophrenic mother
Who worked in the gutter
Would have sold herself
To the devil gladly

What a sad environment
A bug-ridden tenement
And when they couldn't pay the rent
It was 'cause her father was out
Getting liquored
Oh, the stone's been cast
And blood's thicker than water
And the sins of the family fall on the daughter
The sins of the family fall on the daughter

At the age of sixteen she had been around more
Than any girl over thirty
And the high IQs who condemned her
Knew she was a product of poor heredity
It's a fictitious fact when you fall on your back
You can backtrack failure with inspection without exception
The sins of the family fall on the daughter
The sins of the family fall on the daughter

Oh the devil is open to all of us
Heaven selects just a precious few
And it takes an inside pull to get Gabriel to make an angel out of you
One can't live a lie then expect to die
With a soul in paradise
You know you gotta pay the price
Like you oughta
Blood's thicker than water
And the sins of the family fall on the daughter
The sins of the family fall on the daughter

'This Mornin'' was the result of what seemed like a visitation from an angelic Irish spirit. As I was writing the lyric, I heard and felt an Irish lilt to the words and marveled at it, as well as the positivity and insights of the verses. These lines made me aware of only seeming to exist— not really existing—and that life in the world is going to be continually plunged into sorrow: a constant world of worry that we can only bear by finding the light within and helping to change it without.

This spirit was saying to me that one day I will travel and learn the truth. That would happen for me in 1986, on my first of many visits to India to see Sathya Sai Baba. 'This Mornin'' told me that I had awoken to find I was no longer Phil Sloan. It was like the death of a teenaged Phil Sloan and the birth of P.F. Sloan in one song. But I was not through yet with this long, soul-searching night. The spirit told me to continue to write.

Up every morning
In time to see sun's dawnin'
Your body it is yawnin'
And yearin' for more sleep
The problems that have kept you
Awake all night I'll be you
Will disappear this mornin'
And forever they will keep
This mornin' they will keep

I seem to be existing
In a world that will not listen
Like a book with pages missin'
And just blots out the past
One may wake tomorrow
The world plunged in sorrow
Oh everyday I pray
This mornin' won't be my last
This mornin' won't be my last

Someday I will travel
To where life's mysteries unravel
To where questioning and wondering
Don't mean defiance of the law
I hope I get there quickly
Before I am too sickly
And awake one mornin'
To find I am no more
This mornin' I am no more

And so came 'What's Exactly The Matter With Me?' It was written in homage to Woody Guthrie, to whom I had been listening for years. And I was thrilled with the tongue-in-cheek sincerity and honesty of the song.

I didn't care to be a nonconformist—I just couldn't seem to conform like others were doing easily. And within two years, my generation would tune in and drop out.

Why do I deny all that's accepted true?
Why can't I live my life like I'm expected to?
Get a college degree, buy a color TV?
What's exactly the matter with me?

I believe no one's conclusions, I think for myself
I take nothing for granted, my brain ain't on a shelf
I've got my views, though I may sound missed and confused
Oh what's exactly the matter with me?

Why can't I settle down in one little place?
Find me a girl and get out of this race?
But my boots start itching, my eyes they start looking
Oh what's exactly the matter with me?

Why can't I march when the cause is just?
Stamp out oppression, greed and lust?
Oh, inferiority, pent-up hostility
Yeah, that's exactly the matter with me

Why do I 'yes' people that I despise?
Why can't I say 'I hate you' right to your eyes?
Oh, Inferiority, pent-up hostility
That's exactly the matter with me
That's exactly the matter with me

'Ain't No Way I'm Gonna Change My Mind' felt like comic relief to me. I believed in folk wisdom, and I believed in Woody Guthrie. I also believed in the young Bob Dylan, who without my knowing it was opening up my consciousness to what seemed like eternal wisdom.

Now there you go again, foolin' around again
You must think that this poor boy's blind
I've got some news for you
This time we're really through
Ain't no way I'm gonna change my mind

You've played around before so
What's one more guy or more but
I've taken all I'm gonna stand
I'm sick and tired of your lyin' and all your alibin'
Ain't no way I'm gonna change my mind

Maybe you'll believe me when I've left you far behind
I've given you your chances, I've listened to your answers
I think I've been more than kind
So don't start your kissin' up 'cause
Ain't no way I'm gonna change my mind

Don't get down on your knees and
Don't bother with your teasin'
This time I swear I just ain't buyin'
Maybe some other fool will find ya
Just close the door behind ya
There ain't no way I'm gonna change my mind

I had no idea what I was doing with this song. And I couldn't wait to get out of it, because it wasn't experiential. But when I got to the very last lines, I smiled and understood that the song was over, and it ended—for me—on a very tight note. The spirit that was writing the song saved it at the last two lines. And, to this day, I feel OK with the song.

When the lyrics were set I went into my parents' bedroom. It was late, and my father, who worked every day, was sleeping.

'Something wonderful has happened,' I told my mother, as I began reading her the first verse to 'Eve Of Destruction.'

'You'll wake your father,' she whispered. 'Read it to me tomorrow.'

The next morning, I put melodies to the five songs and sang them to myself over and over again. When I played them for Steve, he just threw up his hands.

'I hate that kind of shit!' he said.

After I played them for Adler, he made it clear to me that these songs were unpublishable and rebuked me for wasting his time and mine. Bob Dylan was still considered to be underground, even though he was very popular amongst folk aficionados. But I had been listening to his first album when I was in junior high school.

Adler did not see any future for the folk expression. He was still banking on surf music and girl songs. But the tide of that scene was going into ebb.

It was not until many months later—after Dylan's *Bringing It All Back Home* had gone Top 30—that Adler gave the go-ahead to do demos for these songs. Steve sat in the control booth as I played 'Eve Of Destruction' on guitar and harmonica. I saw him and Chuck Britz in the studio booth laughing and talking.

When I stopped singing, Steve asked, 'Are you done, yet?'

'Was it OK?' I wondered.

'Do the rest of the songs so we can get lunch.'

That session was the birth of *Songs Of Our Times*.

CHAPTER SEVEN

NIGHT OF THE IGUANAS

During the spring of 1965, Lou Adler, Bobby Roberts, and Jay Lasker were drinking in a hotel lounge in Ensenada, Mexico. The house band at the hotel was a local group of four guys playing pop songs. As the alcohol flowed, they figured, maybe for a laugh, that they could sell this foursome as the *Mexican Beatles*.

The drunk record executives offered the group a chance out of poverty and to become, perhaps, international stars, with all of the money and women they could handle. Dunhill worked out the immigration issues for the musicians, who duly arrived in Los Angeles with nothing but hope, some guitars, and no reason to believe they were about to be boiled in oil, rendered down to musician fat, and poured into the furnace of Dunhill.

The Iguanas, as they were now called, were introduced to Steve and me. They struck me as smart, polite young guys who were very scared and rightfully suspicious. None of them spoke English, so an interpreter was secured, though not a very good one. Adler told us that we were to make a record with them as soon as possible. Dunhill had stuck them in some motel down in Echo Park, and every morning a driver would deliver them to the office or the studio. I don't know what they were getting paid—or if they were getting paid at all.

Communication was sketchy at best with the leader, Roy, who understood some English but didn't speak it. I would play them the songs and they would sing them back phonetically. They were giving it their best while we were dancing on eggshells.

Over the course of working together every day for weeks we

naturally began to form a bond. The language barrier disappeared—we were speaking from our hearts to each other. I watched them daring to dream and I wanted the best for them. I wanted them to play their own instruments, but Adler refused. We recorded three new Beatles-esque songs that Steve and I had written for them—'Come And Get It From Me,' 'Don't Come Running To Me,' and 'Meet Me Tonight Little Girl'— as well as Lennon & McCartney's 'Michelle' and Paul Anka's 'Diana.' Roy put his lead vocals on the tracks, and the first record—'Don't Come Running To Me' b/w 'Come And Get It From Me'—was released within a week of our recording it.

The record was very well received in the Mexican communities of Los Angeles, in Baja, and as far away as Mexico City. Maybe Adler and his amigos had the right instincts. I was ecstatic for the guys in the band as they started to sell records and rise up the charts in Mexico. I envisioned them becoming heroes in their hometowns.

Unfortunately, no Anglo pop radio station would play the songs. The partners at Dunhill weren't satisfied with a Mexican hit record. They soon tired of their new toys and arranged for their 'deportation.' The Iguanas thought I had some power to help them stay, and I was able to postpone their departure for six months, by which time they had moved into friends' houses in East LA. In the end, though, brokenhearted and with no money coming in, The Iguanas went back to Mexico.

We kept in touch for a number of months, and they seemed to be getting better gigs at various hotels, which made me happy. I got an email a short time back from one of the children of The Iguanas, who wanted to know if any of it ever really happened. It did. They deserved better. I hope they found it.

MR. TERRY, THE TAMBOURINE MAN

The environment at Columbia Studios was not overly positive for anyone involved in rock or folk music. Terry Melcher was making hits with Bruce & Terry, The Rip Chords, Paul Revere & The Raiders, and soon he would make The Byrds his biggest group of all. But this was not the kind of music Columbia wanted to make. Columbia wasn't into teenage music but geared toward more contemporary adult sounds. The label had decided to dump Terry as a producer, and he knew it was only a matter of time.

Columbia had gotten The Byrds via a convoluted deal with World Pacific Records, a local label that was putting out jazz and early Ravi Shankar records. World Pacific was a classy independent label that didn't sell a lot of records but offered a home to jazz greats like Gerry Mulligan and Bud Shank. Jim Dickinson, who was managing The Byrds, was able to wrangle the band's contract from World Pacific. Given Columbia's lack of interest in rock and folk, though, he felt the best he could get would be a one-shot deal. And true, Columbia wasn't really interested in The Byrds, but agreed to release one single, pending approval of the recording.

Melcher had already submitted one version of 'Mr. Tambourine Man' for release but it had been rejected. He called me at about seven o'clock one evening and told me that he was going to be fired. He had only a few hours to find out what was wrong with his Byrds record and make it right. After that, he was finished.

Jim Dickinson was pushing Terry because he really believed in The Byrds, and Terry believed in Jim Dickinson. And Terry believed in the song itself. Why couldn't it work?

Every Columbia recording had to have a Columbia engineer present, and it seemed like they all had to be anally retentive (maybe that's where the 'A&R' comes from). As I met Terry in the studio control room, time was running out. We listened to 'Mr. Tambourine Man' play through the speakers but there was nothing about it that grabbed you. It sounded flat and lifeless.

'What's wrong with this?' Terry asked. 'What's wrong with this damn record?'

I knew the Bob Dylan song well and considered it one of his very best, even in this truncated version; the lyrics were hauntingly beautiful to me. We started talking about all of the records that we had made and loved and why we thought they worked: the Bruce & Terry records, The Baggys, Jan & Dean, The Beach Boys. We got onto 'Summer Means Fun' and the various versions of it, from the Baggys' to Bruce & Terry's, for which Terry put the song through a number of echo chambers that made my guitar solo pop to the forefront.

Terry asked the Columbia engineer if we could connect together all of the studio's echo chambers—a series of concrete rooms built under the floor of the main studio. The engineer didn't want to do any of that, believing Terry was a kid asking for the keys to his daddy's car.

'You need a written request for that,' he said, 'and another engineer as well.'

'Who's going to care?' Terry asked. 'Nobody's around.'

'I'm around,' the engineer said.

'Look,' Terry went on. 'I think I've got an idea to make this record work.'

'No,' the engineer, said.

Terry had a great sense of humor. I always liked being around him because you never knew when things were going to turn into chaos. He would get a little twinkle in his eye, and when you saw that twinkle you knew things were going to get good.

'Look,' Terry said. 'You know who I am, right?'

'Yeah, I know who you are. And it doesn't mean anything to me.'

'So you feel OK about pissing my mother off?'

'I don't care who your mother is. I've got a job to do, and that's all there is to it.'

'You think Doris Day doesn't mean anything at Columbia?'

'What are you talking about?'

'You didn't know that Doris Day was my mother? I didn't want to have to get into that, but I need access to the fucking echo chambers!'

'OK,' the engineer relented. 'Let me go talk to somebody.'

As the engineer left the studio and closed the door behind him, Terry rushed to the door and locked it. Then we pushed some amps in front of the door, barricading ourselves in the studio.

'All right, then,' Terry said. 'Let's get some damn work done. We're going to have to make this happen with what we have.'

'I think we can do it,' I said. 'How much time do we have?'

'I figure a little short of an hour before they kick us out.'

'Come on, Terry. They're not really going to kick you out, are they?'

'Phil. I'm the *son* of Doris Day … not Doris Day. We're wasting time.'

Terry went to work experimenting with reverb and echo on McGuinn's twelve-string guitar, trying to duplicate the sound of 'Summer Means Fun.' Given the freedom to do as he wanted, Terry was able to tie in to the echo chambers without the help of an engineer.

William Faulkner once said that he wrote as if he would be dead in the morning. That is exactly how Terry and I were working that night. We put McGuinn's guitar through a reverb unit, and then another, and there it was. The guitar popped.

'Let's to the same thing to the bass and drums and tambourine,' Terry said, excitedly, like a wizard who had just discovered that his wand worked.

Terry added reverb on top of reverb on top of reverb to Hal Blaine's drums and Osborne's bass. Finally, we added a triple layer of reverb to the vocals as well. Terry found that perfect tipping point for the sonic signature—not swimming in gravy but just putting in enough to add a unique flavor. The result is what you hear on the record.

'It's alive!' Terry said.

'Open this door, Melcher!' the engineer demanded.

More people started to pound on the door.

'This is security. Open the door!'

'OK,' Terry quietly whispered, sotto voce. 'Now let's see what we've got.'

Terry hit the play button on the tape machine. We looked at each other and realized how great McGuinn's guitar was sounding—how great everything was sounding—and that we were hearing something that would blow peoples' minds. It was great. Terry knew he had something now that Columbia couldn't possibly reject!

He walked to the door and casually opened it.

'What's going on?' he asked.

'You are to leave this facility,' the security guard said. 'And I am here to make sure that happens.'

'That's cool,' Terry said. We're finished anyway.'

And that was the crazy night the sound of The Byrds was created. The night musical history made.

THE SESSION

Barry McGuire had left The New Christie Minstrels, a wildly successful folk group, because he felt restricted and unfulfilled. He had written two hit songs, 'Green Back Dollar,' sung by The Kingston Trio, and 'Green, Green,' which was done by the Minstrels. Now he was going around to publishing companies looking for songs and a label with which to attach himself. But there wasn't really any interest in folk artists.

Barry's vocal style was so unique that he really didn't fit into any mold. Peter Paul & Mary and The Kingston Trio were still popular, but their niche was filled. Folk music in 1964 and early 1965 was still for a small audience of intellectuals hanging out in coffeehouses and Ivy League halls.

Lou Adler had met Barry at Ciro's, a popular club on the Sunset Strip, where The Byrds were performing one evening. Barry was dancing wildly, enjoying the music of his good friend Jim McGuinn. He then showed up at the Dunhill office, where Adler played him a number of songs, but Barry didn't hear anything he liked. As he was about to leave to visit some other labels, Lou suggested that he might go see 'the kid down the hall.'

'Phil Sloan is down the hall,' he said. 'He's got some songs that I don't get but maybe you'd like to hear them.'

Barry walked into the little piano room and introduced himself. I told him that I dug the hell out of 'Greenback Dollar' and 'Green, Green,' and he was sincerely amazed and flattered. *I don't give a damn about a green back dollar, I spend them as fast as I can …* that song was not only a song but a philosophical manifesto about how to have a good time in life. I told him I enjoyed his singing style, too, and he told me how he never really intended to be a singer—it just sort of happened. He was a welder by trade.

'Yeah,' I said. 'I was supposed to be a pharmacist.'

I started piddling on my guitar. I played Barry 'The Sins Of A Family,' but he didn't think it was right for him. Then I then played him 'Eve Of Destruction.'

'I like it, Phil, but it's not what I'm looking for.'

'I've got some other songs,' I told him.

I played 'This Mornin',' knowing in my heart that he had to like that one.

'I like the song, Phil. I just don't think it's for me. Sorry.'

'That's all right,' I said.

I played seven or so more songs with the same reaction, until Barry's face lit up with a grin when I played him 'What's Exactly The Matter With Me?'

'That's what I'm looking for, man!' he exclaimed. 'That's the song!'

We walked down to Adler's office.

'I found the song, Lou.'

'Yeah? Great. Which one?'

'"What's Exactly The Matter With Me?"'

'Never heard of it.'

'I played it for you,' I said.

'You did?'

'Look, Lou, this is the song I want to do,' Barry said. 'What do I have to do?'

'Welcome to Dunhill Records,' Lou told Barry, very pleased.

The session was set up in Studio Three at Western Recorders on Sunset. Hal Blaine on drums, Larry Knechtel on bass, and I was on guitar and harmonica. Chuck Britz, Bones Howe, and Lou Adler were in the booth, and Steve Barri was walking in and out as he didn't care too much for the songs.

We recorded 'What's Exactly The Matter With Me?' and Hal said he thought it was a very cool song. He had never heard anything quite like it, but I could tell he wasn't really that enthused. Barry felt comfortable singing it. We did a couple of takes, took a little break, and then some fried chicken was delivered. After eating the chicken, we recorded 'Ain't No Way I'm Gonna Change My Mind.' That one was pretty uneventful, and we still had twenty minutes left on the clock, so we decided to get one more song in. That song was 'Eve Of Destruction.'

Budhrrm, budhrmm, budhrmm, budhrmm went Hal's floor tom in a military cadence, before my acoustic guitar came in with a D chord. From the very first musical phrase, the song seemed to be shouting, *Listen to me! Listen to me!* It was what kids were shouting all over the land. It was one of those times that magic happens in a studio. At the end of the take, we were all exhausted and floating somewhere in the ether.

'This is absolutely amazing,' Hal said.

Larry just nodded in agreement.

'There's so much energy in it,' he laughed. 'Where the heck did that come from?'

Lou looked confused but intensely interested.

'You've got a hit track here, Lou,' Bones told him.

Steve Barri looked somewhat dejected but was still feigning interest.

The lyric sheet was under the chicken dinners we had ordered and was covered with grease but there was no time on the clock to write them out again. Barry took the paper into the studio and went on mic to put a rough vocal on the song, so Dunhill could fill its quota of songs done in a three-hour date. Barry was struggling to read and sing from the greased sheet of paper, so he added 'ahhhs' and 'mmmms' until he got to a line he could see clearly. He figured it didn't really matter—he just had to get through it so that we could all call it a day.

After the first playback, everyone was totally stunned and silent. We were all in a happy state of denial as to what we had just heard and experienced. Everyone present agreed that this song could never be released as a single, so we all laughed at the absurd irony of recording a great song but knowing it would never see the light of day. That seemed to calm down the incredible excitement we all were feeling.

I think Barry was probably the most visibly relieved at hearing that 'Eve' could never be released.

'I love that line, *my blood's so mad, feels like coagulatin'*,' Hal said. 'You better stay away from chopped liver, Flip,' he joked. 'That's one of those lines you get from eating too much chopped liver.'

'*Hate your next door neighbor but don't forget to say grace*,' Larry said. 'I like that line.'

'The track is great guys,' said Lou. 'All the tracks are great, but this song? I don't think so.'

Steve didn't have much to say. He just nodded at Lou's comments. I felt he was trying to put some distance between him and me, but he was curious about everyone else's reaction. I felt somewhat bad for him, because he seemed to be left out of the scene. I was always trying to include Steve. But now he was the one who was alienating himself from P.F. Sloan.

Lou took the rough mixes home and played them the next day for his partners and promotion men. They all agreed that 'Eve' couldn't possibly be a single, but did suggest that it be stuck on a B-side. So 'What's Exactly The Matter With Me?' came out as the A-side, with 'Eve' neatly dismissed on the flip.

The record was met with stony silence at first, and it seemed destined to disappear from view. Then, one late night out in the hinterlands of Wisconsin, outside the purview of mainstream radio, a DJ flipped the record over and played 'Eve Of Destruction' on a lark. Almost immediately, the phone lines started lighting up with callers asking the DJ to play it again. He played the song over and over again. *Listen to me!* the song shouted, and kids in this tiny market of Northern Wisconsin were hearing it.

Adler called me into his office.

'Looks like you have a hit, Phil,' he said.

'What do you mean?' I asked.

'We sold seventy records in Wisconsin,' he said, with sarcasm in his voice. Now we can all retire. Seventy records!

What Lou didn't know that morning, however, was that the first sales reports coming out of Wisconsin were from a tiny market of only a few hundred people. Other 'nowhere' radio stations started picking up on the record, and there were more sales coming in: twenty-five records here, fifty records there, over the course of a week or two. Some larger stations in the Midwest began playing 'Eve,' but now there were threats from advertisers to stop playing it. Soon the record was officially banned in Boston. New York and Chicago quickly followed.

Adler and Lasker couldn't believe what was happening. 'If people buy this record, it's the end of us,' Adler remarked one day. But the song became a steamroller, breaking through the walls of the cities where it was being banned. Within three weeks it was selling thousands and thousands a day!

The whole country seemed to be in shock about it. It shot to No. 1 in the country and then started to do the same thing all over the world. The BBC banned it, but not the pirate station, Radio Caroline, which broadcast all over the UK from a ship twenty miles offshore, and well into Europe. Sales of the record forced it into the UK charts, and finally the BBC reneged and started playing the song.

When my recording of 'The Sins Of A Family' was mistakenly released during the mild early days before 'Eve' began to create tidal waves, it too was immediately banned. The famous KRLA DJ Casey Kasem played it over and over, and it made the radio station's Top 40. I felt like the man who had released the plague on friends and family and the world, but damn, it was exciting and thrilling. There was little happiness about its success at Dunhill, however, or with Steve for that matter. For the company, it was all about trying to clean up the mess and rake in the money before the mob with pitchforks showed up.

McGuire and I were set to appear on a live national TV show, *The Les Crane Show*, which was part of the primetime Sunday night schedule on ABC. It was meant to compete with *The Ed Sullivan Show*. The execs at ABC had a meeting and told Les Crane twenty minutes before airtime that Barry could sing 'Eve' but I couldn't sing 'Sins.'

'That's fine,' I told Les.

'No, P.F., that's not fine,' Les replied. 'To hell with them—I'm going to put you on even if my job is on the line.'

Les told ABC that if I could not sing 'Sins,' he would no longer work for them. He called it corporate censorship, and he said he wouldn't have anything to do with it. What a hero! So Barry and I appeared together on *The Les Crane Show*, and Les thankfully did not lose his job. And the country continued to exist as it had the day before.

'The Sins Of A Family' hit the American charts at No. 70 with a bullet but Dunhill, severely shaken and scared by the controversy, pulled the record. They ordered their distributors to send back any records they had on hand for a refund, and that was it in America. But RCA was handling the record in Europe, where it continued to fly off the shelves.

'The company is under attack,' Adler said, with sincere fright in his voice.

'What are we running here, some kind of communist propaganda mill?' Lasker asked. 'This "Sins Of A Family" bullshit is pissing people off. The song is about having sex with a fourteen-year-old!'

'It's about my cousin who was forced to go into prostitution to buy school books because her old man was an alcoholic and he wouldn't give her the money.'

'Who the fuck writes songs like that?' Adler replied. He did not want to be known as a threat to society and a curse to decency. He had Jan and Dean to think of.

'Do you know where your place in the world is, Phil?' Adler asked me.

'I don't understand.'

'Are you going to be P.F. Sloan or Phil Sloan? Because I am not sure if there's room in this company for two Sloans.'

'Damn, fucking right,' Lasker added.

'What do you think, Steve?' Adler asked.

'I don't like P.F. Sloan,' Steve said. 'I don't like his writing. I don't think he writes as good as Phil Sloan writes with me. And one thing's for sure, The Vogues would never record a song like "Sins Of A Family."'

'"Eve Of Destruction" makes us look like a bunch of lunatic, subversive, reds,' Lasker moaned. 'Are you a red, Flip? Because if you are, let me know, so we can put a bullet in your head.'

'Look, what I write purely for myself you can choose to publish or not,' I said. 'If you want me to continue to be Phil Sloan, I will, but what I write on my own is my own.'

'That sounds like a load of crap,' Lasker replied. 'What are you, schizoid?'

'P.F. Sloan is doing pretty good,' I said. '"Eve" is No. 1 all over the world.'

'That's great, Phil,' Adler declared. 'But understand this: I don't want this P.F. Sloan to split up the team of Sloan & Barri. It means too much to this company. We need to be well rounded. You know what "well rounded" means? So have your fun, as long as you know that this is a fad, and that you're not going to continue with this line of writing.'

The outcome of the meeting was that I assured Lou that I didn't have a problem with writing popular songs with Steve. I considered all songs—

all forms of music—equally valid. I never considered P.F. Sloan songs to be any better or more valid than Jan & Dean songs. Why did I have to choose? Am I supposed to give up Tony Bennett because of Bob Dylan? No. It's all music. Good, bad, or ugly, I wanted to be able to do the best work possible, with only my own limitations to curtail me.

Brian Epstein called, informing us that he was setting up a world tour for Barry McGuire and myself, and that Dick James, The Beatles' publisher, said artists all over Europe want to record P.F. Sloan songs. Brian Epstein was a man of his word. A lot had changed for him over the past few years, but he did not forget sending me that package of Beatles acetates, or my reaction to them.

THE PRINCE OF PROTEST

After 'Eve Of Destruction' hit I went from backroom follow-up songwriter to the Prince of Protest on the worldwide stage. But Dunhill wanted to know if England would change Phil Sloan for good. Was he still going to be an ordinary guy who they could use for their purposes, or was he going to become a star?

I was going through changes and inner growth. I was a twenty-year-old now, being asked by college and university professors and the world press what my prescription was for the ills of the world. I was being debated over: was I a hack, or a tool of the communists, or the political and social conscience of all young people with an opinion?

If Dunhill could have gotten away without sending me to Europe, they would have, but there were important connections to be made for company business, and that couldn't be negated. They felt fine about using me for that purpose. I found myself in the middle of a phenomenon, akin to Beatlemania but more like Dostoevskymania—there were many levels of intrigue, rather than just one-dimensional euphoria.

Brian Epstein met Lou and me at the airport. He pulled up in a chauffeur-driven white Rolls-Royce. Lou started to get in the car, but after cordial greetings, Epstein very politely suggested that Adler not to get in the car because he had something of a personal nature to discuss with me. The look on Adler's face was that of hurt, embarrassment, and rage.

I got into the backseat and the car drove off. Brian told me how happy he was to finally meet me, and how grateful he was for my believing in the boys when no one else did, and that he always knew this day would come, and would I like some Champagne?

'Uhmmm … sure,' I said.

He asked me to take off my shoes off and then got down on the floor, put my feet on some white tissue paper, and started to draw around the outline my footprints.

'What's this all about?' I asked.

'You'll see.'

About a week and half later, fourteen pairs of boots—white and green and blue suede and leather; short boots, tall boots, and even a pair of boots going up to my knees in exquisite leather with Cuban heels—were delivered to my hotel room. Brian Epstein gave me an extraordinary gift. Beatle boots! Anello & Davide were boot-makers to the Royal Family. They had the royal stamp. But they also made boots for The Beatles.

The British tabloids referred to me as the Prince of Protest. Epstein drove me to Carnaby Street and bought me all the shirts in the latest fashion. I was wearing a suede cap over my short hair with a pair of sunglasses always on, and it felt like I had a disguise to hide behind. As Sir Ben Kingsley once said, 'Show me a man who wears a disguise and I'll show you a man who has the courage to show you his soul.'

McGuire and I did many shows together, including TV shows like *Ready Steady Go* and *Top Of The Pops*. We did concerts in London and Manchester. It was nonstop: business meetings with Dick James and European distributors; endless interviews with the press from all over Europe.

One of the outstanding moments I remember was going to the St. James Club on a Saturday night. It was so exclusive that you couldn't get in without a Top 10 record. I remember The Moody Blues were arguing with the manager outside.

'Our record is going to be in the Top 10 next week,' they said.

'Then come back next week.'

Mick and Keith were there. Harrison, McCartney, Ringo, and Twiggy were there, too, but no John Lennon. The place was blasting, with records being played at top volume. Whiskey and beer was downed and refilled. McGuire and I were seated at a booth with Paul McCartney and Mick Jagger. I thought to myself that I must be here by some Divine plan, but was this really what success looked and felt like? Orgies of alcohol and noise with self-congratulatory stroking and decadent self-indulgence?

McGuire was having the time of his life. Everyone seemed dizzy with happiness. But what was the matter with me? I wasn't getting it. I was trying to have a good time. I really was. I knew I was alive. I just didn't feel like I knew how to survive in this reckless lifestyle.

All these people were older than me, and they were, after all, my role models. If this was what they did to celebrate life then I would need to learn to get with the program.

P.J. Proby stopped by the table and invited me to a party he was having the next night and wanted my commitment that I would show up. I did show up at the party. It was an orgy. There were dozens of naked men and women interchanging partners, drinking, and smoking cakes of hash.

I sat next to Paul, who was waving at George.

'Is it true what you wrote?' he asked. 'That we're on the eve of destruction?'

'Why do you ask?'

'Because if it's true, I need to get my money out of the investments that we have.'

'He's not kidding,' Mick said. 'I'm happy that you finally made it over here.'

And then something strange happened. As if it wasn't strange enough already. The front door opened, and a huge gush of light enveloped the place, like when you open a refrigerator in a dark room. I looked over at Paul and Mick and Barry, and like with my experience with the clerk at Wallach's Music City, when Elvis appeared, they seemed, all of a sudden, not to be there. The rest of the club stood still, as if frozen in time. Then the light dissipated, and everything went back to normal.

'What just happened?' I asked Paul.

'Oh, I think that was John. You know, he told me he thinks your song is rubbish, and he didn't want to be here when you were here.'

Talk about a bring-down. That was quite a kick in the ass. Sayeth the voice: *you are here to witness; you cannot belong*. John Lennon didn't want to be in the same room with me? That was curious, because Epstein had told me that John was so grateful to me for hearing what no one else in the States could hear. He considered me to be one of the guys. Wasn't I? He had even arranged to have my boots made.

Somebody must have got to John. But who? And then I realized: John got to John. John wanted Dylan's approval more than anything else in the world at that time. He assumed that Bob Dylan didn't like the song—but he assumed wrong. When he talked about 'Eve Of Destruction' with Dylan in the backseat of his Rolls-Royce, in the D.A. Pennebaker film *Dont Look Back*, John's take was, *How did you let that little squirt and Captain Barry steal your thunder? I thought you had a better organization than that.*

John didn't care about the idea of the song. He just looked at it as competition for Dylan at that time. And he wasn't alone in that line of thinking. People that I admired and thought would be on my side were panning the song as well, like Pete Seeger or Joan Baez.

Barry wasn't crazy about 'Eve' from the beginning. I had always assumed that he knew what I was trying to say. But that simply wasn't the case. We have laughed about this together since then. How does one fathom the idea that in six weeks from hearing a song, he is now the object of love, hate, resentment, idol worship, scorn, derision, and adulation, considered a prophet, a corruptor of youth, and a voice for a generation demanding a voice? You had to feel for Barry, being thrust into that unwanted role. He was getting death threats and love letters. And with all that going on, he started to buy into the perceived 'dark side' of the song.

One afternoon, shortly before he was scheduled to give a press conference, Barry knocked on my hotel room door.

'What the hell does this song really mean, Sloan?' he asked. 'What are you saying here?'

'Look, Barry. I'm just the son of a pharmacist. And all of this is just a prescription for health. They don't like or want to take the medicine they have to take. Hey, man, it's really a love song.'

When Barry went downstairs to his press conference, one of the reporters asked, 'Why do you hate this society that has given you so much?'

'I don't hate anything. I love you and I love the world. And this is a love song.'

That blew their minds. And then the headline read: 'It's a love song!'

HANGING ON A SCAFFOLD

Ivan's Meads' first single was 'The Sins Of The Family,' recorded at EMI's Abbey Road studio in 1965 and released on the Parlophone label. Ivan's melodic voice weaves its way around the twists and turns of my erratic phrasing with all the skill of an Olympic slalom skier. The harmonica used on my original release was replaced by a Hammond organ, which gave it an unforgettable 60s sound that made it such a success in the soul clubs.

Everybody was still trying to get a handle on the song. 'The Sins Of A Family' continued to climb up the world charts but was not available in the States any longer. How does a twenty-year-old kid create such havoc? What a fragile egg the world is.

Brian Epstein was a sincere and extraordinarily humble man. As we'd all find out later, he loved John most of all, and he desperately needed his approval. But he was following his heart where 'Eve' and 'Sins' were concerned. On another trip to Carnaby Street, Brian informed me that he wanted me to move to England so that he could take over my career.

'You've got a home here,' he said. 'I don't know what your situation is with Dunhill, but if you decide to come here, we will handle everything for you.'

He bought some leather skirts and blouses for me to take home as gifts for my girlfriend Julie and then took me back to my hotel. (I did not know that at the moment of our buying the gifts, Julie was being courted by my partner, Steve.)

The next morning, at about nine, I was having a couple of boiled eggs, stewed tomatoes, and sausages in my room when I heard a knock at the door. I opened it to find a very cool-looking guy wearing a high-quality dark wool suit with a paisley silk scarf around his neck. He had a sophisticated, eclectic cool. I immediately took him for a musician.

'Good morning,' he said. 'I'm Mike McGear.'

'P.F. Sloan.'

'Brian sent me over. He thought you might like to dig London with someone closer to your age.'

'Sure,' I said. 'Thanks.'

'You're called P.F.?'

'Call me Phil.'

'I know where the haunts are, Phil.'

I grabbed my cap and jacket, and we headed down through the lobby and out onto the street where we got into Mike's car—an astoundingly gorgeous red Lamborghini.

'Beautiful car,' I said.

'It's a Lamborghini. But check out the seats. They're real racing seats—hand-sewn. Nobody has these seats.'

'Nice.'

'What do you drive, Phil?'

'Corvette Stingray.'

'Fast.'

'Not as classy as this beautiful car.'

'The leather is from Spain. That's where the best leather is.'

We hopped in and Mike took off.

'Where are we heading, Mike?'

'Soho. Been there?'

'I haven't been anywhere.'

'Brian told me you live in LA?'

'Yeah.'

'Hollywood?'

'It's all Hollywood.'

'You mean, England swings like a pendulum do, bobbies on bicycles … I bet that guy never was in England.

'Postcards from Fantasy Land.'

Mike was driving pretty fast along the narrow streets and he was enjoying it. I was a bit nervous but felt I was in safe hands.

'Are you a musician, Mike?'

'I do comedy mostly. Comedy and photography.'

'You do comedy?'

'My group is called The Scaffold. Goon Squad stuff.'

'I took you for a musician.'

'We're coming out with a comedy record.'

'Good luck with it. Can I do anything for you?'

'Hey, man. Thanks.'

'Anything I can do, Mike.'

'Brian thinks very highly of you.'

'He's a great guy.'

'That he is.'

We pulled into an alley and stopped the car in front of a gallery. We hopped out and entered the space. Hanging on the wall were twenty or thirty extraordinary early photographs of The Beatles.

'What's all of this?'

My eyes bugged out and I was amazed at the shots of The Beatles in various candid settings.

'These are incredible.'

'Yeah?'

'Extraordinary.'

'I took a bunch of photos of The Beatles when they were just starting out.'

Every photograph was better than the last: shots of The Beatles backstage at small venues, fooling around, and engaged in intimate conversation. I felt like I was really peering into the privacy of the scenes.

'Man, these shots are exquisite. Really cool.'

Mike autographed a poster and handed to me. I looked at the poster. *Photographs by Michael McCartney.*

'Michael *McCartney?*'

'Yeah. Cat's out of the bag.'

'You're ...'

'Paul's brother.'

'I thought your name was ...'

'I try not to make too much of a big deal about it. I love my brother, but I don't want to be known as someone who *is* because of who *he* is.'

'I get it.'

'I mean … I'm proud of Paul.'

'I bet.'

'But I have things to do, you know? And I know it sounds crazy, but sometimes that gets in the way.'

'By the looks of these photographs, Mike, you're doing just fine.'

Mike and I hit it off. We went out on the town, going from coffeehouse to pub to gallery. Everyone knew Mike, and he introduced me to his pals, including the playwright Joe Orton. Mike really made me feel at home. He had a tremendous, optimistic spirit.

Mike dropped me back at the hotel at about two in the morning.

'You really made England for me, Mike,' I said.

'The next time I go to LA, you can show me around the Strip. I bet you know some places.'

Mike's Lamborghini peeled off into the damp, English night, and I took the day in, laughing. I hit the sack and tried to sleep, but my mind was racing.

I was twenty years old. I had not been with a woman. England had opened her doors to me, offering love, stability, and creativity. The most famous manager in the world was asking me to come under his wing, but I couldn't tell Lou Adler, as his response would be even worse than it was after the Bobby Darin offer.

Why was I so afraid of that guy? Adler was doing press interviews and enjoying the new celebrity status he had gained as the producer of the record. But he got it into his head that, after witnessing the unbelievable success of Brian Epstein, he could go one better. That one better would happen for him in just a month's time, and he didn't even know what it was going to be yet.

In France, I had the time of my life, performing at the Olympia, having cabbages and tomatoes thrown at us—a sign of respect, or so we were told! Adler and McGuire went to the Moulin Rouge. Women were throwing themselves at both of them. I had a girlfriend at home, or so I thought, so I steered clear of it all.

McGuire got me stoned for the first time in Paris. He used a lampshade as a hookah, and after putting towels under the door he fired it up. We laughed all night.

In Italy, Barry went into the studio to record 'Eve' in Italian and Spanish for release in those territories. There were already cover versions hitting the charts, though. I hadn't seen much of Lou outside of the Italian recording studio, so I knocked at his door one night. Claudia Cardinale opened the door wearing nothing but a towel.

The next morning we were in the elevator together, going down to breakfast.

'By the way,' Adler told me, 'don't get too attached to Barry McGuire.'

'Why's that?'

'We're probably going to drop him from the label when we get back. I just heard that there are so many threats against Dunhill, and they are taking so much bad publicity from your song that it could sink the record company. And while we're on the subject? When we return home, we're going to have a talk.'

At that very moment, I should have gotten on a boat, sailed across the channel, and hid in Brian Epstein's apartment. I didn't. Maybe it was because I was raised a Jew, and I would not believe that a fellow Jew could intentionally hurt another Jew. I should have remembered about the Sanhedrin! Maybe it was because I was a team player at heart— basketball, soccer, and baseball as a kid in school. If you were on a team and did your job, the team won. But this wasn't soccer, and I was too immature to realize that.

Upon our return to LA, Lou had intended to get rid of Barry McGuire, but the demand for an album was great enough that he put his personal fears on hold to squeeze whatever juice he could from the 'Eve Of Destruction' lemon.

The *Eve Of Destruction* album was hastily put together at Western Recorders by Hal, Larry, and myself. Bones Howe engineered it. Lou Adler put his name on as producer, but really he was never there in the studio. It was Steve and me.

It's interesting to me now that it was called a Sloan–Barri production, giving the impression that there was still a team working. Every song on this album that has my name on it—with Steve Barri's name attached alongside it—I wrote by myself.

McGuire chose a number of songs that he wanted to do. Besides two Dylan songs, 'She Belongs To Me' and 'It's All Over Now, Baby Blue,' he sang 'Try To Remember,' an out-of-place but beautiful rendition of the song from the musical *The Fantasticks*. He did 'Sloop John B' the way the Christy Minstrels might have done it, and a few of the songs that I had first played for him in that tiny piano room. The overindulgent six-minute-plus 'Mr. Man On The Street Act One' had lines in it from what Barry had told me about his life prior to the Minstrels, which I then caricatured. And finally I worked on a few lines from a song Barry had written, 'Why Not Stop And Dig It While You Can?'

A series of shots for the album cover where taken by Guy Webster, who also took the photograph on the cover of this book, and was the son of the famous songwriter P.F. Webster. One of the contenders for the album cover was a shot of Barry coming out of a manhole with a rose in his hand, implying he had been through shit and was coming out of it, smelling like a rose. The label used the picture with just his head peering out of a manhole instead, but even that cover caused waves. No one had ever seen anything like it—album covers that told a little story or had some hidden meaning or agenda.

The album was released in the summer of 1965 and made its way into the Top 40, which was respectable enough but somewhat disappointing. Maybe it was because it was packaged as *McGuire Sings Your Favorite Hits*! Lasker and Adler were so paranoid of alienating people that they decided to give the album a vibe of, *It's OK folks, there are no more communists under the bed, and all of these songs are safe and tested with a family seal of approval. Even Grandma will be able to sing along to this fabulously friendly and innocently benign collection of hits.*

CHAPTER EIGHT

HIGHWAY 61 ON SHAG

Bob Dylan was anxious about his *Highway 61* album. *Bringing It All Back Home* had been a critical not a financial success, and the Columbia executives were squirming in their suits, believing that *Highway 61* may be subversive, for it was allegorical poetry, and who knew what he was really saying.

If Columbia had any confidence in Dylan to begin with, they were losing it fast. 'Ballad Of A Thin Man' was a veiled punch at the label, and that wasn't going to help. The executives were a bit behind the curve, still locked into the 50s and early 60s: your A&R man picked the songs, then hired a producer, who picked the musicians, who booked the dates with a beginning and end in mind, with an artist who was grateful. This new 'art' and 'creativity' thing was starting to get in the way of how things had always been done. And whoever heard of an artist writing his own songs with his own publisher?

The market demand for alternative sounds was growing, however, and they wanted to fill that demand—even if they didn't like it. 'Like A Rolling Stone,' which ran over six minutes and couldn't possibly be a single, was in part about a college girl looking to get stoned. Both Dylan's song and my 'The Sins Of A Family' (which had been banned) dealt with the taboo subject of young girls in trouble, and Bob, I suppose, wanted to get my vibe because he understood what kind of damage a song like that could cause.

I had already been labeled as a perverted harbinger of dangerous thinking by the public and by the record companies. Now I was under direct orders from Jay Lasker and Lou Adler not to meet or talk with Bob Dylan, or else I would be severely punished. The reason being, Dunhill wanted to control any potential meeting in order to lure him to sign with their publishing company and label—and use me as a bargaining chip. If he wanted to talk with Sloan, they decided, he would have to pay for the privilege. I didn't know about that. It would have been too embarrassing to bear.

In the early days of Dunhill, I would call Julie, the new secretary, and pretend to either be Ricky Nelson or Elvis Presley.

'Hi, this is Elvis, can I speak to Phil Sloan?'

'I know that's you Phil,' she'd reply. 'Stop it.'

When Bob Dylan really did call and ask to speak with P.F. Sloan, Julie hung up on him a number of times until she realized it was really him. He left a phone number and address and a time and date to meet him and she gave it to me.

I drove over to the Continental Hotel on Sunset and went up to the fourteenth floor. Bob opened the door and greeted me like his favorite cousin. I was confident but a bit anxious, because I was now formally under the threat of career extermination. Bob was looking into that abyss as well.

'Adler doesn't want me to talk to you privately, man,' Bob said.

'Yeah. He's afraid you might be a bad influence on me because you're a subversive,' I said jokingly. 'Adler thinks that I'm expendable and potentially damaging to the company, but doesn't want me to leave.'

'I guess you just have to keep writing hit songs. That should shut them up.'

Bob turned and headed into the living room, and I followed him in.

'I want you to hear something,' he said.

We sat on the tan shag rug with Bob's portable Columbia Masterworks record player. He had the acetate of *Highway 61* in his hands. Acetates were cheap vinyl discs made for the artist that you could listen to five or six times before the grooves wore out.

'Columbia doesn't want to release it,' he told me, 'because they don't know what it is and they don't know what to do with it.'

He gently placed the needle down on the first cut, 'Ballad Of A

Thin Man.' I was aware of his hyperconscious intensity, the way he was focused on my reaction to every line and note that emanated from that magic little box. Halfway through the song, I could no longer contain myself. I started rolling on the shag, laughing uncontrollably.

Bob slapped his thigh and let out a howl of laughter himself.

'You get it!' he shouted. 'Thank God you get it!'

I was listening to a very high level of modern poetry couched in comedy—high comedy with social overtones.

'It's Chaplin,' I told him. 'No—it's Fellini on Chaplin inside Picasso.'

Bob's face brightened. We listened to all of the cuts, rolling on the floor laughing every now and then, and then we lay back on the carpet and listened from the beginning again. He wanted to know about the melodies, and we analyzed each song with more specificity than the first listen. I assured him that the melodies were great.

'Pick a song off this album and do it any way you want, man,' he said. 'It's yours as my gift. Exclusively yours.'

I chose 'Ballad Of A Thin Man,' maybe because it was the most impossible one to do.

About fifteen minutes later, David Crosby (then with The Byrds) appeared at the door, wearing a purple chapeau and a psychedelically embroidered cape. David and I didn't get along very well. He considered me to be illegitimate because I had written surf songs for Terry Melcher and Jan & Dean, and he did not consider 'Eve Of Destruction' to be authentic. He considered me a hack and felt that The Byrds were on a higher spiritual plane of consciousness, so when he saw me sitting on the rug with his idol, listening to music like two teeny-bopping twelve-year-olds, his first reaction was, 'What the fuck is he doing here?'

'What do you mean, what the fuck is he doing here?' Dylan asked. 'Shut up!'

'He's not for real, man!' Crosby said.

'If he isn't real then I'm not either.'

'I'm not saying you aren't, Bob. I'm just saying I know he isn't.'

Crosby didn't like me because of what happened one night at the El Monte Legion Hall. Shortly after the release of 'Mr. Tambourine Man,'

The Byrds were performing for the first time as an established group at the venue in El Monte, California. (History has it that this show at Ciro's, but it wasn't—that was later.) The hall was a haven for doo-wop groups on Friday and Saturday nights: Don & Dewey, Rosie & The Originals, and even the late, great Richie Valens. The town was a Spanish-speaking, happening place, but definitely old school, low-rider rock'n'roll.

Terry Melcher called me and asked me if I would shepherd The Byrds at El Monte and act as a sort of a manager for the night. The hall was packed, and out came The Byrds in full hippie regalia; McGuinn with his granny glasses and full-blown coif, Crosby wearing a fringed suede cape, Michael Clarke playing on his first set of real drums, Chris Hillman with a new Fender Bass, and Gene Clark dressed in black, like Frankenstein's monster.

The Byrds opened with a few Beatles songs and the crowd began to get restless. They had come to hear doo-wop and street music. They had no room in their hearts for long-haired, pot-smoking musical revolutionaries. By the time The Byrds started playing their third song, the manager of the hall grabbed my arm.

'Are you the manager of these clowns?' he asked.

'Something like that,' I told him.

'Look. Get these guys off the stage or I'm going to give them the hook. And we *do* have a hook.'

The hook was an actual pole with a crook that stage managers put around the neck of a performer to physically drag them off the stage during Vaudeville shows, and apparently it was still in use at the El Monte Legion Hall in 1965. When the manager told me about his hook, I was thinking about my original name, Schlein—the German word for a sticky substance put on branches to catch birds. Too bad I didn't have a bag of schlein on that night.

I had to warn them somehow of the dire circumstances they were facing, so I went behind the stage and quietly and respectfully moved behind David Crosby and whispered in his ear.

'The manager wants you off the stage now. Go into "Tambourine Man" or we're all going to be sorry.'

'Hey, man. If you ever dare to get onstage with The Byrds again, I will have you killed. You understand me?'

A simple nod of his head would have worked. A recognition of message delivered, and roger that. Instead, I got threats. I jumped back and nearly fell off the back of the stage as I scrambled my way into the audience, cursing Terry Melcher under my breath. And then The Byrds began to play 'Mr. Tambourine Man.' After all that drama, they took my advice.

As a witness, it seemed that the ceiling had been blown away and the evening stars had become visible, like the opening lines of 'A Whiter Shade Of Pale,' and it truly felt as if a whole new consciousness had been opened. And I believed it would never be the same again. In reality, El Monte enjoyed doo-wop then and they enjoy it equally as much now. But on that night, The Byrds took flight.

Meanwhile, back at the Continental Hotel, Bob told David that he wanted to have a word with him in the bedroom. They walked in and closed the door. I got off the floor and waited on the couch. I felt like a nurse would be coming into the room any minute to tell me that the doctor would see me shortly. I heard Dylan screaming, and it sounded to me like somebody was being slapped across the face. And then I heard Crosby.

'I didn't know! I didn't know!'

Suddenly, the front door opened, and two topless twins with long blonde hair, wearing black chiffon pirate pantaloons, sashayed in like Las Vegas showgirls and sat either side of me on the couch.

'Where's Mr. Zimmerman?' one of the blondes asked. 'We have an appointment with Mr. Zimmerman.'

'He'll be out in a minute.'

'Are you part of it?' she asked.

'As far as I know, I don't think I'm involved,' I answered. 'Maybe next time.'

The three of us sat on the couch in a surreal silence, with an occasional slapping sound coming from the bedroom.

'How was I supposed to know?' I heard Crosby shout.

There was a balcony right off of where we were sitting. A rope dropped onto the balcony, and a man, dressed like Zorro, dropped down the rope and entered the room in a blaze of romantic, swashbuckling splendor.

Zorro looked at me with a great intensity.

'Mr. Zimmerman?'

'He'll be out in a minute,' the girls answered in unison.

'Ah,' Zorro said, and motioned with his arms for the girls to stand up and come to him. They joined hands and began dancing around in circles.

David Crosby rushed out of the bedroom and paused as he was heading for the door.

'I'm sorry,' he said as he left the room. 'I didn't know.'

After Crosby left, the two pirates and Zorro left the room as well, leaving me alone for a moment to contemplate what I had just experienced. It was as though I had just physically traveled through a Bob Dylan song.

Bob opened the door and nonchalantly moved to the record player and sat on the floor.

'Did I miss anything?' he asked.

'Nothing important,' I said.

'I've been wanting to tell you something, Phil. Those guys at Dunhill are going to tear you up. You're not safe there.'

'I'll watch myself.'

'You better,' Bob said.

The next morning it was discovered that I had met with Dylan, and I was immediately fired. Then, when I told Adler that I had an exclusive Bob Dylan song, I was immediately rehired.

THE GRASS ROOTS (TAKE ONE)

Lasker stole the name The Grass Roots from a group performing locally in LA, led by my friends Bryan MacLean and Arthur Lee. They didn't have a contract but they were well known in the underground. After their name was stolen, they changed their group to Love.

Lasker called me into his office. He had a huge cigar sticking out of his mouth, and his bug-eyes, with overly large glasses, gave him the impression of being a large insect with smoke emanating from its mouth. I felt a little like the Herbert Philbrick character in *I Led Three Lives*. Philbrick had to prove that he was not a double agent, and during office hours, I sometimes had to prove that I could be a corrupt, heartless employee, willing to sacrifice anything and anybody to gain acceptance to prove my loyalty to the company. And I truly felt that if I were discovered as being a human being, I would be murdered.

'I don't believe in this communistic Bob Dylan, shit, Flip,' Lasker said.

I hated the name, Flip. My first record at thirteen was by Flip, a name given to me by my sister because she thought I was crazy—flipped out. Lasker called me Flip because of how I felt about the name. Calling me Phil or P.F. denoted a level of respect that he was just not willing to give. (Originally, P.F. stood for 'Philip Flip,' but I had outgrown Flip and decided that my name would now be Philip Faith Sloan.)

'Do you?' he continued.

'Do I what?'

'Do you believe in this communistic shit?'

'What communistic shit?'

'If Dylan's got something to say, why doesn't he just say it?'

'What do you think Dylan is saying?'

'I don't give a rat's ass what he's talking about but his songs are selling. And you've got one of them, and here's what we're going to do. You and Steve are going to go into the studio. I've got a name that we're going to sell it under. I'm going to call you The Grass Roots.'

'But Jay,' I interjected. 'There is already a group known as The Grass Roots, and they are fairly well known.'

'Fuck them.'

'But Jay, I know these guys.'

'Fuck 'em twice. And fuck you if you don't like it. I don't need you. I could throw a rock and hit five of you. Look out the window. All I see is you.'

This is the kind of meeting that frightened me. I edited 'Ballad Of A Thin Man,' which originally had ten or more verses, into a truncated version, like 'Mr. Tambourine Man,' and called it 'Mr. Jones.' I cut the tracks with the Wrecking Crew. I feel somewhat ashamed that I had edited out the most wonderful but most controversial verses. I take full responsibility for doing this, but I was just becoming so tired of fighting these people.

After putting on my vocal, we presented the finished product to Adler and Lasker, who were afraid that this song was going to be a hit. They didn't want to release it with me singing lead. Dunhill believed that this wave of hippie records would destroy the wholesome image the label had started out with. But like the greedy man who sees a gold coin in a loaded bear trap, they were going to take the chance of having their arm cut off to get at the coin.

Lasker and Adler wanted to get a group to be the face of The Grass Roots.

'Why don't you use, Love?' I asked. 'They *were* The Grass Roots, before you stole their name. They don't have a record contract, and they're good.'

'I'm going to destroy them,' Lasker said.

'Why?' I asked

'Because I want to,' he replied, biting down on his cigar. He decided I would fly to San Francisco and find a group who would be willing to not play on their own records. I roamed the streets of San Francisco, from club to club, bar to bar, listening to hundreds of groups, many of whom were starting to make an impact there: Country Joe & The Fish, Moby Grape, The Great Society, The Beau Brummels, Butch Engle & The Styx.

San Francisco was different from Los Angeles. It always has been. San Francisco was considered real, but LA was tinsel and phony. None of the groups I talked with had any interest in going anywhere near LA.

I had met Marty Balin from Jefferson Airplane at a club and we hit it off. He invited me to stay with him so I moved out of my hotel room. Marty introduced me to San Francisco's rock society: Big Brother & The Holding Company with Janis Joplin, Quicksilver Messenger Service, Sons Of Champlain, Dino Valenti, the Dead. I met Jerry Garcia sitting on the steps at his house in the Haight.

'I had a dream last night about the future of the world,' Jerry said. 'Would you like to hear it?'

'Sure,' I said.

'In the future, the idea of a record label is going to be nonexistent. Why should people who are struggling to make a living have to use money to buy music? In the future, everyone will be connected. When an artist comes out with an album, if you like it you will send him what you can afford—a penny, a nickel, a dime, or a dollar! This way the artists can continue to make their way without any censorship or interference. It sounds good, but it hasn't played out well, in my opinion. Labels gouge the artists and the public. As a middleman they should expect a profit for their risks, but they have been greedy.'

We sat on the steps a while and he thought about possible groups.

'I know a group that might fit the bill. His name is Wild Bill Fulton. His band is The Bedouins.'

I called up Bill Fulton and we met at Vesuvio Cafe, over in North Beach—the coffee shop where Lawrence Ferlinghetti and the poet crowd hung out, across from City Lights Bookstore. Bill wasn't particularly interested in coming to LA and putting his voice on a track. He had a band, he said, and he wanted to be loyal to their interests.

I explained that that the song was by Bob Dylan and how I got it, and that he could have a quick hit record and then do what he wanted.

'They're all nuts in LA,' Bill informed me.

'There are some great people in LA, Bill,' I replied. 'It's definitely a different scene.'

'But Jerry recommended you,' he continued, 'and he feels OK about it … and if it's OK with Jerry, it's OK with me.'

Within the week, Fulton and his bandmates had decided to give it a try, having no way of knowing that they were about to step into a horror chamber of band-eating monster maggots.

In the studio, Bill literally sang along to the song with my vocal in his headphones to get the phrasing. And then we erased my vocal. I loved the surety in his raw voice. I blended in the voices of the band as well with my own and Steve's. Dunhill wanted the record out immediately.

'Mr. Jones' came out with great hoopla, but like a Fellini movie on vinyl, it was beyond anyone's comprehension. And though the radio stations were playing the record, they were flipping it over and playing the B-side, 'You're A Lonely Girl'—which barely hit the charts—instead.

This incarnation of The Grass Roots made television appearances, and they were getting a lot of press. Having had their first taste of success without getting any money, all they really wanted now was to play their own music in the studio, but they told by Jay Lasker that under no circumstances would they play their own instruments. They will do what they are told or they can leave.

This was the dirty little secret of rock'n'roll. Record companies did not consider teenage musicians to be professional, and did not allow them, for the most part, to play on their own records. Dennis Wilson of The Beach Boys was not allowed to play on many of their records because Capitol considered him unprofessional. The session for The Byrds' recording of 'Mr. Tambourine Man' was all Wrecking Crew guys except for McGuinn, who fortunately was able to force himself onto the twelve-string guitar. Brian Wilson himself was, at times, forced out of playing the bass. Nobody played on their own records except British groups like The Beatles and the Stones.

And so Bill Fulton and The Grass Roots decided to leave. They went back to San Francisco. Not as The Grass Roots but as The Bedouins. Bill had integrity; he gave up easy national fame because he felt that he was not having any artistic input into the music.

Now Dunhill had a Grass Roots record without a Grass Roots band, and they needed to come out with a follow-up. I had just written 'Where Were You When I Needed You.' I was tired of the professional sound after being in San Francisco. I was looking for a more passionate, unprofessional vibe. It turned out that Bones Howe enjoyed playing drums in his spare time.

'I want you to play the drums on this song, Bones,' I said.

'I can't play the drums on this song or any other song. I can't hit time.'

'That's what I'm looking for, Bones,' I said. It's the passion I want, not the ability to keep time.'

For me, perfection often hid behind the structure of the song. I was always searching for passion in the imperfection of the music. This is not to say that a perfectly crafted, orchestrated work does not have its own unique beauty. I had some of the greatest drummers in the world from which to choose, but I was after an abstract musical feeling, where there is no right or wrong—music that reaches into the soul on a primitive, less contained level.

And so Bones relented and played drums on 'Where Were You When I Needed You.' I sang lead and Steve and I sang harmony. You would have thought that this artistic decision would have been perfectly acceptable, but it was met with hostility and wrath. The slightest change in established, artistic protocol was treated as if I were personally rebelling against the authority, and that I was abusing the gift of opportunity that had been bestowed upon me. This was the beginning of December 1965.

IT'S ALL DUNHILL FROM HERE

Record World, *Billboard*, and *Cashbox*, the three main music publications of the day, had made it crystal clear to Adler that they were under attack for merely charting 'Eve Of Destruction,' and that advertisers were sending an economic message by pulling their ads. Adler was frightened about what another 'Eve' could do to his company. And this was on his mind when Barry McGuire showed up at the office with his troupe of musical hippies called The Mamas & The Papas.

The Mamas & The Papas, formerly The Mugwumps, were John Phillips, Denny Dougherty, Michelle Phillips, and Cass Elliot. The group was there because John had written two or three songs that Barry was going to record as possible follow-ups to 'Eve Of Destruction.' Adler's office always seemed huge to me until Barry, John, Denny, Cass, and Michelle, plus Peter Pilafian (who played the electric violin), Jim Hendricks (formerly with The Mugwumps), Steve Barri, and myself piled in there. Peter took out his violin and connected it to a small amp.

'What the hell is this?' Adler asked.

'Have you ever heard an electric violin?' Peter said.

'No, and I don't want to know what it sounds like,' Adler replied, as Peter began to give a much-needed soundtrack to the meeting.

'Who are these people and what are they doing here?' Adler asked McGuire.

'They are friends of mine from the Village.'

'Maybe you've heard of us,' Cass said. 'We used to be called The Mugwamps.'

'No. I've never heard of you.'

'Well, that's your loss, isn't it?' Cass cooed.

'John has written a couple of songs that I want to record for a possible next single,' Barry said.

'Can we bring in some lunch?' Michelle asked John.

'No lunch,' Adler said, waving his hands wildly in the air.

'Don't you believe in feeding your artists?' Cass asked.

'There are no artists until I say there are artists,' Adler answered.

'Great,' Cass said to Denny. 'Another asshole.'

'This is the kind of day that I wish I had never left Nova Scotia,' Denny said.

'I'm not sure about any of this,' Adler said. 'I don't even know what you people sound like.'

'Buy a Mugwumps record,' Cass said. 'What are you, cheap?'

'You're beginning to piss me off, young lady,' Adler told her.

All of this was a crazy nightmare for Adler. His office was filled with hippies, and all he wanted was to put Dunhill back on track with traditional record fare.

'This place is starting to smell like a bus station,' he continued. 'Do you people ever take showers?'

'I would rather smell like a horse in the meadow,' John mused, to which Cass added, 'than a wilted rose in the window of the queen.'

'Ah,' Denny chimed. 'But the queen doth not smelleth in blue cashmereth.'

'I think we understand each other perfectly,' Phillips told Adler. 'I need a check for $10,000 before this afternoon or we are going to go back to New York.'

'What do I care? Go back to New York.'

'Let's go see my good friend Nick Venet at Capitol.' Cass suggested.

'So we're done?' Adler asked.

'My, my, my. Isn't he heavy.'

'I'm heavy?'

'Yeah. You're way too heavy.'

'OK,' Adler said, pounding his desk. 'We're all heavy, but some are heavier than others. Do I have it right?'

'It's all Dunhill from here,' Cass chortled.

'I'm so bummed,' Michelle whispered to John as they left the stifling office.

'I think you hurt their feelings, Lou,' Barry said as he left the office. 'I don't think they'll come back.'

Adler, Barri, and myself remained.

'What the hell just happened in here?' Adler asked.

'Maybe we should hear them,' Steve said.

'This is completely out of control,' Adler said to me. 'Do you remember what I told you in Italy? This company is bigger than Barry McGuire.'

Steve then excused himself.

'Barry McGuire is a sinking ship,' Adler added.

'He has a No. 1 record,' I reminded him.

'He's a circus freak. And the show is over. Everything that has happened with "Eve Of Destruction" means nothing to me. Including this ridiculous new persona of yours.'

This was the new reality of the moment. The warm embrace that I received as a conquering hero of England and Europe had crashed and burned. I was back to being told that my fantasy was over, and if I were smart I would get with the program or suffer the consequences.

CHAPTER NINE

A TALE OF THREE CITIES

From my very first encounter with Jan & Dean at Arwin Records to writing their last hit single covered a span of only five years. In 1960, Jan & Dean were music gods. And now, in 1965, Jan was looking to me to be able to bring him into the new age. He decided to do an album called *Folk & Roll*. Curiously, Jan had a deep disdain for the new folk-rock scene, which was threatening to relegate him into obscurity. Fortunately for him, he had a lifeline into the folk-rock world—me.

Jan wrote a song called 'The Universal Coward,' which was his version of 'Eve Of Destruction.' He was basically calling his audience communists, pacifists, extremists, crazy, or insane. I caught flak from the folk community again for singing on this album, and this time I deserved it. There was no sincerity behind the project. Jan had sadly attempted to pander to an audience that had left the carefree days of sun and fun for important, meaningful social endeavors; writing an insincere song called 'Folk City' wasn't going to cut it.

Interestingly enough, whether Jan knew it or not, Gerde's Folk City was where Dylan first became known on the New York scene. The magic worked for 'Surf City' and 'Drag City,' but there was no third-time charm for 'Folk City.' Jan was just trying to sell records. He sincerely felt that this style of music was just another fad like surf and hot rod and doo-wop. He was wiping out.

The reason I did the album was that I believe that everybody has a right to their own personal and political opinions, whether I agree with them or not. And I was fiercely loyal to a man I had idolized since I was fourteen. He had given me opportunities, and this was my chance to pay him back. Where I was completely wrong was in helping him capitalize on something in which he didn't believe. Jan wanted the public to perceive him as a person who was deeply concerned and who embraced the values of the progressive politics of the day. But he wasn't that person. That's how I was being pulled. It was when he recorded my actual song 'Eve Of Destruction' and changed a number of lines to reflect his own ideals that my principles demanded that I leave Folk City and never return.

Folk & Roll contained three of my songs: 'Eve Of Destruction,' 'Where Were You When I Needed You' (which I sang and played guitar on), and 'I Found A Girl.' The latter was already a hit from Jan & Dean's *Command Performance*, but Jan felt it added gravitas to the new record, so he included it here, too. Dean wasn't around for any of the sessions. The rift between them had not healed, and Dean was getting involved with other things.

There was never any bad blood between Dean Torrence and me—not on my part. But there wasn't any warmth, either. How could I have told Dean about the many, many times I had asked Jan to please put Dean back on falsetto, to which Jan would always refuse? Dean believed that Jan & Dean were a partnership. And in that partnership, his input into the recordings was a natural thing to expect. However, Jan made it clear that the producing of the records was exclusively his domain, and if Dean couldn't accept that he could leave the session.

Though he loved Dean, Jan made it clear that Dean could be replaced. The brand of Jan & Dean was whoever Jan said it was. Jan believed this so strongly that in the end he even replaced *himself* with me, too. On the Rally-Packs record, which was originally meant to be a Jan & Dean single, Jan replaced his voice with mine, so I was both Jan, Dean, and The Fantastic Baggys on the same song.

I missed Dean. I missed his humor and his lightness of being in the studio. Left to his own devices, Jan was a lovable despot and tyrant. There must have been something lovable about him, because he had the uncanny ability to get people to work long hours for free. He sacrificed efficiency over spirit.

I was happy that it was not common knowledge that Phil Sloan was the falsetto on all of these hit records. I was glad that it was perceived as Jan & Dean. To be honest, my ego would have liked the stroking that came along with singing on major hit records. But it was a secret that I was happy to keep.

In April 1966, Jan wrecked his Corvette on Sunset Boulevard. In my opinion, Dean's loving care of Jan in the hospital and after he was released was a testament to his character and decency. I witnessed it firsthand on my many visits to Jan's house. Dean was always there, helping with the food and the care. He was the most loving friend that one could ever hope for. Often, when I left that scene, I would weep—not out of sadness but out of joy at being around that kind of love.

I had hoped that Jan & Dean being reunited after the accident would have put the tension between Dean and myself behind us. But I realized something from this: I didn't matter. What made me love Jan & Dean was the closeness of their relationship. Like Bobby and Jack Kennedy in a crowded room, even if they were arguing and disagreeing, they had a bond that no one else could penetrate or take the place of. No matter how many records I performed on, or how many records Dean didn't, they still loved each other on a level that few experience.

CALIFORNIA DREAMIN'

Barry McGuire was trying to hold on to the glory that had been happening only a few short months before. In today's music world he would have never had to think about doing a follow-up for at least a year and a half and could tour comfortably by just singing 'Eve,' but at the time he was rapidly fading from sight. That's how fast our world was moving. We lived in a compressed time. The music business wanted to put 'Eve' behind it, and that included Barry McGuire and myself.

Barry wanted to get back to harmless songs like his 'Green, Green.' Who could blame him? He was suffering from overload persecution, having never wanted to do 'Eve' in the first place.

The Mamas & The Papas were crashing on floors in Laurel and Topanga Canyon while Barry was lobbying to be able to record his new single, Phillips's 'California Dreamin'.' Barry convinced Lou Adler to finance a number of sessions that would include the recording of 'California Dreamin'' with the Mamas & The Papas as his backup singers.

We went to Western Recorders. Steve Barri and I were set to produce McGuire's new album and single—Adler wanted no part of any of it. We got the Wrecking Crew together, and Hal, Joe, Larry, John Phillips, and myself laid down the initial tracks. John depended on me then as he had very limited experience in the studio with 'outside' musicians.

John began to play 'California Dreamin'' for us. There was no intro to the song, and to my surprise it had only three chords at best. John was basically into stone-cold folk—simple, three chord songs like 'Tom Dooley,' 'Tijuana Jail,' and 'Goodnight Irene.' I didn't know it then, but Phillips had an extreme hatred for popular music. With the success of his friends like John Sebastian, Roger McGuinn, and Zal Yanofsky, though, he felt more comfortable about getting into it.

The song was tasty and simple, but I didn't find it exciting. I enjoyed the lyric, which was co-written by Michelle and John, but the music really left me cold.

As the song began in A-minor, it reminded me of The Ventures' early-60s hit 'Walk Don't Run.' And I was a huge Ventures fan.

'Have you ever heard "Walk Don't Run" by The Ventures?' I asked John.

'No,' he replied, with great pride.

'Well,' I said, 'The Ventures are one of the great all-time surf bands.'

'Surf doesn't break on MacDougal Street,' he said, and he meant it.

'Yeah, John. Maybe not. But they are one of the greatest bands you will ever hear.'

John seemed a bit stung that I was bringing the game to his face. He was obviously not used to it. He struck me as a guy who had been deeply hurt by something and did not quite know how to process the pain. I thought to myself that one of these days he was going to blow, and I wouldn't want to be around to see it. He wasn't a likeable guy. But I loved Barry, so I would give this everything I had.

I started to play 'Walk Don't Run':

Dun dun dun duh
Dun dun dun duh
Dun dun dun dun
All the leaves are brown …
And the sky is grey …

Barry Mann had unintentionally showed me a suspended chord back at Screen Gems. I was so impressed by this beautiful, simple chord that I called Brian Wilson and played it for him over the phone. The next thing I knew, Brian had written 'Don't Worry Baby,' which had within it a number suspended chords. And then the chord heard 'round the world, two months later, was the opening suspended chord of 'A Hard Day's Night.'

I used these chords throughout 'California Dreamin',' and more specifically as a bridge to get back and forth from the verse to the chorus. *On such a winter's day …*

We still didn't have an intro, but we did have a very nice melody. John began to show signs of enjoying the process.

'Now we need an intro,' I told him.

I told John to hang on to the A-minor chord while I riffed on top of it. We ended up in a suspended E chord. Barry came in and put on his lead vocal. I overdubbed twice for John, Michelle, Cass, and Denny in a slight reverb and echo—this studio had great echo chambers. It sounded good.

Lou Adler came into to the studio. He was wearing a baby-blue cashmere sweater, a nice pair of slacks from Sy Devore's, and loafers without socks. *Oh, God. Here comes father—hide the dope!* Barry was wearing a yak vest and knee-high black boots with his pants tucked in and a striped jersey. John and Denny looked like they had just stepped out of central casting for the roles of disheveled vagrants. Cass was wearing a paisley muumuu dress without shoes. And Michelle was wearing a poncho that she must have picked up at a Venice Beach rathole. Well-dressed collegian meets fashionable hippie hobo.

Lou took control of the sound booth and had us play what we had done. He didn't quite get it, but he did notice half a corned beef sandwich from Greenblatt's that had been left on the table.

'You mind if I have a bite of this?' he asked.

'No, Lou, go ahead.'

'Carry on,' he said, taking most of the sandwich into his mouth. 'Sounds good, let me know when you have something else to listen to.'

I heard from Barry the next week that Phillips had gone into a private meeting with Adler and informed him that they had other offers from various labels, which they were considering unless he could match their offers. Otherwise they would take off. The agreed-upon price was $5,000 and a shot at a single. Adler needed a hit song, and John played him 'Go Where You Wanna Go,' which was about Michelle telling John to go where he wanted to go so she could go where she wanted to go.

Lou called a session for 'Go Where You Wanna Go' with the Crew, plus me on electric guitar. The song was released, and it bombed big time. It didn't go near the charts and hardly made it onto any radio station. I can't tell you why. It was a great song, in my opinion, and it was produced very well. Timing is everything, and I think it holds up today.

Meanwhile, after listening to Barry's recording of 'California Dreamin',' Phillips believed the song could be a hit. He convinced Adler to give them another shot. John went to Barry and told him that he had to renege on his promise that 'California Dreamin'' would be his next single; Barry replied magnanimously that whatever John needed to do to secure his future would be fine. Unfortunately, that left Barry in the lurch.

With little money left for the album, and with no single in prospect, Barry asked me if I had written anything new. I had. 'Child Of Our Times' and 'Upon A Painted Ocean' came out six weeks after 'Eve Of Destruction' hit No. 1 around the world. This time the long knives were drawn and waiting. They had warned us. And when the songs were released, those long knives were used and the blood ran quick. Barry knew that the enemy was lying in wait. But he felt that both songs were so attractive that he had to do them.

'Child Of Our Times' was written to the youth of the world, encouraged them that the world they want, they can create. What will you grow up to respect? What will you grow up to protect? The future's hope is what you'll turn out to be.

Society didn't want to hear that. The song was received about as well as well as the news that typhus is spreading in your neighborhood, and you are the one who has just returned from the swamp infested Panamanian jungle.

The die-hard fans of 'Eve Of Destruction' were doing their best to herald the latest chapter of *The Truth Hurts*. But the forces were too strong, and compelled the fans to flip the record over, hoping there would be a safe haven for Barry McGuire.

'Upon A Painted Ocean' did not offer relief, although the title suggested it might. The themes were racism, and traditionalism versus new thinking—if that belief system is so right, why are we staring at the eve of destruction and oblivion in the eye? The establishment had had enough of this anti-establishment music and wanted an end to it, but the genie was out of the bottle, with no intention of returning.

In 2012, Barry McGuire received a lifetime achievement award from the Far West Folk Alliance in California, and I was asked to give a speech to introduce Barry to the crowd of folksters from all over the country. I had an opportunity to share with the crowd how I felt about him. Here's what I said.

We all owe a debt of gratitude to Barry McGuire. Not just me. For had providence not chosen him to sing the lyrics to 'Eve Of Destruction,' we probably would not have had the twenty-sixth amendment to the constitution of the United States passed so quickly, as the song became a rallying cry for the cause.

Barry's voice spoke truth. When you heard Barry on the radio growl 'you're old enough to kill but not for votin',' you knew that that was not right and had to change. 'Greenback Dollar' and 'Green, Green' were songs I was loving and singing long before I had even known the name McGuire. The Harvard elites were trying to imagine the unimaginable at that time, and that was languishing in a Tijuana jail, while we were singing, I don't give a damn about a green back dollar. The lines were drawn.

Hoyt Axton, Fred Neil, Bob Gibson, Woody Guthrie, Bob Dylan ... heroes all for raising the consciousness of the world's people. And there he was, one of them even then!

But the greatest accomplishment I can think of that Barry has achieved thus far is holding in his heart with love all of God's children. Anyone who has ever spent time with him can tangibly feel the light and joy that pours forth from his heart.

For those who worship at the altar of fame, they use derisive and dismissive terms, caring only for themselves and the temporary advantages that being negative always brings. As Woody Guthrie knew, these people are like lost sheep, no less loved but at the mercy of the wolves in sheep's clothing.

The measure of a man is not only how he deals with success but how he rises from the ashes of defeat. Life is the most remarkable journey when the one who is guiding us is put in charge of the train. McGuire knows who is driving this train. Do you?

WALKING WITH TURTLES

The Turtles had no pretense about their being anything but what they were: lucky, fun-loving, and very talented. They were aware that they weren't a 'cute' group. They had an unusual look. In fact, they looked like the people who bought their records. Volman and Kaylan were a bit heavy, and they didn't fit the mold of rock stars. Al Nichols and Chuck Portz looked like audiovisual guys in high school—guys who had Lionel electric train sets in their basement—and the rhythm guitarist, Jim Tucker, was a tough, insecure, shy kid—and a damn good guitarist. Don Murray was the cute Turtle. The girls loved him. And Don was a good drummer.

As musicians, they were extraordinary. From the opening bass note of 'It Ain't Me Babe' to the strumming of the acoustic guitar, I knew that this was a group with a unique sound. It was a hit for them but they encountered unexpected negativity and flak from the intellectual elite for doing a Dylan song. Dylan was considered sacrosanct, and The Turtles had not earned their folk chops. Even with the success of the record, they didn't want to encounter another backlash of criticism and burning balls of fire being heaved at them from the ivory towers and castle turrets of the philosophical guardians of all things meaningful, artful, and deep. The Turtles had decided that they were not going to do another Dylan song, even though logic dictated that you go home with the one who brought you to the dance.

I had met the Turtles at the Trocadero Club on Sunset Boulevard earlier in this very compressed year, hawking my wares since Dunhill's Trousdale Music did not want to publish any of the P.F. Sloan songs. (Note to the new songwriter: make sure you always have your guitar in the car so you can play prospective clients your songs.) I played them the songs that The Byrds had turned down earlier in the week: 'The Sins Of A Family,' 'Eve Of Destruction,' and 'Take Me For What I'm Worth.' Both groups were interested in 'Eve' and 'Sins' but felt that they were too risky to be considered as follow-ups to their debut hits. Kaylan and Volman were making the decisions and told me they would think about it.

In the fall of 1965, Bones Howe was the unacknowledged producer and technical creative force behind the *It Ain't Me Babe* album. 'Eve Of Destruction,' 'I Get Out Of Breath,' and 'I Know You'll Be There,' a Sloan–Barri song that had been previously done by Shelley Fabares, were recorded. 'I Get Out Of Breath' was being considered as a follow-up to 'It Ain't Me Babe' but they weren't quite sure. Bones called and asked if I had any new songs.

I went down to the studio and played them 'Let Me Be,' a song I had written after a weekend in Topanga Canyon. They decided right on the spot that this would be their follow-up to 'It Ain't Me Babe' and recorded it the very next day. Only 'Eve' and 'Let Me Be' made it to that first album.

I have to admit I was feeling pretty good about myself. I was following my star, and it was shining. After all, 'Let Me Be' was not your average pop song. It was a song for the times, a song with a message—a young adult declaring his independence—and it continues to resonate today. We recently got a letter from a man who wrote: 'As a gay man who was coming to terms with his difference at sixteen in the mid 60s, this song was monumental. I used to play it all the time and wish my family could have heard it and know who I was but I had run away from home and they never knew.' A woman recently wrote: 'This song actually became a personal anthem for me as an abused child. In dysfunctional families, the children are not people but extensions of their parents, and even at a mere nine years old, I could relate.'

'Let Me Be' came out as a single and hit the charts big time. The Turtles were happy, Bones Howe was happy, I was happy. The Turtles were enjoying back-to-back successes, which doesn't always happen, but they feared that they were going to be branded as a group that sings protest songs, even though 'Let Me Be' was not technically a protest song. They made up their minds they were not going to do another P.F. Sloan or Bob Dylan song.

That year, 1965, had been nonstop for me. 'Eve Of Destruction'; my first European tour; ten hit songs in the US and many more in Canada; The Searchers; The Mamas & The Papas; The Byrds; singing harmonies with Jan & Dean; 'Little Old Lady From Pasadena'; 'I Found A Girl,' which was Jan & Dean's last hit single; Barry McGuire's album; searching for The Grass Roots; daily writing sessions with Steve Barri; meeting Bob Dylan up at the Continental Hotel with women dressed as pirates.

I found myself eating large portions of prime rib almost every day at Diamond Jim's on Hollywood Boulevard. I would have this meal with a large baked potato, plus pie or shortcake for desert, washed down with several Cokes. This was considered healthy. As we know today, this type of diet kills. But it is what kept me going. And 1965 wasn't finished with me yet.

In 1965, Bobby Roberts orchestrated a giant billboard on Sunset Boulevard with a cutout of P.F. Sloan. It was an advertisement for *Songs Of Our Times*, an album comprised of my demos, including 'Take Me For What I'm Worth,' 'This Mornin',' and 'Ain't No Way I'm Gonna Change My Mind.' Roberts saw an opportunity for P.F. Sloan as a recording artist, as opposed to Adler's view that these *Songs Of Our Times* should be nothing more than a songwriter's demo.

Curiously, the billboard was near where the Trip nightclub had opened up. The Trip, along with the Whisky and Gazzarri's, was one of the top LA hangouts. African American acts were not performing at the Whisky at this time (although that would change) but they were welcomed at the Trip. It became an important stop on the underground railroad of rhythm & blues. The Supremes, Smokey Robinson, and The Temptations all played there. The folksters were welcome there, too, although we—Donovan, Barry McGuire, P.F. Sloan—were considered among the great unwashed.

Donovan, like me, was considered to be a Dylan wannabe, but Donovan had a team of managers who were shepherding him through the minefield of negative press. That was something I wish I had had, in hindsight. So it goes. Donovan was well protected. His manager, Mickie Most, was grooming him to be a star, and he deserved it: Donovan was a sincere, enlightened, sensitive troubadour whose insightful performances connected strongly with his audience.

Mickie was also producing Herman's Hermits and The Animals. I went to see Donovan on his first LA appearance at the Trip. The place was jammed and the electricity incredible. I had performed there many times but there was something mystical about a British performer. Anything British that was good had a special vibe.

Lou Adler was there at the table with Mickie, and he introduced Mickie to me. Mickie wanted to have a word with me. We walked to a private area near the men's room and he told me that he was a big fan of mine, and that Herman's Hermits were going to do a movie. He explained that he was returning to England in two days and wanted to know if I could write the theme song. The movie was going to be called *A Must To Avoid*.

'Think about it,' he said. 'But only think about it tonight. Call me in the morning and tell me what you decide.'

So much for the show. Donovan came onstage, the spotlight hit him, and he began to sing. Well, I was interested in the job so I wanted to get right on it. I figured Donovan would have an extra guitar in his dressing room, so I headed down to see if that was the case. And there in the little dressing room at the Trip, I wrote most of 'A Must To Avoid,' while listening to Donovan singing upstairs. I demoed the song the next morning and sent it over to Mickie.

Mickie went back to England with the song and then, to my surprise, arrived a couple of weeks later at RCA to record it with the Hermits.

He called me up and asked if I could come down and teach the guys the song. You wouldn't expect it with a major, successful group, but the Hermits were insecure about their musicianship. They wanted me to play acoustic and lead guitar on the record. I told them how absolutely superb they were. They were pleased. They felt that they had gotten authenticity.

I showed them the riffs and how to do the acoustic part. Keith Hopwood, the guitarist, had a beautiful guitar—a Gibson J-200 with a tobacco sunburst finish—and I was playing a cheap Harmony Sovereign guitar with the strings so high off the frets that you literally had to force them down to play a chord. (I believed that in order to write a song, there had to be physical pain.)

At this time, the movie was still called *A Must To Avoid*. It would later be changed to *Hold On!* out of fear that, if it were panned, the critics would say it was 'a must to avoid.' Steve added a few words to the song so that it could be a Sloan–Barri composition. 'A Must To Avoid,' the song, was released in the UK in the last week of 1965 and became a hit in early 1966, before the film's release.

Herman's Hermits were sharp, smart, streetwise young men. They were working-class Manchester musicians. They were good musicians and were very particular about their choice of songs. They were a very tight band. When I first heard 'I'm Into Something's Good,' I knew that this was a great band. And their songs—the arrangements, the musicianship, and the singing—were first rate. To this day, some elitist rock types consider them to be fluff. I never did. I will always defend the legitimacy of Herman's Hermits.

THE ONION TRUCK

I decided to drive my Corvette to San Francisco to reconnect with the music scene. I was driving with my good pal Gino Daniello, who was from New York and was Sonny Bono's assistant. Actually, he was Sonny's fiercely loyal muscle and fixer. He was seriously streetwise. He first found work in LA as a bouncer and a bodyguard. He was real New Yorker: square-jawed like Dick Tracy, muscular, quick to anger. You didn't mess with him. But he had a heart of gold.

I once told Gino about the problems I was having with Jay Lasker.

'Hey!' he said. 'I can bust his face into a million pieces! His dog won't recognize him.' And that would have to be pretty unrecognizable.

Gino loved me and acted like my bodyguard—in restaurants, in parking lots, even trying to get a ticket to a movie.

'Hey!' he'd say. 'This is my friend. You do something against him and I'll bust your balls.'

Stephen Stills was a great singer and songwriter, and a sincere and brilliant guy. I met him at the time the Buffalo Springfield—Steve, Richie Furay, Bruce Palmer, Neil Young, and Dewey Martin—were playing at the Whisky A Go-Go as an opening act and headlining on weekdays when there was no business. I went upstairs to the dressing rooms and told them how great they were. They wanted to believe me but they had been turned down by everyone. Neil was telling me that this show was going to be his last and he was heading back to Canada.

'Can't you do anything for us?' Stephen Stills asked.

'You guys are going to be as big as The Byrds,' I said.

'How's that going to happen?' Neil wondered. 'It's impossible.'

'I don't know how,' I said, 'but it's going to happen.'

Stephen gave me the rough demos they had made of 'Nowadays Clancy Can't Even Sing' and 'Hot Dusty Roads.' 'Clancy,' written by Neil, was such an extraordinary song. I recognized it right away as a full-blown movie, completely coordinated from start to finish, with a message that was cynical and hopeful at the same time. It was a commentary on the world written by someone who hadn't even gotten into the business yet.

I played the songs for Jay Lasker and told him that the Buffalo Springfield were going to be as big as The Byrds.

'If you think this is what music is supposed to be, you don't belong here.' Lasker bellowed, and he fired me then and there on the spot.

I went to Stephen and told him that I had been fired from Dunhill. As far as Stephen was concerned, that was the end of the Buffalo Springfield. They were going to break up. But I still had my friend Gino on hand.

'Don't worry, Phil,' he said. 'I'll take these songs to Sonny Bono. Are they any good?'

'I think they are, Gino.'

'OK, then,' he said. 'Leave it to me.'

Sonny listened to the Buffalo Springfield but he didn't get them and politely passed. Disappointed, Gino collected the demos and began to leave. However, Green & Stone, Sonny & Cher's managers, had heard the music from their office next door—just as Al Nevins had heard mine back at my Screen Gems audition—and kind of liked it. They sent the demos to Ahmet Ertegun at Atlantic Records, the label Sonny & Cher were signed to, but he too passed on the demo.

Here's where it gets magical. An Atlantic employee who worked as a second engineer was walking down the hall and heard the music coming out of the speakers. This fellow told Ertegun that there was something there and that he thought he could fix the record if he messed with it a bit, and maybe he'd be able to make something special out of it, if he could get the masters. So Stephen Stills got me the masters, and I gave them to Gino, who gave them to Green & Stone, who gave them to the engineer, and the result was the finished 'Nowadays Clancy Can't Even Sing.' The Buffalo Springfield had their record deal with Atlantic, and the song was released. Deal done. All because of the persistence and connections of Gino.

I have no control over how the event is remembered by some today. But that is how it happened.

The problem for me now, though, was that I was out of a job, so I thought I'd head up to San Francisco with Gino to see if I could rustle any work.

We didn't make it to San Francisco. About two hours out of LA, up around Salinas, a truck loaded with onions smashed into us. Gino had hung a little crystal on the rearview mirror. The last thing I remember before the accident was staring at that little crystal. There was nothing left of the car except for two bucket seats with Gino and me sitting in them amid a heap of white fiberglass. Pieces of the car were all over the highway. The guy driving the onion truck wasn't hurt but the truck was pretty smashed up. There must have been a million onions rolling like marbles on the road.

I sat there in shock as Gino unbuckled himself and took off into the brush. He was holding, and he didn't want the cops, who were bound to come soon, to find the bag of weed on him. In those days, you went to jail for carrying a little grass—and I don't think Gino ever carried a little grass.

Gino made it back to LA somehow and spent a couple of days in the hospital. I was pretty banged up but more freaked out than anything. The Highway Patrol drove me to a bus station, where I boarded a bus back to LA and hobbled into my parents' house.

'What happened to you?' my father asked.

'I got hit by an onion truck.'

'Where's your car?'

'I'm afraid it was totaled, but it wasn't really my fault.'

'Was the driver hurt?'

'I was the driver.'

'I mean the driver of the truck. Was he hurt?'

'No, he wasn't hurt, thank God.'

'Thank God is right,' he said.

'Have you given any thought as to what you're going to with yourself, now that you are out of work?' he asked.

'I'm thinking about moving to England!' I replied. And I was. A week later, however, Bobby Roberts intervened, and I was reinstated at Dunhill, back into the blender.

CHAPTER TEN

FROM CRESCENT HEIGHTS TO LAUREL CANYON

Being as I was underage at the time, all my royalties were collected by a court-appointed judge, and Dunhill had an accountancy firm handle the monies. I petitioned the court for $25,000—a large sum in 1965—to present to my parents so that they could pay off their mortgage, as my father was going through rough waters.

I was very excited about this. I presented the check to my father, and my father ripped it up in front of me.

'Who do you think you are, Elvis?' my mother asked.

'Of course not. This is just my way to show you both how much I love you and how grateful I am for all you have done for me.'

'Believe me, we were doing well before "Eve Of Destruction" and we will do well after "Eve Of Destruction,"' my mother informed me.

To me, earning money was not a symbol of success. It was a way to prove to my parents that I did not have to become a college graduate to gain their acceptance and not be a burden. And this seemed like a realistic use of it. The make-believe amount of money that was available to me was beyond my parents' comprehension. But giving money to my family, I found, was not as easy as I had imagined.

Striking out with my parents, I headed to my sister's house. Her husband had just recently been fired from his position as a mathematician at the Jet Propulsion Laboratory and was now drinking himself into space without leaving his chair. What better way to cheer them up then to buy them a brand new Chrysler 300? I told them that I was going to order the car and it would be delivered the following week. But my sister refused my gift, chewing my ear off about how I was trying to show off. I recalled my childhood lesson of not making waves and not bringing attention to the family. That was what it was like in those days.

Up until this point I had been living comfortably at home. My meals were provided and my clothes were cleaned and pressed. My parents' house on Del Valle had turned into a happening place. It was there where I entertained people from all over the world—rock stars, university intellectuals, interviewers, European record executives. It was where Steve Barri and I worked on songs at the breakfast table—the room that had such a great echo. It was not uncommon for me to walk into the house and find my mother sitting at the kitchen table, drinking coffee with people like Hal Blaine or Phil Ochs, or somebody from the *LA Times* or a KRLA DJ.

When I walked into that environment, it was like, *excuse me, I'm just going to get a glass of milk and then go into my room.* Eventually, though, I guess I started to feel a bit cramped, so I came to the conclusion that it would be a good time to find my own place.

I thought I'd check out the Canyons, Topanga and Laurel. I had taken long drives through Topanga many times to clear my head and get into nature. I wrote some of the lyric to 'Let Me Be' out there. People in Topanga had the attitude of, *I don't care what you do, just let me do what I do, and don't bother me while I'm doing it, and have a good life.* And the musicians who lived there—the artists and actors and directors—were all just a little bit different. A little more eccentric. A little more against the status quo of being hip. Down on the Sunset Strip, people were into acting hip. They were acting as if they were out of the norm, but in Topanga they really were. Canned Heat, Little Feat, Taj Mahal, Emmylou Harris, Etta James, Neil Young, Crazy Horse—they all lived in Topanga. It's where you lived when you had an 'edge' to your head.

Laurel Canyon was sex, drugs, and rock'n'roll. But it was also more than just a party canyon. I had the intention of doing great work there. I figured Laurel Canyon might be a place where I could explore the character of P.F. Sloan without derision or interference. I felt that P.F. Sloan was my doorway to adulthood, while others thought that this was just a phony persona—a crazy stage I was going through.

People were telling me not to bet on P.F. Sloan. They were telling me to stay with who I was, not who I had become. But the poetry and insight that came from those first few songs is what I was going to bet my life on.

I decided I would make my stand on Wonderland Avenue, in Laurel Canyon. I rented a three-bedroom house patterned on an English Medieval castle. I had a lot of room to move around, and at first I enjoyed it. I went to clubs on the strip looking for a love with whom to share my castle, but I wasn't having much luck with that.

Then one day an odd fellow showed up at my door. He told me his name was Kip and that he was from India. He told me that his Guru, Babaji, a 2,000-year-old Enlightened Being, had instructed him to find me, and that he was to be my yoga teacher.

'Well, if that's what he told you, come on in,' I replied. 'Make yourself at home.'

Kip took up residence while a lady friend of his showed up every morning with fresh blueberry muffins and orange juice laced with the tiniest bit of LSD—not enough to send you on a trip but enough to make things look a bit more vivid. Kip slept on a mat in the living room and answered the door like he was my manservant, and I soon grew used to it. He was very polite and helpful to anyone who visited me.

There were always parties in Laurel Canyon. Denny Doherty of The Mamas & The Papas would have dozens of people at his house at any given time. There were cases of Chivas Regal, bags of grass and hash, and people rolling on the floor, dead drunk. John Phillips had a place up there, too. Cass Eliot had a place off of Kings Road, and Phil Ochs lived off Lomita Drive, although there were no parties at Phil's place. Usually stoned, we'd wind up sitting at an outdoor table at the Country Store and watch a movie director with his starlets, or Jim Morrison struggling with the change in his pockets to buy a pack of cigarettes. Everyone seemed to run out at almost the same time of night, and there was a relaxed, friendly atmosphere. *Yeah man, you know it.*

That table was a great place to catch up on what people were doing. Occasionally, I'd get lucky and find a woman who I thought I could relate to, but after a month or so I'd find that it wasn't working out on that score. I was beginning to become a little full of myself, but it happened so gradually that I never noticed until my friends Bob and Jerry pointed out to me that I was acting like a 'prince' and pontificating to them as if they were the 'little people.'

This was deep water for a young man. I knew myself to be a strong swimmer, and I didn't want to live my life at the shallow end of the pool. The problem I was having was that the rock'n'roll lifestyle at the deep end of the pool was drowning me, and there was no lifeguard on duty.

SECRET AGENT

There was a very popular spy show on television in the UK called *Danger Man*, starring Patrick McGoohan. CBS bought the show for American television and planned on debuting it in 1966. They needed a new theme song as the British show had a harpsichord playing. CBS wanted something more definitive. There was a worldwide contest—not unlike the *TAMI Show* competition—so a good number of songwriters throughout the world submitted songs. The new song was going to be placed over the opening titles for the show, and it had to be less than a minute long.

I wrote a guitar riff first, then Steve and I worked on a single verse and chorus while I created the melody. The chorus ran *Lookout Danger Man / Lookout Danger Man / This life you lead is a deadly game*. Then the producers came back with a name change—the show would now be called *Secret Agent*. I threw away the old lyric and started writing it on my own. The lyrics came together fast and furious. I wrote three verses and a new chorus. I kind of wondered where the line about *bleeding in a Bombay alley* came from, but I liked it and decided to leave it in. Many years later, that line would prove significant in my life.

I went into the studio with Hal and I think Larry Knechtel to demo the minute-long version of the song, and while I was there we decided to do a full instrumental version as well. The lyrics to the second and third verses were written for fun. Dunhill submitted my demo to the producers, and we were given the thumbs up. All agreed that the project was a great one. Adler enlisted Johnny Rivers to sing the forty-five-second song for the show, and when it was done he was glad to be done with it. Johnny was working at writing his own songs, and he felt this type of thing was a step backward.

Hal Blaine loved the song, however, and pleaded with Adler to release the demo we made as a Hal Blaine single. Adler agreed, and the demo became the follow-up to his chart record 'Topsy 65,' a remake of the late-50s hit 'Topsy' by Cozy Cole. *Secret Agent* aired on CBS, and within a month it was a top-rated show. Rivers was asked to come out with a full version of the song but he didn't want any part of it and repeatedly turned down the idea.

The Ventures heard an instrumental demo at their record label, Dolton, a sister label to Imperial-Liberty. Three weeks after the show became a hit, The Ventures released their version of 'Secret Agent,' calling it 'Secret Agent Man,' and it began burning up the charts, entering at thirty-eight. It was their fastest selling record since 'Telstar.'

Lou twisted Johnny's arm to do a full-length version of his own and a session was called. The plan was to do the song in front of a live audience at the Whisky with Mickey Jones on drums, Joe Osborne on bass, and Johnny on a black Gibson ES-335 electric. They nailed it after a number of takes, Johnny taking the solo live and then overdubbing a rhythm electric under it. The record came out and made so large an impact that the Ventures were driven from the charts—but only after selling a cool half-million copies. Johnny's version stopped just shy of No. 1, which was pretty good going for a guy who had to have his arm twisted to do it.

The show went on for several seasons and spawned a follow-up called *The Prisoner*. In an interview, McGoohan revealed that the new show was inspired by a line from 'Secret Agent': *They've given you a number and taken away your name.* And everyone agreed it was a cool show.

Over the years, lots of people have taken credit for writing the guitar riffs for 'Secret Agent.' It was only when Carey Mansfield, the president of Varese-Sarabande Records, decided to release an album of my demos called *Trousdale Sessions*, which includes the original demo of 'Danger Man,' that it became clear without a doubt that I had written it. And I never get tired of hearing it.

A CRY IN THE WILDERNESS

Phil Ochs was one of the pioneers of the modern folk movement, navigating American culture through the unknown wilderness of self-expression. Along with acts like Ian & Sylvia and Fred Neil, he was at the point of a musical scene that had at its core a conscience and point of view nourished by incitement, intellect, and an appreciation for the human condition and the human comedy.

Woody Guthrie, with his cutting phrase 'This Machine Kills Fascists' scribbled onto his guitar, was arguably the spearhead of this movement, as to an extent was the tall man with the banjo, Pete Seeger. Woody came out swinging an ax; Seeger came out wanting to confront his enemy with a heartfelt plea for justice. Phil Ochs seemed to bring both of those worlds together, as did Bob Dylan.

Phil Ochs, David Blue, Eric Anderson, and myself would meet occasionally for songwriting and guitar-picking sessions at Phil's little house in Laurel Canyon, which was purchased for him by his former wife Alice. I was living right nearby on Wonderland Drive.

I had been a fan of Ochs before I met him, and he was intimidating. He wore the mask of an intellectual just beautifully, but you always felt he was a little child who enjoyed letting his curiosity run amok. He was a brilliant actor, but you felt his heart was breaking on the inside, and anyone who loved him knew this. He tried to convince people that it was part of the act of the heartbroken poet.

'It is what makes me,' he once told me. 'You are witnessing the disillusion of the artist. The crucifixion of the poet.'

The crucifixion of the artist was one of Phil's favorite analogies. You wanted to shake him and tell him, *c'mon, just talk to me*. But his intellect would not allow the walls to come down.

Phil loved to play the laureate professor of intellectual poetry—a position I began to emulate but dropped when I learned it was distancing myself from those I loved and respected. The guys who met at his house were the only ones Phil would occasionally let in, and even then only on a casual level, as it exposed him to criticism and self-doubt.

Phil held these songwriting get-togethers because he was trying to uncover what he was missing. And what he was missing was his heart.

Phil and I would talk for hours and hours about Elvis. Or rather I would. I brought over all of my Elvis records, and he'd listen to them over and over again. In a moment of unusual trust in me—or perhaps only out of curiosity as to what I might say—he asked, 'What does Bob Dylan have that I don't?'

'A love of Elvis Presley,' I told him flatly.

'Bob loves Elvis?'

'Yeah. Elvis is one of Bob's biggest dreams in life. Elvis is an incredible interpreter of music—to the point of supernatural. And it's not only Elvis. It's his band. Elvis has one of the greatest bands that ever existed. When you are listening to this band, you are hearing eternity. Elvis plays his part beautifully, but his band is as good as any jazz band that ever was.'

Phil's heart began to get excited about music—the glory of music that was Elvis Presley and his band. Scotty Moore, Bill Black, D.J. Fontana. We discussed what made music wonderful and magical, and why it seemed to bring the soul closer to God. I thought he was getting it, but he only got it on a guerilla-intellectual level. Maybe this is why he wore Elvis's gold suit on his *Greatest Hits* album. Phil actually went to Nudie, the famous tailor who made Elvis's suit, and had another made just like it.

I was stunned and awed and not just a little bit envious. But to envy Phil Ochs was to love him. He had a disarming smile. A disguise. When you saw him smile, you knew that something was happening in his brain. It was as if intellectually he was putting heaven and earth in a nice package that Phil Ochs, like Moses, could bring to the world—a Lewis & Clark expedition to discover the true roadmap of humanity, and the meaning of it all. I think Phil believed he had the only map. This poet of opposites had a disdain for the mundane, which included everything that makes us human and the love of humanity, where he, like an eagle, could perch high above it all and point us in the right direction. That is what makes me continue searching for words that will set me free of him and finally understand him and his deep longings for love and adoration.

To love Ochs was to adore him with all his faults. But Phil, like a scientist with a microscope, wanted to know what made P.F. Sloan tick. He wanted to know how I could write so many different styles of songs. That made me feel somewhat insecure in his presence. So Ochs, in the spirit of scientific investigation, started hanging around my parents' house on Del Valle and talking to my mother. I would go over to visit my folks, and there would be Phil Ochs, sitting at the kitchen table, eating dinner with my father or in the living room watching television. Finally, he moved into their garage, sleeping on my old bed.

I'm not bringing this up to flatter myself in any way. It was somewhat scary to me. Phil was doing this as some sort of cosmic mind-meld. He explained to me that he wanted to get under the skin of P.F. Sloan. I hoped he would learn whatever he was trying to uncover and move on.

Phil was invited to play Carnegie Hall in 1966 but didn't want to do it. We talked about it for a couple of months, and finally Phil agreed. On opening night, he played to a sold-out house of adoring fans but he could not take it in. He rejected their love as inferior idol worship. His fans should know better than that, he said. What a conundrum!

'Why can't you let the love in?' I asked. 'People love you so much but you push them away.'

'I can't,' he said.

But why couldn't Phil Ochs feel it? He wanted so desperately to be loved, and people certainly loved him, but he could not let them. Sadly, what he loved the most was the slow dance of suicide, not realizing that enlightenment of the intellect was only the first step toward the total enlightenment of the heart. So Phil Ochs became a willing tragic figure. I spent a good number of years by his side. He ran every note of *Pleasures Of The Harbor* through me, gleefully, like a little child running his fingers over a shining jewel he had dug up from the dirt.

'Do you think they'll get it?' he asked fearfully.

'I don't know, but it is so very beautiful.'

Pleasures Of The Harbor was as beautiful to me as the exquisite melody he wrote for 'Changes.'

It was amazing how many people showed up after the end to get in line to be called his friend. They came to idolize him and worship him, and he got the dues that he deserved, but for me it all seemed hollow. It ignored his tragic crying in the wilderness.

Love to you Phil, and brother Michael.

RUNNING WITH TURTLES

In 1966, Steve Barri had two favorite songs in the world: The Lettermen's 'The Way You Look Tonight' and The Vogues' 'It's A Five O'clock World.' We sat down at the kitchen table on Del Valle one afternoon with the intention of writing a follow-up to 'It's A Five O'clock World,' largely to satisfy Steve. Hopefully, we thought, we would be able to get it to the band.

Our relationship had changed since 1963. P.F. Sloan had charted with many songs in 1965, but when I was working with Steve, I had to put P.F. Sloan away. Fortunately, there was a part of me who dearly loved pop music. I needed to express that part of my personality rather than kill it off.

The song we came up with on this occasion was 'You Baby (Nobody But You).' It was upbeat and catchy, but there was a blues element and a sadness hidden in the song, particularly in the line, *Who makes me feel like smiling when the weary day is through ... nobody ... but you, baby*. It may seem like a miniscule point, but to me that gave it authenticity. I needed to have something in the song I could relate to personally. I wasn't going home to see a smiling face, telling me everything was going to be all right. No, not me.

We submitted the song to The Vogues and they turned it down, though they did record it a few years later. Interestingly, in the 1966 *Billboard* Top 100 songs for the year, 'You Baby' was 87, and The Vogues' 'Five O'clock World' came in at 88. Peas in a pod.

Meanwhile, The Turtles had decided that they were being pigeonholed as a 'message song' band. They feared the idea of carrying the burden of heavy songs on their shoulders for all of the teenagers who yearned to be unshackled. The band wanted to become a Lovin' Spoonful-type band. They felt that would fit their personalities better. Howard and Mark were fun-loving guys, always clowning around and giving the impression that they were not deep, serious thinkers—which they were.

The Turtles' *It Ain't Me Babe* album had included two songs of mine,

'Eve Of Destruction' and 'Let Me Be,' and between Mr. Dylan and myself they had more than enough message-folk-rock. Imagine their surprise, then, when Bones Howe told them that he had another song from me for them. *Oh, please, Bones, not another P.F. Sloan song!* But then they listened to the demo I had made of 'You Baby' and absolutely fell in love with it. It was exactly where they wanted to go. They could not have been more pleased and excited.

'This is exactly what we want,' Kaylan told me. 'How did you know?'

The truth is that I didn't. It must have been a Divine gift that was good for them and good for Steve and me. Soon the song was recorded and it sounded great. Everybody was happy. But Steve was the happiest of them all—or as happy as he could be, with not having The Vogues do it.

'You Baby' became a big hit in a matter of weeks. It went to No. 1 in New York, Los Angeles, Chicago, and Philadelphia, but the band's label, White Whale Records, couldn't seem to keep up, as was the case with a lot of smaller imprints. Instead of hitting all over the country at once, the song would go from city to city. Kaylan said he felt he was robbed by White Whale's incompetence. He wanted the legitimacy of a No. 1 record to cement the group's new sound.

While Bones was searching for a follow-up record, Steve and I got together and reworked a song we had written for Betty Everett, 'Can I Get To Know You,' retitling it 'Can I Get To Know You Better.' I changed it from a blues song to a pop song and demoed it for Bones. Again the group loved it, and it was released as the follow-up record. By now, however, White Whale Records was beginning to implode. After the problems with the distribution of 'You Baby,' it only got worse with 'Can I Get To Know You Better,' which was getting played and selling like a Top 10 record but literally died on the vine. It went to No. 50 on the charts and then started falling. Kaylan again felt he'd been robbed. But three hit singles in a row with The Turtles was a good ride for me. It showed me that I was doing a fairly good balancing act between Phil, Steve, and P.F. Sloan. That was how I saw it.

The Turtles were a great band, but man were they minimalized. No matter how many hits they had, they were always considered second-rate. Every group in LA was considered second-rate, as crazy as that sounds today. LA groups didn't even get respect in their hometown. Buffalo Springfield, The Turtles, The Byrds, The Doors … LA groups were not real, not like The Beatles or the Stones. That was the purist's mantra. When Howard told me that he met John Lennon and John told him how much he liked their records, he was shocked.

'If they knew this in LA we would be given the keys to the city instead of being called Beatles wannabes,' he said.

The Turtles went through changes because of these perceptions. Chuck and Don left, and Jim quit the group too after being insulted by John Lennon. At various points they were replaced by John Barbata, Chip Douglas, Joe Ponz, and Joe Larson.

The Turtles eventually got their No. 1 hit with 'Happy Together,' but in the end Howard and Mark, who were best friends, decided they couldn't take this lack of credibility anymore and instead became supporting players in the Frank Zappa circus as Flo & Eddie. *Forget the Turtles*, I suspect Frank told them. *You're now The Florescent Leach and Eddie, and you'll take a lot more acid and be embraced by the Grateful Dead crowd who know how to make you feel loved, and I won't let anyone screw with you …*

Today, the Turtles are loved and celebrated for their music, and rightly so. But the deep hurt and scars remain from all of the years that they were considered second-rate. They were never second-rate. They were always first-rate.

MISSING THE BEAT

Don Murray was the original drummer for The Turtles, and something very strange happened that drove him into the depths of hell for thirty years that I would like to set forth in this narrative. As we were working on 'You Baby' in the studio with Bones Howe and The Turtles, I played them the demo I had made with the unique drum intro on it by Hal Blaine. Don went back into to the studio to practice it while Howard, Mark, Al, and Chuck were figuring out their parts in the booth.

Chuck Portz was a cool bassist and had figured out a bass part for himself that we liked. When we were ready to record the song, Don thought he heard me say that his drumming was messing up the record, and that we needed to use Hal in his place. But I had said nothing of the sort. If anything, it was just the opposite! I said that Don's creative riff was much better than the one I had done and we should use his take on it. But he seemed to have heard the exact opposite of what was said and kept quiet about it. From that moment on, his confidence and joy left him. Don thought I wanted to get rid of him. I was unaware of any of this at the time, but looking back I can't help but conclude that the reason Howard and Mark tossed him out of the group was because he had lost something inside. It seems the seeds of his destruction were somehow planted that day and began to feed on Don's soul. He journeyed through hell for the next thirty years.

In the meantime, I had begun my long journey into healing, and had become romantically involved with a redheaded woman who I was not able to break off with, no matter how hard I tried. She just wouldn't let go of me. I had traveled to India a number of times to see Sathya Sai Baba, and everyone was encouraged at how I was steadily getting stronger. But she believed that my Guru was a cult figure, and she wanted to free me from that. I appreciated her fanatical caring, but she was way out of line. Seven years later, I was still trying to detach from her. We weren't living together or anything like that, but she was still in my life.

One afternoon, she told me about a show at Surf City that she thought we should attend. Jan & Dean were there alongside a lot of other surf bands, including The Surfaris, for whom Don Murray was the drummer. After the show I met with Don backstage after so many years and introduced him to the cherry-haired girl.

'Phil,' he said. 'I have had dreams about this redhead for twenty years now. In the dream we fall in love and are happy forever. And she is the real love of my life.'

They fell in love in real time, on the spot, and the redhead finally left me for Don. They couldn't have been happier, and I couldn't have been happier. They were together for a couple of years until his death in 1996 from complications following surgery on a stomach ulcer. Before he died, we reignited our friendship, and we spent many an evening on my back porch, gamming about the old days. For that I am grateful.

CHAPTER ELEVEN

TWELVE MORE TIMES

Steve Barri was a likeable guy. He didn't drink or smoke grass or go on weekend LSD trips at Joshua Tree or commune with nature. He was a transplanted New Yorker who loved the simple things in life: sex, TV, and a good deli. He also loved music, too, and he had a talent for it. He had his own magic but it was magic without any risk. He wasn't a creative risk taker and he distrusted any one who was. He was in this game for the long run.

Steve thought I was like him, and God knows I tried to be. These differences played out not only in our writing songs together but also in the studio. I wanted cutting-edge sounds and feelings, while Steve was looking for middle-of-the-road, don't-piss-anyone-off kind of music. The battles began with the early Grass Roots records and Steve pretty much acquiesced to my demands. But as with the Baggys, where I had to force him to sing a song on the album, I had to make sure I gave in to his tastes.

Adler and Lasker gave in to Barri's demands to produce an album on his own. Who could he produce? Well, he produced the first P.F. Sloan album. That's how *Twelve More Times* was born. Hal and Joe, John Phillips, Larry Knechtel, and myself got together and knocked the album off in a week. It was basically a songwriter demo album, as I was still considered to be a make-believe recording artist.

Of the twelve songs on the record, eight became chart hits. Of course, Steve got his name on a number of them. That worked like this.

'Phil,' he'd say, 'this doesn't really sound like a P.F. Sloan song. I want my name on it.'

'Well, it is a P.F. Sloan song.'

'C'mon Phil, you can't have all the songs to yourself!'

'Why? Which one do you want?'

'"I Found A Girl," "Here's Where You Belong," and "This Precious Time,"' he said.

He had done this to me with half the songs I wrote for my first album. And though I said no, his name seemed to get on the label anyway. Today, on the internet, he is listed as cowriter on many of my songs, but I guess that's the price you pay when you disappear for such long periods of time, like I did. The vultures come and steal every little piece they can get. You have to fight to hold on to every little thing, and you get tired of fighting all too quickly. I was disgusted by it, but then I grew up hearing Little Richard say that even though writers put their names on his songs as cowriters, a quarter of a penny was better than nothing. And since the Dunhill lawyers had drawn up all the contracts for these songs, there was no going out of house unless I wanted to start a war.

I hid my feelings in songs like 'The Man Behind The Red Balloon,' referring to Steve as *the man with the little black case who may forget his tie but never his face*; to Lou Adler as *the man walking down the street looking great—how his fragile ideals, he thinks are concealed*; to myself, *hiding behind a Batman cape and pretending to be a spy*; and to McGuire, *singing with a golden disc scotch-taped to his lips*. Steve didn't get it and Adler didn't get it. Nobody got it really and nobody cared. They thought it was meaningless poetic drivel from the mind of a madman.

I searched for the meanings behind conformity and non-conformity in the song 'On Top Of A Fence.' Again, nobody cared. I searched for spiritual truth in 'From A Distance,' and all they said was, 'That's pretty.'

On second thoughts, they got it. I wasn't getting it. The label believed that songs were simply created to sell records and not to explore the inner psyche or soul. Leave that to F. Scott Fitzgerald or John Steinbeck or Bob Dylan. It's like the line in the Dylan song: *My God, am I here all alone? And you know something's happening, but you don't know what it is, do you, Mr. Sloan?* Mr. Jones, I mean.

The folk-rock movement was happening now all over Europe, Australia, Canada, South America, and would soon be hitting in Japan.

The week after the album wrapped I went in and demoed a new song called 'City Women' with the usual crew, including John Phillips. It would become the basis for Phillips's 'Monday, Monday.'

FOUR HIPPIES IN A BATHTUB

John Phillips felt that, since I played guitar on the tracks for 'California Dreamin',' I should continue on guitar for The Mamas & The Papas' first album. And so, aside from everything else I had going on, I became the lead guitar player and in-studio arranger for them.

In the studio, the group was insecure. They had an initial distrust of Lou Adler or anybody in authority. But John was having the time of his life. He took to the studio life as if he were made for it, and in no time, he was taking control of the musicians—Hal, Joe, Larry, and myself. At first, he spoke a language the musicians couldn't understand, so I translated. John did not speak LA studio *musisicanese*: only Greenwich Village *folkese*.

Hal didn't cotton on to Phillips at first but he realized he had talent and was going to be a star. Joe rarely showed any like or dislike for any song or musician. He was there to work. Larry wanted to make everything better.

Michelle was kind of bored. She didn't have much faith in the project. She was sweet but distant. Cass was just distant. She had not yet grown into the gregarious Mama Cass that we would learn to love and appreciate. Denny was the glue that held it all together. He had jokes and stories, and he was having fun. He was going to have a good time whether he was a Papa or not.

I was all business, and so was Lou, who was in the booth with Steve. My job was to get four tracks done in three hours and translate the songs into *musicianese* by interpreting the sound that John heard in his head and making it happen by communicating that with the musicians. The musicians themselves immediately started to come up with ideas, which I would approve or disapprove.

These were truly creative, high-energy sessions. What was unique was this feeling of excitement that this was going to be a major event. Listening to the songs, I knew that this group was going to be big. They had a much bigger sound than Peter Paul & Mary, and a hard beat with it. Though

'Go Where You Want To Go' had failed, I knew 'California Dreamin''
couldn't. We had cut the instrumental tracks a month before with Barry
McGuire. Now we took Barry's vocals off and rerecorded them.

As confident as I was in the songs, you really never know. It's just
a gut feeling really. When we started working on 'Monday, Monday,'
John asked if we could get the same drum and guitar riffs I created for
'City Women.' And so we did. You can almost sing the entire 'Monday,
Monday' over the 'City Women' track.

It took three or four sessions to do the basic tracks for the album.
We rushed through overdubs of tambourine, woodblocks, extra piano,
and electric guitar, which was the mentality of the time. Bud Shank, the
renowned flautist from World Pacific Records, came in to do the flute
solo on 'California Dreamin'.' When he heard the guitar solo that I had
put down on the original, he told Adler that he thought it was great and
that the song didn't need a flute. But Adler insisted, so Shank followed my
lead and played the same notes I had done on the guitar. If you listen real
closely to the flute solo, you can hear my guitar underneath.

With the tracks completed, the group came into the studio to sing. It
was just a matter of finding that magical, sweet place where their actual
voices melded together. A physical place: how close or far they would
stand from one another and the mics. Denny and John were on one mic
and Cass and Michelle were on the other. Then we needed to find a mic
that worked magic for their voices, and the perfect echo and reverb for
them. Without it, their voices didn't seem to fly.

After we put their voices on, they were double-tracked to get a fuller
sound. Denny loved 'You Baby.' Adler didn't want them to do it, but
Denny and John had worked up a new interpretation of the song. This
would also gave them the creative permission to use other songs on future
albums that already were hits—'Dancing In The Street,' 'Do You Want
To Dance,' and 'My Heart Stood Still.' I found this interesting, because
it meant Trousdale Publishing would have to give money, rather than
receive money. But Adler was beginning to believe the group was worth
it, and he let them do what they wanted to do. Not unlike The Beatles
doing 'Money' or 'You Really Got A Hold On Me.'

I liked working on this album because the group was tight, they were involved and interested, the studio was drug-free, and the creativity was focused and high. Everyone was intent on getting the best possible music, as opposed to what The Mamas & The Papas turned into later, which was getting the best possible drugs that would then hopefully give them the best possible music. Of course, that wasn't possible.

'California Dreamin'' was released in November 1965 but didn't hit as a single until 1966. It looked like it was going to go where 'Go Where You Want To Go' had gone: nowhere. Interestingly enough, when the record finally broke, it was Boston that was responsible for creating The Mamas & The Papas' career. That market really ate it up. The city was loaded with college students who dug the hell out of anything about California, since it was cold there most of the year and this type of song allowed them to dream of escaping to warmer climes. Like Greenwich Village, Boston also was very accepting of folk-rock. And what Boston heard quickly spread throughout the hundreds and hundreds of colleges across the States, which are basically small cities. The song made people feel good. That feeling spread across the country, and then the world, beckoning expats living abroad to return home.

Jay Lasker hated The Mamas & The Papas, however. He hated hippies. Adler on the other hand was becoming enthralled with the charisma of this group—especially the young and nubile Michelle. He was still wearing cashmere sweaters at this point—he was curious about the new lifestyle but not yet willing to cross the line and become one of them. Bobby Roberts was put off by the group. He hadn't had a great experience with Barry McGuire, and in his mind, hippie equaled controversy. Lasker's relationship with The Mamas & The Papas would continue to worsen until he got what he wanted—the end.

PRECIOUS TIMES

John Phillips had pulled 'California Dreamin'' out from under Barry McGuire just as Barry was struggling. We had already cut the tracks for the song and The Mamas & The Papas had sung background parts behind Barry's powerful vocal. But it wasn't going to be his follow-up to

'Eve.' Barely a few short months earlier, he had been singing on the world stage. In today's world, he would have been touring for two years or more before even considering a follow-up album or single, selling T-shirts and coffee cups and records to sell-out crowds. But in the compressed time of the sixties, Barry started to look washed-up after only three months!

Barry was trying his best to have a good time, but his heart wasn't all in it because the label basically wanted him to disappear. He knew that he was just going through the motions of making an album. That album contained 'Upon A Painted Ocean' and 'Child Of Our Times,' but there wasn't anything you might call new and exciting except for 'This Precious Time,' a new song I had written, with The Mamas & The Papas singing backup. It would be released as a single in 1967, and it actually hit the charts, but the recording of this album was bittersweet. The Mamas & The Papas were getting ready to enter the limelight, but Barry was preparing to leave. The joy of creativity was not really there. You could feel the boot heel of Dunhill on our necks. Nobody cared about Barry McGuire.

THE BLACK PLAGUE

The Black Plague was a collection of Terry Black's greatest hits. It was released in 1966 and went flying up the charts in Canada, solidifying Terry's position as an authentic recording star. However, Terry became persona non grata at Dunhill when his manager Buddy Clyde asked Jay Lasker for the money that was owed for the records sold. I was in the office when it all went down.

'Fuck you,' Lasker told Buddy, taking the cigar out of his mouth, shocking Buddy with his vile crudeness. 'Who the fuck do you think you are? Go back to fucking Canada and take that fucking *Black Plague* with you.'

Buddy started to shake and looked like he was going to collapse.

'What, are you going to have a fucking stroke?' Lasker continued. 'Get the fuck out of here before I have you thrown out.'

Buddy left the office, shaken and humiliated. I started to leave with him to help him to his car.

'Hold, on Flip,' Lasker growled. 'I'm not finished with you.'

Buddy left, and I stayed in the office, ready to have it out with Lasker, but I held my tongue and waited as he snuffed out his cigar and lit another.

'Be honest with me,' he said. 'Do you think I was too rough on that maggot?'

Here was my chance, I thought, but before I could answer, Lasker went on a ten-minute diatribe about how Terry Black was finished and would never be heard from again.

'And by the way,' he said, suddenly turning friendly. 'How are The Grass Roots doing? Is there anything I can do to help?'

'Jay,' I replied, 'The Roots are out on tour.'

'Good for them. Are they having fun? How's everything going in the hinterlands?'

'Not so good. They don't even have enough money for food. We're getting calls from the hotels. We owe them money.'

'Go and tell fucking Muriel to call their manager to set up a meeting with me. I'll take care of that bastard for good.'

'OK, Jay.'

'And everything else is good?'

'Never better.'

Terry Black never made another record for Dunhill. He was devastated and beaten down so bad that I barely recognized him when he left to go home to Vancouver. It would take him nine years to recover. He reemerged briefly with his beautiful 'Moondust,' which was featured on the soundtrack of Bill Murray's *Meatballs* in 1979.

Daniel Rutherford is a Canadian who grew up loving Terry Black records. After he married Marilyn Wilson (Brian's ex-wife) in the mid 90s he got me on Terry's case. We spent years trying to get his album *The Black Plague* released on CD, but Arc/Tollie said they didn't know where the masters were. The album had been bootlegged for years, earning no money for Terry.

Finally, through endless persistence, Arc found the masters and rereleased *The Black Plague*. His career was instantly resurrected. He began touring and performing all over Canada as a hero. He got his own radio show and was listened to all over the country. He remarried and reconnected to life and was truly happy and doing well. We remained friends until he passed away in 2009 after suffering from multiple sclerosis.

Coincidentally, another early Canadian star, Patrician Anne, who was also on Arc would have a hit with a song I had written when I was sixteen called 'Blue Lipstick.' A small cult following for her and the song continues to this day. Perhaps the subject of the song—a Bohemian girl loses her boyfriend and starts to wear blue lipstick to let the world know just how blue she is—was ahead of its time.

LITTLE BIG SONGS

This was an extraordinarily prolific time for me. The songs kept coming and coming. They were being recorded, and they made a difference in the lives of the artists involved. Some of these songs, though not gigantic hits, were as important to me as any of the more well known songs. They were important because they kept some of these artists in the game, and that was a big deal for me. I felt like I was contributing.

Freddie & The Dreamers released their version of a demo I had sent to Dick James in 1966. The song was called 'I Wonder Who The Lucky Guy Will Be' and got Freddie and his group back onto the charts after people felt they were finished. Around the same time, The Searchers released their version of 'Take Me For What I'm Worth' for a ride on the British and American charts. It was seen as a major comeback record for them, as they hadn't been doing so well until then. And then Dev Douglas recorded 'What Am I Doing Here With You,' which hit the English charts in 1966, just before Twinkle did the same with her version of the song. After that, Bev Harrell got onto the Australian charts with her take on the song. Johnny Rivers had actually been the first person to record the song in 1964, but he didn't really dig it.

Johnny Tillotson was considered to be a has-been teen idol by Dunhill. He had written and sung numerous Top 10 records like the great 'Poetry In Motion' and 'Send Me The Pillow You Dream On' but had fallen on hard times as of late. Basically, anybody who still wore their hair in a pompadour was sent out to the back roads of rock'n'roll.

Johnny wrote me a letter, telling me that he loved my songs and wanting to know if I had one he could record. I was thrilled. I had grown up watching him on *American Bandstand*. I showed Adler the letter and was promptly told that Johnny was nobody and didn't warrant a P.F. Sloan song. Adler was now taking full credit for both creating and discovering P.F. Sloan, and this moneymaking machine wasn't to be wasted on trivial artists. No siree! I went into the studio and recorded a simple guitar demo called 'Cling To Me.' I sent it to Johnny, who recorded it, and it became his biggest hit in three years.

'You're lucky, Phil,' Adler said. 'I'm not going to fire you, because the song was a hit.'

Tony Thomas was the son of Danny Thomas, the well-loved comic, singer, and television producer. American kids grew up watching his show *Make Room For Daddy*. Tony had been bitten by the rock'n'roll bug, possibly because of the success of his friends in Gary Lewis & The Playboys. Gary was the son of Jerry Lewis, and had recorded three or four of my songs. The bug was traveling up and down the well-manicured streets of Beverly Hills and biting every son and daughter of the Hollywood elite. Nancy Sinatra was bitten. Dean Martin's son Dino and Lucille Ball's son Desi were bitten pretty seriously and formed Dino Desi & Billy with their pal Billy Hinsche; they recorded 'Let Me Be' in 1966.

Tony played the drums in The Thomas Group. He and his pals Greg Gilford, Marty Howard, Robert Wallerstein, and David Goldsmith had formed the group in Tony's garage. They were a garage band—a *Beverly Hills* garage band, but a garage band nonetheless. His sister Marlo was a popular actress in her own right and the star of the television series *That Girl*. Adler was interested in Marlo, and for some reason The Thomas Group soon found themselves signed to Dunhill. Tony's dream of moving out of his garage and onto the stage of *The Ed Sullivan Show* was only one date with Marlo away.

Steve and I were assigned to take over the group. We produced them, wrote some songs for them, and shepherded them into the spotlight. And I enjoyed doing it. Tony was a great guy. He was serious about his music and very protective of his band. We had a lot of respect for each other. They had played together and they had rehearsed. They performed publicly a number of times at Hollywood parties. But when they got into the studio, they were shocked to find that they could not be on their own records. I fought against this for just about every band that came through Dunhill. Professional musicians gave the records a tight, professional sound, but it also took away the rawness—and oftentimes the life—of the record.

Steve and I wrote 'Penny Arcade' way back in 1964, when we were doing endless demos—*I can be a millionaire with my baby at the penny arcade.* I played guitar and piano, and Steve and I sang harmony. The record came out, and The Thomas Group did *The Ed Sullivan Show* and sold enough records to earn a follow-up.

It was fun hanging out at Tony's house. We played basketball in the backyard, and sometimes Marlo would hang out or make cookies and brownies. Every once in a while, Danny would come out and fool around on the court. It was stargazing in Hollywood, and who doesn't like that?

It was also around this time that Adler started discussions with ABC Records, which was keen to buy Dunhill. I was told that there might be big changes afoot.

THE GRASS ROOTS (TAKE TWO)
One day, a promotion man mistakenly gave a demo of 'Where Were You When I Needed You,' with me on vocals, to the top LA radio station KFWB. They put it on the air and it became the 'pick hit' record of the week. Dunhill were livid because there was no group attached to it, and they didn't want me going out on the road as The Grass Roots (or as P.F. Sloan). The record had to be pulled immediately. Every group in the world was trying to get a hit record, and here we had one without a group.

I was asked to get Bill Fulton back, with Dunhill promising to play ball with him this time. Bill agreed to come back on the condition that he would get the money owed to him, and his group would be able to record in the studio with their own instruments and do their own songs. Dunhill agreed. Wild Bill put his vocals on 'Where Were You When I Needed You,' and the record was officially released.

At the time, Steve Barri was still connected to Norty's Record Store, which was one of ten record stores in Los Angeles that KFWB would call to find out what was selling and then put together the charts accordingly. The station was angry at the way Dunhill had pulled the original record, however, and didn't want anything to do with The Grass Roots. But Steve's reporting that the single was selling very well forced the radio station back to the new record, which then became a hit on its own. It was pretty much the same trick Brian Epstein had used to get The Beatles going in the UK from his own record store.

My intention was to keep the label's promise and allow the band to play and be a real band. They had appeared on several national television shows and had done a bit of touring but were ridiculed when it was discovered, through interviews, that they did not play on their own records—especially in their hometown of San Francisco. They were referred to as musical puppets. So I decided on my own to take the band into the studio and record them playing four songs of their choosing.

Lasker was furious and withheld their royalties. After a few weeks on the road, Fulton decided he'd had enough and left, realizing that everything Lasker and Adler had promised him had been a lie.

The album came out with no picture of the band on the cover—just an empty chair. It featured the four songs the band had recorded, plus eight more that I did. It was moderately successful, though for me it just barely passed in a creative sense. The problem now—again—was that there were no Grass Roots. The demand was high for a follow-up single, and 'Only When You're Lonely'—with me singing lead—would have to fill the void until a new band could be found. The record just kissed the charts and said goodbye.

In the meantime, the early Beatles publisher Dick James had secured a deal with RCA Victor to put out all of the P.F. Sloan and Grass Roots records in the UK. Dick promoted all of the songs, so it was no surprise that The Grass Roots hit the British charts. Now Dunhill needed a group. Badly.

I asked The Robbs—a great regional group from Oconomowoc, Wisconsin—but they weren't interested. I asked dozens of groups from Los Angeles, but none of them wanted to sell their souls for fame and become the playthings of a sociopath. The word went out, asking any group willing to take on the burden of a new album and hit single to send in a tape.

Eventually a group calling themselves The Thirteenth Floor responded. They were Creed Bratton, Warren Entner, Rick Coonce, and Kenny Fukomoto, who was soon called up to the army and replaced by Rob Grill. Rob had a penchant for being able to capture my vocal phrasing, so Dunhill signed the group. As ever, however, they were not allowed to play their own instruments.

I did one more single for The Grass Roots in 1966 and sang the lead vocal. The song was called 'Tip Of My Tongue' and was a sort of Rolling Stones knockoff. It did make the charts but disappeared around a corner and was never heard from again. The Grass Roots went on tour and were successful at recreating the studio sound onstage, thereby gaining acceptance. Nobody questioned the band's ability again, and the charade worked.

By late 1965, listeners in United Kingdom were starting to respond to songs that came from an introspective point of view, which was not the mainstream. What I had started—and been rebuked for—was now becoming popular, in the form of songs such as John Lennon's 'In My Life,' from *Rubber Soul*, which came out in December 1965.

This was one of the seminal moments in rock'n'roll. A generation was waking up to its potential and its place in history. Dylan's clarion call had been somewhat heeded by some, but he could still be written off as an eccentric poet-troubadour; Lennon, on the other hand, had the ears of the world. When Lennon went deep, kids across the world began to join him, realizing for the first time that there was more to life than dancing. They started listening to music as they would read books. They had their favorite writers—the ones with whom they could most relate—and they found that their stories became alive in music, rather than on the page. I believe that this was when people first accepted the singer as songwriter and storyteller. This was the beginning of the end of the Brill Building mentality. But the record companies would not give up easily, and they would continue to fight it.

Meanwhile, The Grass Roots had turned into an *American Bandstand* version of The Beatles. Steve was not going to let them do any of my more introspective songs, and Dunhill wanted to keep it that way. Within a year, The Grass Roots had become a hit-making machine.

As P.F. Sloan, I had garnered a modicum of legitimacy. Many people sought my songs, but I was beginning to break apart. I started to feel isolated, and stretched thin by working on mediocre projects that had little relevance to me. I began to compartmentalize my talents, thinking that in so doing I could avoid sinking. I had no idea of how much water I was actually taking on.

This would have been a good time to have somebody I could talk to—somebody who was looking out for me. A Brian Epstein. But Dunhill owned me. I couldn't talk to my parents. Who was I to complain? *You've never had it so good.* There I was, twenty years old, enjoying great success and thinking to myself, *can I make it through another week?*

CHAPTER TWELVE

THE 'PAINT IT BLACK' SESSION

I was living back in Del Valle. I could no longer sleep at my house on Wonderland after discovering that my Brazilian landlord was living in a secret room under the floorboards and stealing food from the refrigerator. It was a very creepy situation. Also, there was so much action going on around me—people coming and going—that it was difficult to get any work done. And really, P.F. Sloan was all about work.

One evening around midnight, the phone rang and my mother answered it, then knocked on my bedroom door.

'There's a phone call for you,' she said.

'Who is it?'

'Do you realize that it's after midnight and your father is asleep?'

'Who is it, ma?'

'I don't mind that you've moved back, but please tell your friends to respect our lifestyle.'

'Who is on the phone?'

'He says his name is Jagger.'

'*Mick* Jagger?' I asked, jumping up.

'I don't know. But he better be as important as Frank Sinatra to be calling at this hour.'

'He is, mom,' I said. 'He is.'

I got out of bed and took the phone. My mother stood next to me to listen, but I waved her off and she reluctantly retreated to her bedroom.

'I hope I'm not calling too late,' Mick said.

'No, not at all,' I replied. 'How have you been?'

'Was that your mother?' he asked.

'Yeah. Yeah. That was my mother.'

'Look, man. The reason I'm calling is that we have an emergency at the studio.'

'What studio, Mick?'

'RCA on Sunset.'

'What's the problem, Mick? What can I do?'

'I need you down here immediately,' he said. 'We just locked out our producer.'

'Oldham?' I asked.

'Yeah. And I need you to take over. How soon can you get over here?'

'Twenty minutes, Mick. I'll be right there.'

The last time I had seen Mick was in London, at The St. James Club. At the time he had expressed his gratitude to me because he was aware of my dealings with Brian Epstein and The Beatles, and how I had supported the Stones as well.

The reason Oldham had been thrown out of the studio was perhaps the same reason Murray Wilson was thrown out of the studio by Brian Wilson: the music had outgrown management. Oldham was suddenly in the way, and Jagger and the Stones needed to express themselves with as much freedom as possible.

About twenty minutes later, I walked into a darkened studio. There was just a small light on in the booth where Mick Jagger was sitting alone. The rest of the Stones were in various stages of dormancy.

Until this time, even The Mamas & The Papas were doing three-hour unionized session dates. Here, though, was a whole other level of freedom and creativity. Mick greeted me, asked me to sit in a chair, and told me the story of how he had to lose Andrew Loog Oldham because they had different visions. He said he was interested in my input, and that they had the studio to themselves for as long as they wanted it.

After relating this to me, Mick kicked up his feet, closed his eyes, and went into a period of meditative sleep. A long but indeterminate length of time seemed to pass, and then he suddenly reached over for a guitar that was leaning against the wall and began to play a song for me.

'This is a song that Keith and I wrote about six months ago. I want to know what you think about it.'

He began to play 'Paint It Black.'

'What do you think of the song?' he asked.

'God, man, that sounds like a No. 1 song.'

'Really? You think so?'

'Yeah.'

'You like it, then.'

'Very much,' I said.

'Good,' Mick replied, turning on the lights in the studio. 'Let's get to work.'

Keith was sitting in a chair closest to the control booth. Bill Wyman was sleeping standing up against the soft studio wall. Charlie Watts was sitting at his drums reading a paperback novel with a flashlight. And Brian Jones was sitting in a chair, facing the booth, wearing a purple cape and dozing off.

Mick dropped down on one knee and started to play 'Paint It Black' for Keith.

'Do you remember this song?' he asked.

'Yeah,' Keith said, and then he noticed me in the booth. 'Is that Sloan?'

'Yeah. He's going to help with the session.'

Mick went over to Bill, who was still groggy and only semiconscious, and played the song for him. He then went over to Charlie.

'Never mind,' Charlie said. 'I've got it.'

Mick returned to the booth.

'Phil,' he said. 'Go over to Brian and ask him if you can use his guitar on this song.'

I didn't realize I was being set up, but it would be like going over to George Harrison and asking him to use his guitar on a song. But I followed Mick's direction … sort of.

'What a fantastic Cape,' I told Brian. 'Where can I get one?'

He looked at me and snarled.

'Who the fuck are you, coming over to me asking where I bought my cape? What are you doing in my space? Get the fuck out of my face.'

Mick and the others started laughing and I returned to the booth.

'Good job,' Mick said, and then left the booth to call in the engineer. We took about twenty-five minutes to test all of the instruments and set up the levels. The engineer asked if all was satisfactory, and I told them all was fine.

'"Paint It Black," take one,' Mick announced from the booth.

Charlie Watts went into the iconic drum riff, Keith Richards strummed his guitar lick, and Bill went into a bassline as if they had been performing the song for twenty years. Brian's pot—the dial that controlled his track—was kept low. Mick did not want to hear his guitar.

These guys were amazing and perfect. At the end of the take, Mick called for a break, and I asked for a backup take. They did the song again, exactly the way they did it the first time. After the second take, Mick told the engineer to leave, and the lights were dimmed again.

After what seemed like a long period of meditation, Mick asked what we should do next in relation to the track. At that point, Keith thought that there should be an opening before the drums, so we recorded Keith's opening lick as an overdub.

I noticed a big case at the back of the studio and was told it was Keith's sitar. He had become interested in the sitar through George Harrison, who of course was learning it from Ravi Shankar. Keith wasn't anywhere nearly as accomplished as George on the instrument and protested when I suggested using it on the song. He was absolutely averse to the idea, weighing the strengths and weakness over in his mind, but he seemed to be changing his mind as he took it out of its case and began playing on it for his own pleasure for a little while. The rest of the Stones went back to relaxing. Keith overdubbed the sitar and seemed happy with the result. Mick thanked me profusely, and they called a wrap to the session at about 5:30. (Received wisdom has it that Brian Jones played sitar on 'Paint It Black,' but that's not what I saw. It's possible that on a future session, Keith's sitar part was replaced with Brian's. I don't know. But on that night, Keith was on the sitar.)

'Hey, Phil,' Mick said. 'I want to tell you something.'

'Sure, Mick.'

'The Doors.'

'What about them?'

'They're legitimate. I want you to tell Morrison for me. I think they're a legitimate band, and we want to promote them whenever we can.'

'That's cool.'

'I want you to find Morrison and tell him that.'

'OK.'

'I want you to tell him that The Doors are all right with us.'

It was drizzling rain outside when I left the studio. I felt great but I knew nobody would believe me when I told them what had just happened. I started driving west on Sunset, exhausted but exhilarated. It was a recording session like no other that I had ever experienced, and one of the most rewarding. I discovered how music should really be done.

One school of thought says that pressure brings out the best in you, and the other says relaxation brings out the best. This was a case of the latter, and it was magical and unforgettable. A lot of people assume that drugs were involved in the session, but there was only one, and that was the drug of music—plus a little exhaustion. And sometimes exhaustion brings out the best in an artist.

I saw a young woman hitchhiking in the light rain on my drive back and felt that I should get her out of the weather. She got in the car and introduced herself as Kim Canoe. She was a beautiful woman.

I told her my name.

'I've met P.F. Sloan,' she said, giggling. 'You're not P.F. Sloan.'

'Yes I am,' I replied.

'OK, you're P.F. Sloan,' she said, smiling mischievously.

'What are you doing hitchhiking on Sunset Boulevard this late?'

'Or this early,' she replied. 'What is so strange about being out on a beautiful morning? Where I come from, people would have already eaten breakfast and be on their way to work.'

'Where's that?' I asked.

'Oregon.'

There was something about this girl. She had a mystical and charming quality to her. Her eyes reflected a superior species.

'Where would you like me to take you?' I asked.

'Where would you like to take me?'

I felt an immediate attraction to this woman. She had long dark hair and large black eyes and there was an American-bohemian-Indian vibe to her. She told me that she was half Cherokee and had the gift of second sight. She was a free spirit, in control of the moment.

'Where are you coming from?' she asked.

'I just came from a recording session with The Rolling Stones.'

'Are you trying to impress me?'

'Maybe I am.'

'I thought so.'

'I didn't really mean.'

'Are you retarded?'

'No. But maybe I was trying to impress you.'

'I am.'

'What?'

'Impressed. I really am. I just got picked up by P.F Sloan, who is coming back from a late night session with The Rolling Stones. I can tell that story for years.'

'It's not that big a deal.'

'Oh, I see. Now we're going to get humble.'

'I ...'

'Which is just as deadly as pride, you know.'

'Look ...'

'This is going to look good in my diary. And maybe even my novel someday,' she said convincingly to herself and me.

'Oh, are you a writer?' I asked.

'I dabbled with it in college, before I got married and had kids.'

'You have kids?'

'Yes. Do you think less of me? Have you heard of Mars Bonfire?'

'Mars Bonfire? No.'

'Strange,' she said, shaking her head. 'Maybe you *are* retarded, after all. Mars is a very talented songwriter and will eventually be very famous.'

The conversation had taken a strange left turn, and I was reeling from it.

'Where can I drop you?' I asked.

'Why don't you turn around and drop me off where you picked me up?'

'Do you always speak so abstractly?' I wondered.

'Let me out here,' she told me.

'Are you sure?'

'I'm not sure of anything, P.F. Sloan.'

I stopped the car where right where the Strip ends, before it dips down into Sunset and Beverly Hills. She smiled at me, making me believe this morning would go on for a bit longer, but at the moment when I was about to continue with whatever was happening, she got out of the car and looked into my eyes with more sincerity and love than I had seen in a very long time.

'I loved "You Baby,"' she said, and walked into a coffee shop.

I kind of wanted to stop the car and join her, but I was tired and needed sleep.

THE MILLIONAIRE'S CLUB

I slept very well. I had my breakfast and began making a few phone calls to find out where I could find the mysterious Jim Morrison.

I had met Jim before at a small party, when he was living in Venice, a super funky beach town in West LA that was originally supposed to replicate the canals of Venice, Italy. Now, however, the Love Canal had transformed into nothing more than shabby bungalows along a semi-stagnant swamp runoff that barely flushed away the garbage at low and high tide. There was a hip quality to Venice but also a sense of danger. It was a paradox. A good place for Morrison to hang.

Jim was friendly and outgoing, spur of the moment and in the now, definitely conscientious and playful. I was finally able to get tip from a friend of his that he would be at the Millionaire Club that evening. The Millionaire Club had, at one point in time, been a fancy fish restaurant on La Cienega. Since then it had been converted into an exclusive club for wealthy hipsters. I had never had a problem getting in because my friend Gino knew the doorman.

The action took place on the first floor. This was where the cream of LA's rock, art, and fashion world went to unwind. It was a hub for movie stars and music types who could make connections for drugs and business. They came to the club looking to get stoned, get laid, and find their next big deal. Since everybody else who was there was famous or rich, it was a safe place to hang out. Nobody bothered them.

I was walking around the ground floor, taking it all in, feeling not quite in but not out of place. I *could* belong but I knew that I didn't belong. This was a room filled with people celebrating their own lives. I was at the castle because I had a message from the archduke for one of his knights.

I heard a voice calling my name from two stories above my head.

'Sloan! Hey, Sloan!'

I looked up and I saw Jim Morrison hanging over a rail, bottle in hand.

'Take the elevator,' he said. 'Take it up.'

I got in the elevator and took it up to where Jim was. I went over to where he had been standing but he had moved and was now sitting on the floor with his back up against the wall.

'Did you know that Cousin It was covered with fur and was actually a member of the Royal Family of England?' he asked. 'Yeah. He was, he really was and he lives in Scotland. Do you want a drink?'

I took a swig from an almost empty bottle of Johnny Walker Red. Morrison had a willing audience. He started flailing his arms like an inebriated ballet dancer.

'*When I went up to Boston, they served me fish with frostin' … but it was too much a-costin' for the likes me of me.* You know what that is, Sloan?'

'No, Jim,' I answered.

My heart was hurting for this guy. I had a message from one of the most important people in music, and Morrison seemed to be wallowing in a poetic sense of self-pity, which I recognized as being an idle state where one travels to avoid the harsh realities of life.

'I'm the bearer of good news, Jim.'

'Good news for me?'

'I was with Jagger last night.'

'He's a fuckin' phony,' Morrison said. 'Don't you think he's fuckin' phony, Sloan?'

'He gave me a message to give you. Are you OK, Jim?'

'That, Sloan, is not my deal. What the fuck does Jagger want?'

'He considers you and your band to be authentic blues artists and is going to state that in his next interview. They're going to back you 100 percent.'

'The bastard. You believe that? He's pulling our legs.'

Suddenly, Morrison began to weep.

'It's too late,' he told me. 'He's too late.' With that, he passed out.

Feeling shattered and elated, I decided to join the party downstairs. A woman who looked like a model approached me as I was moving to the bar.

'You're P.F. Sloan, aren't you?' she asked.

'I wouldn't put any money on it,' I replied.

I sat down and asked the gorgeous model what she was drinking.

THE INFAMOUS SUNSET STRIP RIOTS

In the 1940s and 50s, the Sunset Strip was an exclusive playground for the wealthy and the entertainment community. Gowns and tuxedos wandered in and out of fashionable supper clubs. The drink of choice was the martini, and wit and wisdom of cool permeated the candlelit tables as Ella Fitzgerald moaned the blues into contented souls. Life was good. The Strip was a private club for the rich and famous. And then along came *77 Sunset Strip*.

During the opening credits of the show—which starred the epitome of style, Efrem Zimbalist Jr, alongside Ann-Margret's husband Roger Smith, Connie Stevens, and Edd 'Kookie, Lend Me Your Comb' Byrnes—you could see a club across the street called Dino's Lodge—an exclusive haunt owned by one Dean Martin. People crowded into Dino's to get close to the heat of his cool. Tourists from around the world started to wander up and down the streets looking for celebrities. And they found them.

Business was good on the Strip through the early 60s. The Peppermint Lounge West opened up on Sunset, followed by the Whisky, where jazz was played, and Trini Lopez was over at PJ's. It was still a suit-and-tie environment, but there was an air of modern privilege. And then the hippies started to make a play for the atmosphere.

With the onslaught of the British Invasion and the birth of folk-rock—followed by the introduction of marijuana and the culture of non-materialism—the Sunset Strip became an obvious place to hang out. It was clean and attractive, and you could meet your friends for coffee or walk up and down the street, digging each other's energy.

The club scene started to draw more and more people. Kids had started to hitchhike across the country, and they invariably wound up on or the near the Strip. It became a magnetic center for likeminded young people. The Strip allowed a sense of freedom from disapproving parents and what they expected. It became the Greenwich Village of the West, albeit without the tradition and history.

In the beginning, retailers started to cater to this new culture. New singing groups like The Byrds, who dressed in capes and velvet and granny glasses, started to appear in the clubs, which drew even more people out at night to roam the Strip and feel the spirit of the times—the strange nights filled with the scent of patchouli oil, sweat, and the faint aroma of orange Owsley.

The Sunset Strip became a mecca for expressing one's individuality. In Red China (*think of all the hate there is in Red China*), individualism was punishable by death, or worse, long prison terms. The style of Mao had no place on the Sunset Strip, but here, though, the police and merchants were beginning to view this parade of unique examples of humanity as one endless Halloween party.

In late 1966, I had read of radio disc jockeys telling their audiences of planned protests against repressive actions and curfews that had set in place weeks before. I, however, was unaware of such plans.

My companion that night was Steve Stills. We were at Pandora's Box to see our friend Bryan MacLean perform with Love. The place was packed and the show went on. At some point during the show, however, somebody ran into the club and shouted that there was a riot going on outside, and that the police were on their way to arrest everyone in the club. Absolute panic ensued. Arthur Lee jumped off the stage and ran for his life, leaving his band. Bryan seemed to be getting a kick out of the whole thing and began jamming with the band as kids ran in terror.

'I think we should get out of here,' I said to Steve.

'Nothing's going to happen. We're peaceful people just listening to music,' he replied.

'We've got to split,' I told him. 'I'm not going to spend another night in jail.'

On New Year's Eve 1964, I had been playing music on the back of a pickup truck with a lady and a group of musicians out near Bakersfield. We felt it was perfectly OK to be driving down the freeway at 70mph, doing a concert. It was New Year's Eve, after all. Eventually, though, a highway patrol stopped us, arrested us, and put us in the Bakersfield jail, making a statement that they did not want our kind in Buck Owens country.

With Bakersfield in mind, and with Steve still displaying an uncomfortable sense of naiveté, I grabbed him by his poncho and pushed him out the side door. We were momentarily free, but then we heard the whistles blow.

Steve felt a cosmic pull toward the street. And that turned out to be a cosmic pull toward destiny. He was transformed into a correspondent, as if someone had suddenly put a microphone in his hand and he was reporting live for network news.

'There's something happening here,' he said, excitedly. 'Look. There's a cop with a gun over there.'

'What do you think is going on?'

'I don't know. It's not exactly clear to me.'

He was actually speaking the lyric that would become the song 'For What It's Worth.'

The Strip was now crowded, and there was mayhem—kids running, chanting, standing their ground, and many being arrested and loaded into buses. The arrests infuriated the crowd, which began to rock a city bus and eventually turned it over. And then things became even more frantic.

The cops started to draw a line in chalk along the boulevard.

'Anyone who crosses this line will be arrested or shot,' one of them shouted through a bullhorn.

'This isn't right,' Steve said. 'The cops are making this worse.'

We were out of the action by now because we were standing on the other side of the street. We watched for a long time until things calmed down a bit. We were both in shock at what we were witnessing. And I was feeling exhausted.

'I'm going back to the house,' I said. 'I've got Shelley Fabares coming into the studio in the morning. What are you going to do?'

'I'm going back to the apartment.'

Steve went back to his apartment, which was down on Doheny Drive. At some point during the next couple of days he wrote 'For What It's Worth.'

Some people claim that the riots continued until demolition of Schwab's drugstore in 1972, but to be honest I was only aware of that one night. Sunset was closed for a couple of weeks, and after that things quieted down. In the end the curfew was abandoned because the music clubs were losing money. But something had changed. There was a feeling—a misplaced feeling—that the kids had won; that they were there to stay, and the adults would have to get used to it.

The reality was that the freedom to walk and congregate had gone. Intimidation became the norm throughout the city. Neighborhoods that had had nothing to do with the rioting became the target of police brutality, which created an overwhelming fear of the Los Angeles Police Department.

Arguably the most significant aspect of this action was that white, middle-class teenagers had felt—for the first time in their lives—the effect of oppression because of how they looked. *Paranoia strikes deep, into your life it will creep, it starts when you're always afraid, step out of line, the man will take you away ...*

CHAPTER THIRTEEN

JIMMY WEBB (A PRELUDE)

One day, I received a request to meet with a young songwriter at the Hollywood Hills home of Madeline Baker, who ran Audio Arts Recording Studio on Melrose and a small music publishing company. It was a beautiful house overlooking the city. I rang the bell and was greeted by a Mexican maid who escorted me into the living room, which overlooked a garden of topiary and fountains. For the most part, the room was empty, except a high-gloss black grand piano and a beautiful brocade couch.

I was here as a favor to Madeline. I had recorded at her studio a number of times, and she was always giving me breaks, so I owed her one or two. A long skinny kid with shaggy hair entered the room and seemed happy to see me, although we had never met before.

'P.F.?' he said, with a slightly drawl. 'I'm Jimmy Webb.'

'Good to meet you,' I replied.

'I just want you to know how grateful I am that you took the time to come to listen to an unknown songwriter,' he continued, 'and whether you like my tunes or not, I appreciate it.'

'My pleasure, Jimmy. Madeline's told me a lot about you.'

'She's great,' Jimmy said.

'She sure has helped me.'

Jimmy sat at the piano, toying with the keys as he spoke.

'Yeah … well … I won't waste too much of your time.'

'You're not wasting my time, Jimmy. I'm here to listen.'

'I'm from Oklahoma,' he continued, 'and I've come out here to seek my fame and fortune, but apparently all of the people I've played my songs for just don't get me, so I'm thinking about going back home. I was at Motown for a little while, and can you believe it, I actually got a song recorded by The Supremes, but the record bombed and they let me go, and since then I've been rejected by nearly every publisher in town, man. I don't know if you know what it feels like, but I'm just so weary and worn down from my songs being rejected.'

'My publisher rejects nearly every song I write,' I told him.

'P.F., you've got to be joking. Who's your publisher?'

'Trousdale, out of Dunhill.'

'Sounds like a racehorse.'

'More like the racehorse's ass.'

'I've got to get some songs out,' Jimmy said. 'I've got an awfully nice girlfriend, but it's not going to last if I can't bring in some money.'

'I'd like to hear the songs, Jimmy,' I said.

I liked Jimmy, but I was kind of nervous, because 99 percent of what you hear from songwriters is generally not very good. I want every song I hear from a new songwriter to be great. Most, however, are unrealized.

I grew up listening to songs like 'Somewhere Over The Rainbow,' 'This Land Is Your Land,' and 'Nature Boy.' I studied lyricists like Hammerstein, Hart, Porter, Goffin & King, Leiber & Stoller, Mann & Weil, and Lennon & McCartney. A good songwriter never stops learning, be it from poetry or novels or movies or relationships. You are like a surgeon on call, twenty-four hours a day, to the muse. You are writing songs in your sleep. You are constantly trying to connect the dots. You are aware of your faults, your ego, and the filter that tells you something can't be written, even though you feel that it must be. There is a natural sensor in that filter.

One of the filters during this period of time was that a song couldn't be any longer than two minutes and twenty seconds. The radio stations had a strict formula so they could fit in advertising. If your song was longer than that, it might still get played on a few college stations, but it wouldn't be a hit.

Jimmy hunched himself over the keys like a tiger ready to pounce.

'This first song is called "Wichita Lineman,"' he said.

Jimmy tilted his head back as if he were about to sing to the sun and moon. He played a couple of chords and began to unload. I was aware immediately that I was listening to a songwriter's voice. It was filled with feeling and emotion. Most songwriters don't have a voice, but this one was haunting and unusual and raw and wonderful. There are singers and there are songwriters, and only rarely is there something known as a singer-songwriter. Singer-songwriters were a threat to the establishment. And I was one of them.

Jimmy's voice was soul-deep, like a moan—a howling lost angel—as he let out the first line of 'Wichita Lineman.' As he continued to play, I became relaxed at first and then on edge, figuring that he would screw the song up in some way. But he didn't. The song got better and better.

Without asking what I thought, he went into 'Up, Up And Away,' but turned to speak before the first verse.

'This song is not what it seems,' he said. 'It's not only about balloons.'

This song had a different style—sort of a jazz opening with a pop feel. It was different to anything I had ever heard. It was so well crafted, so well done—a concept that never lost sight of its origins.

When I'm listening to a song, if it doesn't keep me constantly captured—if it needs a different chord here or there, or there's a phrase out of whack—I lose interest. It's hard to hear songs sometimes because I am trying to figure out how to make it the best it can possibly be, which gets in the way of enjoying it. It doesn't happen often that I can just *listen*. It happened when I heard The Beatles acetates for the first time.

A songwriter's energy and passion will sometimes push a song past the analytical reasoning of the listener. Take a song like 'Tutti-Frutti,' which may not be a perfectly constructed song, but when Little Richard sings it there is no doubt you are hearing perfection. When you listen to Pat Boone's sanitized version, without the songwriter's passion, you are aware of it as a flawed piece of work.

Jimmy carried on without stopping, wanting to use every moment of our time together. He was going to empty his barrel without reloading, hoping that one bullet would hit its mark, but in fact the bullets had been hitting their mark since the first chord he played.

He went into the minor prelude of 'MacArthur Park.'

'This song is called "MacArthur Park" but it's really not finished,' he said. 'And here's the thing, P.F., I've written a three-and-a-half-minute instrumental in the middle of the song, and obviously I can't do that.'

'Why not?' I asked.

'Nobody will play it.'

'Play it from the top,' I told him, 'with the instrumental section.'

Jimmy had the look on his face that a kid gets when presenting his mother with a present he has bought with his own money. This time I was transcended as he was playing, and left speechless when he stopped.

'Could I please play you one more song, P.F.?' he asked.

'Jimmy, I have a feeling you're going to play it anyway.'

'I realize that your time is valuable, but I just have one more song in me.'

There is not a songwriter alive who, if given the opportunity, will not say, 'Can I play you one more song?' given the opening.

'I'm not leaving,' I said, putting him at ease.

Jimmy started playing 'By The Time I Get To Phoenix.' And by the time he had finished, there were tears in my eyes.

Jimmy was exhausted.

'What do you think?' he asked.

'Jimmy,' I said. 'Pick a tear. Any tear. They're all diamonds.'

'What do you mean, P.F.?'

'Songwriters don't cry tears, they cry diamonds.'

'Does that mean you like my stuff?'

'I think every song you played me is a major hit.'

'Even the long one?' he asked.

'Especially the long one,' I said.

The Mexican maid entered the room with a plate of sandwiches and coffee. She left the tray on the table, and I reached for an egg salad.

'Do you think Dunhill would be interested in me?' he asked.

'Why would you want to go to Dunhill?'

'I want to sing what I write, like you're doing.'

'I think you can do better than Dunhill, Jimmy. All of those songs are going to be Top 10 records. The right place will open up. Let me see what I can do.'

I left Jimmy with a plate of egg salad sandwiches and a heart full of hope.

A couple of weeks later, Johnny Rivers called and asked me to meet him over at his label, Soul City Records, on Sunset. There was a rivalry between Johnny and Lou Adler, even though Adler had been responsible for getting Johnny on Imperial and guiding him through his early years at the Whisky A Go-Go. After the success of 'Poor Side Of Town' and 'Secret Agent Man,' Rivers felt that he needed to take control, and Soul City was the right place.

Rivers had signed a group called The Fifth Dimension, and curiously enough their first record was 'Go Where You Wanna Go,' as written by John Phillips. The song should have been a hit but had bombed with The Mamas & The Papas singing it. Now The Fifth Dimension's version was starting to look like a hit. This must have given Johnny a lot of satisfaction as he was succeeding where Adler had failed. Adler had created this feeling in people of wanting to outdo him.

Johnny and I met at his office on Sunset. I told him about Jimmy Webb and how I felt that this guy was extraordinary, how he had magic. Johnny then offered me a shot to write a song for the follow-up to 'Go Where You Wanna Go' for The Fifth Dimension. Maybe that was Johnny's way of thanking me for 'Secret Agent Man.'

Now that Johnny had started his own label and was taking control of his life and career, he was officially out of Adler's good graces. In agreeing to do this for Rivers, I was now officially consorting with the enemy. At this point, Adler was very busy trying to keep The Mamas & The Papas buoyant, and his personal prestige was on the line. His attitude toward me, now, was 'do what you wanna do.'

Jimmy Webb was hired as an arranger for 'Another Day, Another Heartache,' the song I had written for The Fifth Dimension. Rivers had gotten the song to him. We met up with each other in the studio for the first time since the Hollywood Hills. Jimmy seemed nervous and ill at ease.

'I hope you like the arrangement of this song, P.F.,' he said. 'It's a bit different than the demo you made.'

The record came out and was a respectable hit. The Fifth Dimension's follow-up to 'Another Day' was Jimmy's 'Up, Up And Away,' while Johnny Rivers recorded 'By The Time I Get To Phoenix.' As beautiful a song as it was, though, Johnny's version was met with stony silence, which only goes to show that every song has its own time. Glen Campbell recorded the same song later, and while his version was not superior to Johnny's, the time was right, and it turned into a mega hit. It brought Glen and Jimmy to the forefront.

My opinion of Jimmy's talent had been accurate. All of the songs that Jimmy played for me that day at Madeline's would become Top 10 hits, and Jimmy became as famous as the people who recorded his songs.

LET'S LIVE FOR TODAY

Jay Lasker called me into his office and he informed me that I was to make a record.

'Look, Flip. We're going to make a record,' he told me, with that cigar hanging out of his awful mouth and his glasses falling down on the bridge of nose. 'We're going to fuck your pal Dick James and his new group, The Living Daylights. The song is called "Let's Live For Today." I need the record out in two weeks and we're going to fuck him good.'

This is not exactly the way a good song should come about, but then again, how does anyone know how a song comes down unless they're in the room? However, if you're ever faced with this moral dilemma—a monster sitting across a desk telling you that you're going to make a record for the mere purpose of hurting somebody—you should leave the field and find another rainbow.

'You mind if I think about it, Jay?'

'All right. Sure. Think about it. And I'll think about it. And I'll think about things like you not showing your face here anymore. And I'll think about taking every fucking dime you and Steve have made. I might even think about your parents. But what I'm really thinking about is a little bastard like you coming in here and telling me that he's going to think about anything! I don't want you thinking about shit, Flip. Tell Muriel to set up the session.'

'Dick James has always been good to me and to the company.'

'Dick James is in the way of expanding our publishing into England. You got a problem with that?'

'I'll need to finish up a …'

'What do you think you're dealing with here, the Bay of Pigs? What do you need to think about? We're making a fucking record.'

'I brought you The Beatles at Vee-Jay. I brought you the Buffalo Springfield and you weren't interested, I brought you The Mamas & The Papas and you thought they weren't worth your time.'

I could see that Lasker was starting to boil.

'And what's the point, Flip?'

'The point is that you're not always right.'

'You think you're some kind of genius? You don't seem to understand that I'm looking out for you. Artists come and go. I can piss out this window and hit five artists. Does what I'm saying mean anything to you? I have your future in mind—one that goes beyond this moment in time. Look. I know you think I'm crude and gruff. I know. But believe me when I tell you that I'm looking out for your best interests. So go make a record, will you please? Or I will fuck you up so badly, you won't be able to write a greeting card,' he said, and then started to laugh at his own joke.

Muriel was Lasker's secretary. If there was a happy face to smallpox, Muriel was it. Muriel was the kind of woman who could run the complaint department at Auschwitz. And after you complained, you somehow felt better. Nothing changes, but you feel better.

Muriel set up the session at Western Recorders with Hal Blaine and Joe Osborne, and I told The Grass Roots I would be calling them in for the date. Steve and I listened to the song over and over again, and I recognized that the chorus of this song had been lifted from The Drifters' 'I Count The Tears.'

'How in the world did the writer of this song think they could get away with stealing the best part of "I Count The Tears"?' I wondered.

'It's fine,' Steve said. 'It's four or five bars.'

'Wait a second. We're going to steal a song that was stolen from The Drifters and record it with a group whose name was stolen from another group? How good can this turn out?'

'What's the big deal, Phil? It was a good song for The Drifters, and it'll be a good song for us.'

'Steve. You want to attach yourself to this level of business?'

'You worry too much. You'll see. Everything is going to be fine. Let's produce a record.'

I called Rob Grill and the rest of the Roots to come in for the date. As far as the instrument track, I really wanted their opinion. But I made a dangerous creative decision. I put Rob on the twelve-string and I played electric. We cut the basic tracks like that, along with Hal and Joe. We went into overdubs and doubled the drums and bass as well as putting on another electric part. Steve and I and Warren Entner and Creed Bratton did the background vocals, and Rob Grill took the lead—*sha na na na na live for today.* Nobody ever knew about Rob being on the twelve-string. Management assumed it was me.

The record was released at breakneck speed and was on the radio before the vinyl cooled. Lasker got what he wanted. He succeeded in destroying the relationship between Dunhill and Dick James—a very nice and sincere man—thereby freeing him to make his own publishing deals in England. Lasker thought that he and Adler were now bigger than Dick James, and they were going to show him a thing or two.

'Who needs The Beatles when we've got The Mamas & The Papas?' Adler once boasted.

Because of the success of the single, it was decided that an album had to come out as soon as possible. We started recording the *Live For Today* album right away.

One of the songs that I had written for The Grass Roots was called 'Out Of Touch'—*she looks so good on the outside but inside she's out, somewhere … can she be reached … no … she's out of touch.* This was going to be one of the songs on the album.

I made another risky decision. The Grass Roots were a great bunch of guys, and I decided that they should start to play on their own records. It is what they wanted most in the world. All of the groups wanted that. I felt that this was my opportunity to do something for music—to change the status quo and move the creative ball down the field for other groups to come.

In this inconspicuous little song, not meant to be a single, hidden in the stacks, buried on the B-side, under the radar of the prying ears of management, Creed Bratton took a thirty-second solo, and in my opinion was astoundingly good. The riff was a simple but brilliant, and I was very pleased, so I put it on the record.

The next thing I knew, I was called into Lasker's office. As I walked in the door, he dropped the needle down on the acetate of the record. We both listened to the record and, having not yet had all of the optimism sucked out of my brain, I foolishly thought that I may have, in my naiveté, pleased Jay Lasker and his musical taste.

The song finished and he placed the needle back in the cradle.

'Is that you playing the guitar?' he asked, poker-faced.

'Do you like it?'

'Is that *you* playing the guitar?'

'Yes. It is me playing the guitar.'

'I don't believe it is you playing guitar.'

'Why do you say that?'

At that moment, Lasker exploded like I had never seen him explode before.

'Because that is the worst fucking guitar I have ever heard, and I want the truth right now or you are fucking dead. You are a fucking dead man! Do you understand me? You are a fucking dead man!'

'All right, Jay,' I said, suddenly calm. 'That is Creed Bratton on the guitar, and I think it is brilliant. So I put it in.'

'OK. So. You put it in. And you can take it out.'

'What is wrong with letting these guys play on their records? It's what they deeply, dearly want. They have given you so much.'

'Look what I've given them! They should be grateful. And if they're not grateful, we can find someone who is. Are you with us or are you with them?'

'I need to give The Grass Roots a feeling that they belong.'

'I'll tell you what. I have a better idea. I'll tell Steve to take the riff out of the record, and you can get the fuck out of Dunhill Records and never show your face again. How's that sit with you?'

I left the office and went back to Del Valle and went for a swim in the pool my father had recently installed. Steve Barri called me that night.

'What is so important about Creed being on the record?'

'Did Jay tell you to call me?'

'No. I did talk to him but I'm calling you on my own. And there is a way we can work this out.'

'What is so important about Creed's little solo is self-respect. They're artists. They want to be involved with their music.'

'Don't give me this "artist" bullshit. We're not artists. We make pop records. The Grass Roots are not artists. We're lucky to be doing what we're doing. And you're going to blow it. We have a good deal here and you're going to blow it.'

'I'm not going to blow anything.'

'Look,' Steve said. 'Let me handle it. Stay away for a week and this will fade away. I'm going to go into the studio and do some mixes and all this will be forgotten.'

'Don't touch Creed's guitar,' I said, thinking to myself that Steve couldn't mix a Caesar salad.

'I won't. I promise.'

Steve realized, way down deep, that there was an artistic level to producers, writers, and musicians, and even though we did it on a daily basis and it may get lost at times in the humdrum of redundancy, it existed. This energy beats in the soul of everyone in the artistic community. The rap that Steve got in his solo career as a producer was that there was no artistry. But when Steve went into Screen Gems that day with Carol Connors, trying to sell his record, he had creative hopes. And I believe that at this time, he had that creative spirit again, for a moment.

After a few days the workload started to pile up again and I was called back. Steve was right. Things just blew over. Meanwhile, Creed's solo stayed on the record, and you can hear it there still today.

GRAND FUNK KNIGHTS IN CLEVELAND

LA was feeling small and hot. When the opportunity to get out of town presented itself, I grabbed it.

I was given the chance of four exquisite days in Cleveland with a local group called Terry Knight & The Pack. They were making regional hits and wanted a P.F. Sloan song, and for me to come out and produce it. Dunhill nixed the idea, of course, as Terry Knight was not a major player, so I bought my own ticket to Cleveland.

I arrived in Ohio, checked into a second-rate hotel, and caught a cab to the studio. Terry was amazed that I had showed up. He was a street brawler with a good heart. He was the type of guy who could punch your lights out and feel sad about it later. The Pack were all hip guys and eager to please. They were totally into music. I played them 'This Precious Time' and they dug it. The band couldn't figure out why I was so happy to be there, in Cleveland, but what was cool for me was that I was working with a band who played their own music.

I asked Terry if he could take me around town to talk to people and see things. Sandusky was near Cleveland, and I wanted to see it because Marilyn Monroe had a line in *Some Like It Hot* where she proclaimed, 'Imagine Me, Sugar Kowalczyk from Sandusky, Ohio, on a millionaire's yacht.' I wanted to see Lake Eerie, too, and freshwater waves. I wanted to see Cedar Point, the famous amusement park. I wanted to see it all.

'Why would you ever want to leave this place?' I asked Terry.

The record came out and lingered just under the Top 100 but was a Top 10 record for the band in their hometown, as well as across the rest of the Midwest, so they were happy.

Terry Knight went on to form Grand Funk Railroad and then became their manager and producer. He was murdered in 2004 while trying to defend his daughter from her boyfriend. He was a legend.

THE GOLDEN KEY

Julie was a blonde-haired, blue-eyed Jewish princess bombshell and the secretary for Dunhill Records. The label was in the process of being sold to ABC/Paramount, and Steve and I were expecting a very large bonus. She informed us that we were to wait in the conference room for Lou Adler and Jay Lasker, who wanted to explain what was happening. We assumed the best.

The conference room was used primarily as a holding pen for those with appointments. It was made of glass, giving one the feeling of being in a fish bowl, and furnished with a large wooden conference table that seated twelve. Whatever happened in there could be seen by everyone.

'What do you suppose this is about?' Steve asked.

'What did Julie tell you?'

'Julie doesn't know anything,' Steve said.

She never did, I thought. 'I think we're here because they've sold Dunhill and we're going to get money or thrown out on our asses.'

Steve became animated and very optimistic.

'This would definitely be the time when they would show their gratitude and their appreciation, don't you think?' he said. 'Don't be crazy, Phil. They are not going to kick us out. We're too important to the company.'

'We can't be sure of anything,' I told him. 'How much do you think we'd get?'

'They're going to make millions. They would have to pay us … $50–100,000?'

'OK, Steve. Yeah. That sounds right.'

Julie walked into the conference room looking like she had already ordered a mink from David Appel. I have often been asked how Steve and I could have worked together after she changed me out for him. The answer is music. Nothing else mattered to me. This is how I convinced myself that I could go along with this new arrangement. I would adapt to this new normal. But I felt wounded.

I told myself that I needed Steve more than I needed Julie. Steve was older and more security-minded. I was creative and impetuous. He was always trying to convince me that we were a great team, but the fact was that we were not a team at all. I think by trying to convince me that we were a partnership, he was trying to convince himself that he was relevant. I was trying to convince myself that I had someone who would watch my back if I went too far out on a limb. The partnership between Steve and me was nothing more than an arranged marriage by Lou Adler. Steve and I were trying to make the marriage work because the parents were wealthy, and he assured me that we would be getting the blessing and the inheritance if we played the game.

In a successful writing partnership, there must be an understanding of the difference between compromise and being told what to do. In the very early days, Steve and I attempted to be a partnership. However, that compromise quickly dissipated into each of us doing what we wanted, and feeling hindered when the other made a suggestion. Steve got his name on many, many songs that he didn't write, and he got 50 percent of everything. I think that he felt that he was taking something that didn't belong to him, and maybe that made him feel guilty. But his ego was big enough that he was able to convince himself that he was worthy of all of it.

'Phil?' Julie called. 'Lou is ready for you.'

'I'm supposed to wait?' Steve asked.

'For a minute, honey.'

Lou Adler was standing up behind his desk.

'Take a seat,' he said. 'I have some news. And by the way, congratulations on "Live For Today." Looks like it's going Top 10. You're something else, Phil.'

I sat down on the hard-backed wooden chair that Adler would offer his associates, trying to make them as uncomfortable as possible so that they would want to end the meeting quickly.

'What's up?' I asked.

'We've all decided that the best thing for the company is to sell to ABC/Paramount.'

'How much can you get for something like this?' I asked.

'Look. Everything is going to stay exactly the way it was. We're going to run the company but we will be able to do it now with a pocketful of cash.'

'This is great, right?'

'Great for you and great for me,' he answered, cheerfully. 'And I've got something for you. A small token of appreciation. You've helped give this company great value.'

With a smile on his face, Lou opened the top drawer of his desk, rummaged around a bit, and pulled out a tiny, gold-colored cardboard box with a silver ribbon wrapped around it. He handed it to me and I accepted it, thinking that it was a strange box to contain a check but also remembering the old adage, *good things come in small packages.*

'Before you go and open your box, Phil, I've got something to tell you that you're going to get a big kick out of.'

'Yeah?'

'You'll never guess who stopped by the office last week.'

'I have no idea.'

'Bob Dylan and Phil Spector came up last week for a little talk with Jay. They wanted to buy your contract.'

'What happened?'

'Jay threw them both out of the office.'

I couldn't believe what I was hearing.

'Jay Lasker threw Bob Dylan and Phil Spector out of *this* office?'

'Yes, he did,' Adler said. 'The both of them are finished. You know what Lasker told them? *You guys don't have a tenth of Sloan's talent.*'

'Lou. Jay is insane.'

'If Jay weren't my partner I might agree. Look. I understand. We're both songwriters, and I know how you feel. Don't worry. I'll protect you from Jay. This is a new beginning of good things happening. Now I know you want to open that box, so get the hell out here,' he added, jokingly. 'And tell Steve to come in.'

I went back into the conference room and told Steve that Adler wanted to see him.

'And?' Steve asked.

'And nothing. I'll wait here.'

I slowly opened up the little box, truly believing and hoping that it might contain something of value. Inside the box was a small, gold key, stamped with the word 'Dunhill.'

I thought about what this key could possibly mean. Was it the key to a car? No. It wasn't a car key. It didn't look like a house key, either.

Steve returned with a smile on his face.

'What did Lou tell you?' I asked.

'The future looks great, just like I told you.'

'Open your box.'

Steve opened his box and found the same key.

'It's a blank key,' he said. 'What do you think it opens?'

'Nothing,' I said. 'I think it opens nothing.'

'I don't get it,' Steve said. He sounded confused and hurt, and was checking under the key and wrapping to see if he had missed anything.

Just then, Julie burst into the conference room.

'Did you guys like it?'

'Like what, honey?' Steve asked. 'It's a key. There's nothing in the box but a key.'

'It's just a key to nothing,' I told her.

'I picked it out,' Julie said. 'But there wasn't a check with it?'

'No. Just thank you very much, and here's your key.'

'It's got to be a joke,' Julie said. 'Lou's joking!'

'This is no joke,' I replied. 'We've got to get out of here, Steve. I feel like I'm slowly being choked to death.'

'Let's give it some time,' Steve said. 'Maybe we're misreading this. Let's not do something we're going to regret.'

'I don't know about you but I'm going home. My mother is making roast beef.'

I left Steve and Julie in the conference room and decided to walk. I needed fresh air in my lungs because I felt like I had been raped in a prison shower. I was clean but screwed.

I decided to head over to Rodeo Drive to Dunhill Jewelers. Maybe I could find something out about the key that I didn't know. I walked in. Everything in there was monumentally expensive, so my hopes went up a bit. I walked up to the counter and showed the gentleman the box with the key in it. He held the key in his hands as if looking at a fine stone and then put it gently back into the box.

'I'm sorry,' he said. 'This is not one of our keys.'

'Is it at least gold?' I asked.

'Gold?' he chuckled. 'No. It's not gold. It's not even gold plate. It's gold-painted bronze. Nice paint job, though. A real quality piece of work. It's hard to make paint look this good. How much did you pay for it?'

'It was a gift.'

'Well, it's a gift, and that's a good thing. But I'm sorry to say, it's practically worthless.'

On my walk back, I deposited my key into a trashcan. I'm pretty sure Steve kept his, though, and he did seem to be able open doors with it.

CHAPTER FOURTEEN

IF YOU'RE GOING TO SAN FRANCISCO ...

In 1967, race riots were breaking out across America. The Vietnam War was raging, and Lyndon Johnson had lost control of the presidency. Robert Kennedy's star was rising. Kids from all over the country had started to migrate to San Francisco. Los Angeles seemed oppressive compared to the clear breezes and free thinking spirit of Marin County and Golden Gate Park.

'San Francisco (Be Sure To Wear Some Flowers In Your Hair)' was a song written by John Phillips and sung by Scott McKenzie to promote the upcoming Monterey Pop Festival. I played guitar on the record but I was uncomfortable in the studio with Phillips, who was enjoying being in control and wasn't asking for any opinions on how to make the song better. And that was fine. He told me to play it as written and keep my ideas to myself. Fine!

The studio musicians were embarrassed about Phillips's newfound power trip but knew how to accommodate those rock stars with ego-eccentricities and a penchant for acting like King Rat. Drugs were starting to make a serious play on John's mind, and I wasn't the only one who would feel the wrath of that madness.

'San Francisco' was an immediate success and seemed almost literally to empty entire towns of their youth. Hoards of young people from the East, South, and Midwest were descending upon the pristine, peaceful little city of San Francisco. They arrived without money or shelter and with just the clothes on their backs, expecting to enter the golden gates of utopia. They slept in the parks and on the streets. Jerry Garcia and Peter

Coyote formed a group called The Diggers that became sort of a Red Cross, feeding and clothing these nouveau hippies. Bringing them down from bad trips was the role of Hugh Romney, known as Wavy Gravy, who claimed to be the only person in the world to smell like Albert Einstein.

Kids were arriving by the thousands each day, and the city did not know what to do. In the song, Phillips wrote, *when you come to San Francisco, be sure to wear some flowers in your hair ... you're sure to find some gentle people there.* What they found instead were cement sidewalk beds and urine in their shoes. It was nothing like it was a year earlier, when you felt you were in a separate city that respected your right of self-exploration. All that had changed. The Haight-Ashbury District was merely eight blocks long and it quickly became a ghetto for hippies who for the most part didn't have any place to sleep or wash. Sixteen-year-old Midwestern girls who only a week before were milking cows and complaining that their parents didn't understand were now prostituting themselves for food and shelter.

Until that song came out, Haight-Ashbury was a cool, tight, clean community. When kids arrived, they would stand at the corner of Haight and Ashbury looking for hippies like tourists looking for celebrities on Hollywood and Vine, not believing it was just an ordinary street corner but rather a magical rendezvous where they would be whisked away on a magic carpet.

Most of San Francisco was very conservative and didn't want anything to do with these 'new' hippies, so they were relieved when the spillover ran across the Bay into Berkeley—another sleepy university town, which became Dante's inferno in about two months. What went wrong? The idealism of all of these kids, ablaze with the possibility of a new and better world, was dashed on the rocks of the reality of having to be able to survive.

When they crossed over the Bay Bridge into the quiet enclaves of Berkeley and Oakland, these kids expected to be met as conquering heroes of peace; instead they were met with police and jail. The naive hippies of the East Bay did not arrive with political agendas. They wanted to spread love. But as they were spreading that love they created urban blight and political anarchy, much to the concern of an establishment that first fought it tooth and nail and then, in losing desperation, embraced it in total defeat.

The new order, intoxicated by its own power, turned fascistic to protect the ground that had been won over. In San Francisco, the old guard was not going to give up the high ground of Telegraph Hill; they were going to stamp out this tie-dyed plague. This was the battleground for the Summer of Love.

SECRET PLANS AND THE MONTEREY POP FESTIVAL

In the midst of all this, Lou Adler and John Phillips were planning an extravaganza musical event in Monterey, California—the Monterey Pop Festival. Jimmy Webb and I were invited up to John Phillips's house in Trousdale Estates in Beverly Hills to discuss the creation of the festival. The idea was for it to feature many different acts but with The Mamas & The Papas as the main draw, closing the show. Their star had started to fade, however, and Jimi Hendrix, Janis Joplin, The Who, and Ravi Shankar were thrust upon Adler and Phillips as attractions that would bring more people to the festival. Adler didn't really want any of them.

Jimmy and I drove up to Phillips's house together. By the time we arrived, most of the others were there already—Paul Simon, Art Garfunkel, David Crosby, Steve Stills, Lou Adler, Cass Eliot, and Derek Taylor, the press rep for Brian Epstein and The Beatles—and were involved in a very animated discussion. Lou Adler was trying to press Derek Taylor for a commitment from The Beatles to play.

'I can't give you a yes but I can't say no,' Taylor told him. 'I know that Paul expressed interest in doing it, but I don't know yet about John or George. And I don't know where Ringo is.'

It was as if Jimmy and I were simply two Jewish newspaper reporters who had walked in on a private meeting of the German High Command, looking for a scoop. We were made to believe that our input would be worthwhile and helpful, but apparently the invasion of Europe could go on without us.

I looked at Stills but his eyes seemed vacant, as if he was suddenly pretending to be somebody he wasn't. Phillips seemed high-strung and irritable, perhaps out of his element in the role of rock entrepreneur. His living room was palatial—more suited to a Moroccan king than to a folkster from the Village.

I had never met Art Garfunkel or Paul Simon, and it would have been a courtesy for someone to introduce us, but that was ignored. I thought Simon was a very talented songwriter, and I would have enjoyed getting to know him, but I don't think he thought much of me. (In fact, I had heard that he considered me to be a two-bit hack.)

Jimmy and I didn't know what to do, and we felt a little humiliated, so we slipped out of the door and onto the porch.

'I don't know what I'm doing here,' Jimmy said. 'These guys are big stars. We're just a couple of songwriters.'

'I don't think that Phillips cares that we're here,' I told him.

'I don't think I want us here, either. You want to split and grab a burger at Norm's?'

Just then, Phillips appeared at the door. He was an imposing figure—about six foot four—and tonight he was wearing a Russian fur hat. He was beginning to morph into his alter ego, which he called the Wolf King.

'You guys smoking a joint?' he joked.

'We're not sure why we're here, John,' Jimmy said.

'Be patient. Be cool. We're working out a few things. Phil, can I see you in the kitchen for a minute? I've got a few things to ask you. Jimmy, would you mind?'

I thought John wanted to talk to me about something relating to the show, or maybe he planned to apologize for being demeaning to me in the studio.

'I'll wait here,' Jimmy said.

I followed John into his grand country kitchen and waited as he puttered around the cupboards for a bit.

'Would you like a cup of coffee?' he asked.

'That would be great,' I said.

'I've been thinking about your contributions to the group,' he said. 'And I've decided we'd be a lot better off without you. Your guitar playing is holding us back—frankly, it's second-rate.'

This really made me angry. I wasn't going to stand there and take that from him. I decided right there and then not to give him the chance to fester into a boil on my ass.

'Fuck you, Phillips.'

'Fuck me?'

Phillips looked like he had just been sucker-punched on a street corner.

'Yeah, fuck you. I helped to create your sound.'

'Any studio hack could have done what you did.'

'If it weren't for those studio hacks, as you call them, you'd still be singing background for McGuire.'

At that he spun around holding a large carving knife, slashing wildly at the air in front of my face, coming threateningly close to my neck.

'Get that knife away from my face, John,' I demanded.

John acted as if he didn't hear. He carried on toying with the knife as if he was getting a thrill out of terrorizing me. Who was this person in front of me? Gone was the man I once admired—the man I had learned to respect in the studio.

'Do you think I called you here to my home to get your opinion on our festival?' he asked, lowering the knife to his side. 'I called you here to give you fair warning that I'll have you killed if you show up in Monterey. Are we clear?'

'You know, man, I'll go where I fucking wanna wanna go,' I said.

Phillips gave a kind of demonic chuckle.

'Don't try me, man,' he said, throwing the knife down on the counter.

Phillips lumbered back into the living room, where I heard him talking to Paul Simon, who was excited about a platter of cold cuts. I stood at the counter, frozen in time. My legs were wobbly and I felt like throwing up. When my reasoning returned, I got the hell out of there. My first thought was to find Jimmy and scram but I couldn't find him.

I jumped into my car and took off. I drove down to Santa Monica and took a walk along the pier to try to clear my head and make sense of what I had just happened. I started asking myself questions. *Was Adler in on this? Should I tell Steve Barri?* No. He wouldn't believe it. Even *I* couldn't believe it!

It turns out that Jimmy Webb was looking for me, while I was looking for him. When he couldn't find me, he etched the scene in his mind, and a couple of years later, he started writing a song.

> *I have been seeking P.F. Sloan*
> *But no one knows where he has gone ...*

A GATHERING OF BEAUTIFUL THINGS

I had been invited to play at a music event called the Fantasy Fair on Mount Tamalpais in Marin County, California, on June 11 and 12, a week before the Monterey Pop Festival was to take place. It was to be the first ever event of its kind—two days of music, with over thirty acts on the bill: The Doors, Jefferson Airplane, The Byrds, Captain Beefheart, Steve Miller, Country Joe & The Fish, Tim Buckley, Moby Grape, Wilson Pickett, Smokey Robinson & The Miracles, Hugh Masekela, Spanky & Our Gang, The Fifth Dimension, The Grass Roots, and me, P.F. Sloan.

Perhaps because it was filmed, Monterey Pop continues to be remembered as the seminal musical event of 1967, but the Fantasy Fair was the first major rock festival in history, with over fifty-thousand people in attendance over the course of two days. It was put on as a benefit for the Hunters Point Child Care Center.

A gathering of beautiful things, created and collected by the artisans and craftsmen of Northern California, and represented by the exhibitors listed on the Fantasy Fair Map ... a variety of 'happenings.' When you arrive at the Fantasy Fair, you will immediately be surrounded by color and motion, the good vibrations of thousands of people flowing with the natural beauty of Mt. Tamalpais. The major happening is you—your feeling of good will, and your knowledge that the Fair and the Mountain are a part of you, therefore yours to enjoy. The woods and meadows are an open invitation to wander and enjoy yourself to the limits of your imagination.

Stan Owsley was there, of course. He was known for cooking high-quality LSD. It was Stan who provided the acid for The Beatles during the filming of *Magical Mystery Tour*. As the acts were going onstage, Stan administered communion with all who wanted to partake, putting a tab of his Owsley acid under each waiting tongue. I took the wafer and then the stage, unsure of what I was going to play.

The crowd seemed happy to see whoever appeared on the stage. I started off with 'I Can't Help But Wonder Elizabeth.' It was an extremely difficult song to play, but when I had asked Creed Bratton what song I should open with, he suggested this one. He might as well have suggested I open with Beethoven's *Seventh Symphony*. I was told after the show that I did a twenty-minute guitar solo, but I do not have any memory of such a thing. The only memory I have of the show is the wave of love that I received from the crowd. None of us had ever performed in front of such a large audience. With most of the performers under the influence of LSD, including myself, it was difficult to maintain the separation between performer and audience. You wanted to jump into the crowd and be swallowed. A few years later, that would become the norm, rather than the exception.

I left the stage as Jim Morrison and The Doors were going on. I remember looking at Jim, and he looking at me, and both of us wanted to say something but knew not what.

Tom Donahue, one of the promoters of the show and a well-known disc jockey, grabbed me and threw me into a limo.

'Get some rest,' he said. 'You're playing the Fillmore tomorrow night.'

One of Donahue's assistant's then whisked me off to the St. Francis hotel in San Francisco.

I went into the Haight for breakfast. I was sitting on the stoop, hanging out with a couple of guys from The Sons Of Champlain, one of the greatest and most respected and loved of the San Francisco groups, and Phil Lesh from the Dead. At this time, there were rumors that bad LSD called STP was being fed into the community by the government to cause hippies to commit suicide. How's that for a conspiracy theory? Within weeks, people started overdosing on bad acid, and it became a real nightmare. Overnight, The Height turned from bad to worse.

A Rolls-Royce pulled up on the corner of Haight and Ashbury and out stepped George Harrison.

'Hey, George! Over here!' Phil Lesh shouted.

George looked in our direction and waved.

'Get the fuck out of here, George! Quick!'

'What?' George shouted.

Suddenly the street scene was transformed into *Night Of The Living Dead*. George, slow on the uptake, thought the approaching zombies were Beatle fans. They weren't. They were zombies.

'Get in the car and get out of here,' I yelled.

George jumped into the car as the zombies started pushing and trying to roll the car over with him in it. They started crawling on the car like hungry lizards. As the car sped off, the zombies looked around for something else to crawl onto, before dissipating into their own self-imposed madness. George went back to London, and must have reported to the others that San Francisco had turned into a rathole, and to stay away.

A QUEEN OF RAGS

The headliners at the Fillmore West were Big Brother & The Holding Company and Quicksilver Messenger Service, with two special guests: Kris Kristofferson and me. Once again all of the performers—and, as far as I could tell, the entire audience—were tripping to some degree.

I opened the show. I did a well-received forty-five-minute set and then joined the audience to watch Kristofferson and the rest of the night. The audience loved Kris and so did I, but it was when I was listening to Quicksilver, under the influence of LSD, that I began to appreciate the wondrous discordance of an un-tuned guitar. That evening would lead to my great appreciation of punk music, and to some punk musicians being appreciative of P.F. Sloan.

After the show I was sitting on an old beat-up couch between Janis Joplin and Kris. Janis was drinking her Southern Comfort and kept asking me to drive her to West Texas.

'You seem like a nice fella,' she said. 'Will you drive me home? I'm tired of all of this.'

'She means it, you know,' Kris told me. 'She wants to go home. They hated her there but she wants to go home.'

I tried to say something humorous but I really had no idea how deeply sad this girl was. And though I had my own level of sadness, Janis was swimming in the deep water. Janis was a girl that you wanted to spend the rest of your life protecting. She really brought out the knight in shining armor in you. She was a queen—a queen in rags. When Janis put her head on my shoulder, I felt like I wanted her to crawl inside of me so she could feel safe.

Relating this story, I feel even after all the years as though I am betraying some sacrosanct experience. I'm not sure why it resonates so deeply within me. And I'm wondering. If Janis had not achieved superstardom with *Pearl*, would I be writing about this? She really disliked the world of celebrity. She hated being thrust into any role that she could not herself control. She could moan and scream and wail without any danger, but it was only when the world wanted her to do it on command that she became nothing more than a caged tiger, her audience demanding that she rip off the head of her trainer.

The lure and promise of great wealth must have given her a modicum of plausibility that she could do it. But Janis was never meant to become the celebrated wild woman of blues and rock'n'roll. Out of all the artists I ever met, Janis struck the deepest chord. Maybe it was because I knew that what she was going through was lurking in me. And if I couldn't heal her, how would I ever be able to heal myself?

When I heard that Janis had died, I felt relieved that she had ended her suffering, as strange as that might seem to say. Janis belonged to the people, and she sang her heart out for them. When the corporate types got their claws into her and tried to turn her into Barbara Streisand, she said, 'Fine.' And then she died.

BEWARE … THE WOLF KING LURKS

The Monterey Fairgrounds were set in bleak, dusty, dried-flat landscape, in stark contrast to the beauty that is associated with the Monterey Peninsula and the gorgeous Northern California coastline. I arrived knowing full well that I was under threat from the Wolf King.

The festival area was surrounded by temporary fencing. Not many people had shown up as yet. The word was slow in getting out. I was waiting around the entrance, bound and determined not to buy a ticket out of principle. Aside from really wanting to see The Who, Ravi

Shankar, and Janis, I had no other business at this festival. The last thing I wanted to do was to see The Mamas & The Papas with some other guitarist on the stage, playing parts that I wrote. I knew I would get in, though. I always got in.

A limousine pulled up near where I was standing. The rear window opened and Jimi Hendrix popped his head out.

'Aren't you P.F. Sloan?' he asked.

'I was yesterday,' I said.

'Hey, man. Do you know where the artist's entrance is?'

'No, Jimi,' I replied. 'I'm not really here.'

'That's cool,' he said, beckoning me over to the car. 'Get in.'

Jimi Hendrix had not yet hit in the America, but I was aware of his music and influence in Britain, where he had had three Top 10 songs and was thought highly of by Eric Clapton and Chas Chandler of The Animals. Jimi was in full hippie-rock sartorial splendor, wearing a purple velvet suit and black hat and bedazzled with layers of silk finery and jewels.

I got into the limo. Jimi was sullen and quiet. He seemed sad. I sat back in the seat and took a deep breath. The driver started to look for the artists' entrance. Jimi took out a pack of Gauloises cigarettes and offered me one. He lit mine and then his own. They were strong but smooth. I began to relax.

'I just found out that this woman who I loved with all of my heart and all my soul has been making plaster casts of my dick and selling them to her friends,' Jimi said.

As he told me the story, his eyes welled up. I could tell he was deeply hurt by this.

'I'm so sorry, man,' I said.

'Yeah, man. Yeah.'

Jimi's spirits seemed to pick up as we drove in through the VIP gate.

'I'm looking forward to playing tonight,' he said. 'It's going to be a great show if the promoters know what they're doing. Are The Beatles going to be here?'

'I heard something about it.'

The limo stopped in front of the hastily constructed press office and I hopped out.

'Have a great show, Jimi.'

'Thanks, man. Catch you later.'

I was looking to get lost—and quick—but I noticed Derek Taylor sitting alone at a desk and speaking on the telephone. Aside from seeing him at John Phillips's house, I had been introduced to him by Brian Epstein, who had referred to me as 'one of the lads.' Derek represented The Beatles and Epstein with charm, wit, and intellect. He was simply the best.

He looked up from his phone conversation, waved me inside, and signaled for me to sit on one of the chairs. He covered the phone and whispered to me.

'John is on the phone.'

'Phillips?' I whispered.

'Lennon,' he whispered back, and then went back to the phone. 'P.F. Sloan just walked in and he's not supposed to be here. John Phillips is trying to kill him.'

At this point in time, Phillips had lost all sense of reality. I motioned to Derek that I would see him later, but he signaled for me to stay.

'John,' Derek continued on the phone. 'This thing feels so dark. I don't want you coming here. At this moment, I don't want to be here. Yeah. OK. Hold on.'

Derek handed me the phone.

'What?' I asked.

'John wants to say something to you,' he said.

I put the phone to my ear.

'Hello, John?'

'Hello, P.F.,' he said. 'Look, I just wanted to let you know that I think you are a good man, and I take back what I said about your song. Don't worry about anything. Stay if you like. Leave if you like. Just take good care of yourself. Don't do anything foolish. Put Derek back on the phone.'

As I handed the phone back to Derek, I could hear John yelling.

'Tell those pieces of shit, Phillips and the other guy, that there's no way The Beatles are showing up for his money-grubbing-ego-fucking-festival.'

'Right,' Derek said. 'I'll grab the first plane out to London.'

Derek hung up the phone.

'I'm getting out of here, Phil, What about you?'

'Derek, I just got done performing at the Fantasy Fair outside San Francisco and they put me up at a great hotel for a week. I did the Fillmore and some clubs, and you know, rather than going home I thought, you know I'd really like to see The Who.'

'The Who? Really? The Who? What are you, nuts? Come to London. We'll spend the weekend with The Who. You have got to get out of here. Phillips is going crazy. I don't know what's wrong with him.'

'Oh, man, tell me about it, but I'm not going to let Phillips stop me from having a good time.'

'That's fine, Phil, but I'm leaving. If you decide to stay, you're on your own. I can't protect you.'

'I understand.'

Derek gathered a few things into a briefcase and we shook hands.

'Be careful,' he told me.

'Give my regards to Brian,' I said.

'I will. You should have moved to London,' he replied, and rushed out the door.

People started milling about the press office. The field was starting to fill up with thousands of people. A VIP section had been set up in front of the stage but was still being worked on by carpenters, technicians, and roadies. I decided I had had enough of fear and was going to put myself right out there and do what I wanted to do.

I spotted Cass Eliot. I thought for sure that she would not have anything to do with John's craziness. I went in and sat next to her as if everything was normal. Brian Jones was with her.

'Are you crazy, Phil?' Cass asked.

'What do you mean?'

'You know that John doesn't want you here.'

'I know.'

'So what are you doing here?'

'I want to see The Who.'

'John Phillips is trying to kill Phil,' Cass told Brian.

'Then keep him the fuck away from me or I'll be trying to kill him myself.'

'You can't sit here,' Cass told me. 'I won't tell John that I saw you, but you need to get lost.'

'OK.'

'Really, Phil, you need to go.'

Cass Eliot knew that the dream of The Mamas & The Papas was over. A couple of weeks before, on *The Ed Sullivan Show*, Cass did the unthinkable on live television. She announced to the world—with the words, 'Roll the tape'—that they were lip-syncing to their own song.

With that, Cass broke the myth of The Mamas & The Papas. Things were not as they seemed. In John's mind, Cass knew that I was part of that lie.

I moved into the crowd and became invisible as I waited for the music to begin. I was happy to spot Kim Canoe in the crowd. We hugged and reconnected and enjoyed the performances together. I felt that I had found someone who loved me and that things would be OK. She wasn't going to stay for the second day, though, and she made me promise that I would visit her in her new apartment when I got back to LA.

YOUR MONEY OR YOUR LIFE

Dunhill released 'Things I Should Have Said' as a single from the *Live For Today* album, plus any demos they could find lying around. They made up names for imaginary groups like The Imaginations and The Emergency Exit just to pump records out into the market, to make the company look like they were overflowing with creativity and product.

It was a time of transition for the company. People were coming in and going out. 'Things I Should Have Said' hit the Top 20. I was called to a meeting with Lasker in early September, just before my twenty-second birthday. He had a dead look in his eyes.

'I've come to a very important decision,' he said, waving me to the couch.

'OK.'

'We both know that you are doing all the work—the producing, the arranging, the singing and the writing in this partnership of yours. Phil? I think you're carrying Steve Barri.'

'We both do what we can do.'

'There's no reason why he should be receiving half of your royalties.'

'What are you getting at?' I asked, curiously.

'I think we have to get rid of Steve.'

'How do you mean … get rid of Steve?'

'I mean lose him. Look. You go one way; he goes another way. You stay here; he goes somewhere else. You feel good about giving Steve half of what you do?

'No, but …'

'You feel loyal to this guy?'

'We started together.'

'You don't feel loyal to me.'

'I never said that.'

'But you *think* that.'

'I wasn't thinking that.'

'Excuse me,' Lasker said. 'I'm going to take a leak.'

He got up from his desk and headed for the door.

'You want a Coke, Flip?'

'No, thanks. I'm good.'

Lasker left the office and closed the door.

I have thought about this scene many times over the years. It was obvious that Lasker was setting me up to agree to throw Steve under the bus. But I did not think that I was in any physical, financial, or professional danger. I was used to this sort of rhetoric. This was the way Lasker spoke to everyone—he had a manipulative personality, to say the least. And he enjoyed his own perverse nature.

When Lasker returned, he seemed buoyant.

'Now I can think,' he said, moving to his desk, lighting a fresh cigar and leaning back in his chair. 'You know the feeling you get when a song is really working?'

'Yeah.'

'Come here. I want to show you something really interesting.'

Jay opened the top drawer of his desk and removed several eight-by-ten photographs of what looked to me like police crime photos. He laid each photo out very carefully.

'What do you think these are?' he asked.

'What are you showing me here?'

Jay was enjoying the moment. He took a long puff from his cigar and smiled, mischievously.

'I lived a long time in Chicago. Made a lot of friends there. And when I ran into trouble, I could always find people to persuade the other party to see my point of view.'

The photographs were grotesque pictures of murder victims—blown-up, burned, hacked to death.

'Not a pretty picture, is it?' he said.

I was shaking. I was now starting to be truly afraid of him. Until now, it was a game that I could play. My self-confidence had carried me through, but now I was in unchartered territory.

Jay stood up, opened the window, and took a breath of fresh air before turning to me.

'You must have heard the stories about Jackie Wilson being hung out the window until he gave up his publishing royalties.'

'Yeah. Everybody has heard that.'

'Crazy, huh? Well, I'm not like that. I'm not going to hang you from the window to save your partner.'

Jay closed the window and sat back at his desk. From the top drawer, he pulled out a paring knife he used to cut the tips off his cigars.

'Here's what I want you to do,' he said, very matter-of-factly. 'I want you to pull down your pants, take this very sharp knife, cut out one of your testicles, and put it on the desk. Then everything will be the way it was before this conversation. You good with that? Just one testicle. One little, old testicle, and everything is perfect for a very long time.'

The line had been crossed. I was now in the presence of a monster. I was mentally scrambling to figure out the ending of this play.

Jay replaced the knife in the drawer.

'No? OK. Go out and tell your partner I want to talk to him.'

I left the office and found Steve waiting outside.

'He wants to see you,' I said.

'What's it about?' he asked.

'Just go in.'

About fifteen minutes later, Steve came out of Lasker's office. He seemed distant as he walked toward me. He had a strange sense of confidence that I hadn't seen in him before. I almost didn't recognize him.

'I had no choice,' he told me as he walked away. 'He wants to see you again.'

I walked into Jay's office, and there was a look of satisfaction on his face.

'I just had a nice chat with Steve,' he said. 'Here's what's going to happen. You're going to leave Los Angeles and never come back. You're going to do this within twenty-four hours, or your parents or your sister or anyone else you care about may come to regret knowing a boy named P.F. Sloan.'

'I want to talk to Lou,' I said.

'This has nothing to do with Lou, Sloan. This is about you and me … mostly you. I've had the papers drawn up. Before you leave the office, you're going to sign it. It relinquishes all of your interests in your music—yesterday, today, and tomorrow. It's your choice. It's not like I'm threatening you.'

I felt like I was caught in a whirlpool of poisoned Jell-O. I knew that the partners, my parents, Steve, Julie—everyone had had enough of P.F. Sloan, but I couldn't fathom the situation getting this perverse.

'We own your contracts for the next ten years so you can't record anywhere else. We're not firing you. We're just telling you that you can't work here or anywhere. It's sort an anti-competitive clause.'

'Jay. Why? Why are you doing this?'

'All of the money that will come into Dunhill Records from P.F Sloan will be split between the three partners. Oh … one more point. I'm pretty sure that I own the name P.F. Sloan and that we can have any writer we want to be P.F. Sloan.'

It was simple: it was all about money. They wanted to get rid of either Steve or me so that the songwriting royalties for one of us could be split amongst the partners. And this represented millions and millions of dollars.

What has plagued me after all of these years is this: Should I have played Lasker's bluff? Should I have said, *fine, kill whoever you like, but I'm not signing anything?* Most normal people would say that you don't take the chance. I remember having a conversation with a rabbi friend of mine and he told me that my parents should have been willing and proud to sacrifice themselves for my God-given talent.

I wasn't about to take that chance over a song. I took the pen and signed the paper. I walked out the door. On my way out I walked past Julie, who had a blank, sick, embarrassed look on her face. I got into my car, drove to Del Valle, and told my parents that I had to leave Los Angeles.

'What did you do to them that makes them hate you so much?' my mother asked.

'Nothing, mom. I have to leave, and I can't tell you why. I'll be in touch, OK? Pray for me, will you? I love you!'

I got into my Jaguar, filled it up, grabbed a map, and headed east to New York. I had grown up there and had relatives there, and I guess I was being drawn back. I don't know. I drove. That's what I really wanted to do. I never wanted to stop. Drive and cry. Just drive. I needed to cry for the first hundred miles and I was angry for a thousand miles.

I remember very little of the actual trip. I felt that a good part of my soul had been ripped out of me. For the first time, being P.F. Sloan was no longer a game. Being P.F. Sloan had cost me everything. To say I was angry at God wouldn't begin to describe it. I felt I had been cursed. I examined every little thing I had ever done to deserve such a fate. Had getting a glimpse into the beauty and insightfulness caused this to happen? Did I need to get rid of P.F. Sloan and see what others perhaps saw—an ego trip, a phony?

Maybe I needed to get back to being Phil Schlein. Why did my being P.F. Sloan disturb so many people? Why the negative tidal wave against this kid who was only trying to make music and mend a few fences?

In 1967, the world was starting to fall apart. And so was I.

Book Two
1968-2014

CHAPTER FIFTEEN

NO ONE WILL BE ABLE TO LEAVE ONCE THE DOOR IS CLOSED

It was snowing when I checked into the Chelsea Hotel in the winter of 1967, next door to a room permanently occupied by Arthur C. Clarke. I'd see him every morning when he walked down to the street to get coffee and a newspaper, wearing a Japanese kimono. His room was filled with exotic plants. He wasn't a particularly outgoing person and I was in no mood to talk to anyone. I spent my days in sorrow and contemplation.

Under the safety of night, I would venture out to the streets of Greenwich Village, covered in scarves, hat, and a heavy pea coat I had picked up in a second hand store. One night, in an alley off of McDougal Street, I ran into Bob Dylan. He recognized me but didn't seem to want to stop and converse. We were both wrapped up from head to foot, and the temperature was close to freezing.

My initial feeling was that of elation upon coming in contact with a much-needed friend. Dylan looked dazed and bewildered, as if he was battling his own demons on that cold night.

'Bob?' I said.

'It's really getting dark, man. It's really getting dark.'

'Can you tell me everything is going to be all right?' I asked.

'No. It's just getting darker. I know what happened to you, man. I told you what kind of guys they were. How come you didn't listen?'

'I listened, but I couldn't believe.'

'Where are you staying?'

'Chelsea. Arthur C. Clarke is in the room next to me.'

'That's not good, man. You've got to get out of the Chelsea. It's a dark place, and you don't belong there, man. Just keep moving. Don't let anything sneak up behind you.'

Bob stopped and pointed his finger at me, as if to portend doom, like Elijah in *Moby Dick*, as Ishmael and Queequeg are about to board the Pequod.

'No one will be able to leave once the door is closed,' he added.

'Are you going to be around?'

'I'll be around, man. I'm not going anywhere.'

With that, Bob turned and disappeared like a waft of smoke into the cold, New York, winter night.

THE LOFT

I started hanging around blues clubs in the Village and was beginning to drink a bit too much. One night, Van Morrison pulled up to the bar next to me, and we started talking.

'What does success look like for you in New York?' I asked.

'Knowing that the next drink is paid for,' he replied.

I had to laugh. Morrison had his 'Irish poet' intact and understood the art of small expectations. There's nothing new about drinking away your sorrows, but I thought if I could somehow justify it by convincing myself that the poet in me needed alcohol, like mother's milk, and I was sitting in a bar because I had a visitation from the spirit of an Irish poet, I should drink and drink hard. But after seeing what alcohol had done to my uncle Harry and my cousin Barbara (the subjects of 'The Sins Of A Family'), I felt uneasy about it.

I had been using mind-expanding drugs up until then—mostly for learning's sake, I told myself—and I felt all right with that, but this was the Village, and the bone-chilling cold with the dirt and grime stole into my soul. In drunken binges, I would wonder, *did P.F. Sloan abandon me because I was no longer worthy?* Lately I had been writing more pop songs than meaningful, insightful songs. Or was I abandoning P.F. Sloan because pop songs were easier? Maybe my destiny was to sacrifice it all and wind up dead in the gutter with a crumpled poem in my hand, to be published immediately in the *New Yorker* upon my death.

One thing was for certain: I was out of my mind, or rather lost inside my mind, and it was getting worse by the day. Fortunately, I met a woman. Her name was Miki St. Clair. She knew me from a few of the songs I had written but didn't know if I was for real or just another wannabe folksinger.

'I am an undercover agent for the CIA and I can't reveal anything to anybody,' I told her, in all seriousness.

'You need to get your head together,' she told me. 'Where are you living?'

'The Chelsea.'

'Let's go to your place,' she said.

We grabbed a cab and she stayed the night. In a matter of days she had moved in with me and we were inseparable. She knew everybody in the Village—the musicians, the poets, the shopkeepers. She knew the stay-away-from and the trustworthy cops on the beat. On one trip to Times Square, I bought her a 3D picture of a winking Jesus that followed you around the room. She bought me a full-sized American flag to use as a bedspread. We would drink coffee at Chock Full Of Nuts and ate lunch at the Horn & Hardart automat.

Miki was going out of her way to make me feel at home. I felt safe with her. Before me, her boyfriend was Buzzy Linhart, a singer-songwriter who had been on the scene for many years. He had been John Sebastian's roommate, too, and was well respected as a musician. It was through Buzzy that Miki became pals with Bob Dylan and Fred Neil. She idolized Fred and couldn't wait to introduce me to him. But she had some work to do on me before that could happen.

After a few weeks at the Chelsea, Miki took me to see a realtor, and I rented a loft on West Broadway. It was late 1967, and I was twenty-two. By now Greenwich Village had lost some of its romance, but it was still an active and vibrant place. The folk-beatnik days of Fred Neil, Lenny Bruce, and Phil Ochs had been replaced with the hippie element of hard blues, rock, and psychedelia. The old folk scene was still going on in Washington Square, just not in the clubs.

Miki introduced me to Howard Solomon, the owner of the Café Au

Go Go, who gave me a weekly gig there. The Go Go had some great lineups—John Lee Hooker, Canned Heat, The Steve Miller Band, Jimi Hendrix, Dave Van Ronk, Moby Grape, The Blues Project, Ian & Sylvia, Cream, and so many more all played there. It was absolutely the hippest stage in Greenwich Village, and directly across the street from the famous Bitter End club. I was usually the opening act but I also headlined on occasion.

Howard Solomon ran the club by the book. No drugs or alcohol allowed. The City of New York didn't want his club to be open, and the authorities were looking for any excuse to shut him down. This was the club where Lenny Bruce performed each night and was arrested for obscenity so many times. Howard bailed Lenny out every time he was hauled in and then put him back on the stage.

I was actually earning money as a performer by now and seemed to fit in as an accepted creative spirit, although I still felt like a Californian living in exile. I was no longer *in* my life but rather witnessing it. The Jag I had driven across the country was my LA trophy, and when it mysteriously burned to the tires I realized that my connections to my old life were not going to work for me here.

'What are you so upset about, Phil?' Howard assured me. 'Nobody drives in the Village.'

He was right. I got a Yamaha 180 motorcycle.

Miki took me to Andy Warhol's Factory, and we became friendly with Andy, Nico, Lou Reed, Tennessee Williams, Edie Sedgwick, Salvador Dali, and Truman Capote. These folks were also regulars at the Go Go. A fan of mine from Brooklyn introduced me to his friend, the poet W.H. Auden. He was in his sixties by then, and although homosexual was still with his wife Erika Mann. I visited him often at his apartment on St. Mark's Place. We would sip brandy together, and when the brandy took hold he would recite a poem and then ask me to recite what I was working on. At the time he was working on *City Without Walls*. He may have seen a bit of his younger self in me.

Before long, our loft became the stomping grounds for musicians passing through town and regulars like Kenny Rankin, and even Buzzy and his new girlfriend. All this was great! I seemed to be succeeding in what I thought of as my resettlement phase. I loved New York and felt like I had an instinctual local knowledge of the place. I had grown up on the streets, and I even had my own gang that used to steal apples and oranges when I was seven. If I could take care of myself then, I could certainly do so now. Maybe I was returning home! And God knows, the food was great. The delis and Italian restaurants were like nirvana to me.

Miki was supportive and loving. She taught me the ropes as best she knew. If there was a dark side to this life, it was keeping its presence hidden.

Sid Bernstein was a manager and entrepreneur. He managed Laura Nyro and The Young Rascals—he is the one who took the 'young' out of the Rascals—and had brought The Beatles to Carnegie Hall when nobody believed in them. We had that in common. One night he came backstage at the Go Go after I finished a set and told me that he wanted to manage me. I told him that I had a lot of scary problems, not wanting to go into the Dunhill nightmare with him.

'We'll straighten everything out,' he told me. 'Don't worry.'

Sid connected me with his attorneys, who assured me that what Dunhill had done to me was illegal, and that there was no doubt that they would be able to overturn the contracts. Sid brought me over to Atco Records, where the Rascals were, and got me a five-album deal as well as some much needed money.

The reason I needed money now was because my bank account had been raided. Jess Morgan was the brother-in-law of one of the Dunhill partners, Bobby Roberts, and had an accounting firm that controlled my earnings under the terms of my original agreement with Dunhill, back when I was underage. Even though I was no longer receiving any royalties, due to the contract I was forced to sign by Lasker, I was still owed a sizeable amount in back royalties. But just like that, it had taken off to Rio in Morgan's briefcase. First class all the way. Now, though, I figured the record deal would allow me to prove to myself that I could leave all of that Dunhill business behind and survive on my own.

Miki was happy about me signing to Atco and wanted to celebrate. She decided that the best way to do that was with heroin, which she felt would give me 'Village chops' like her friend Fred Neil.

Heroin was and is the number-one taboo that you hear about as a young musician. It might kill you, or it might instill you with what they call 'genius.' Heroin gave me a sense of not being in my body, of 'feeling' without any pain whatsoever. I could think normally. I was aware of the horror stories of people selling guitars or souls for a fix but I thought, hey, James Baldwin, William Burroughs, and Lenny Bruce—writers I admired—were using. I had just signed an album deal with a major label that believed in me, I had a famous manager, and I was performing almost every night in a nationally recognized club in Greenwich Village. I was hanging out with Paul Butterfield, Tim Hardin, and Richie Havens. I was playing with Ian & Sylvia, who were so sincere and real and sang so beautifully together that they brought a sense of grace to this whole crazy world.

After my car burned, Loretta, my insurance agent in Los Angeles, told me that she had given my *Twelve More Times* album to a movie producer at Columbia who was impressed by my photo and vocals. He knew of me and wanted to sign me for a hot-rod/motorcycle movie called *Wild Nights On Ventura Boulevard*. My character was named Vince. Vince rode a motorcycle and played the guitar, which sounded good, since I had been riding a motorcycle and playing the guitar. Loretta gold me they wanted to send me a script and contracts and that I needed to return to Los Angeles to do the film.

When the script arrived, Miki and I read it aloud.

'This is crap,' Miki said. 'I can't let you do something like this.'

Miki knew something about the movie business—her stepfather was Mike Todd, the producer of *Around The World In Eighty Days* and the man who, with his then-wife Elizabeth Taylor, had let me sit next to them during the world premiere of the film at the Carthay Circle Theater.

'Here's what we should do,' Mike said. 'I'll tell them that you'll do the film but we will have the right to make changes in the script.'

Miki spoke to the producers and told me that they would do everything they could to accommodate our desires. It was all good. She was looking forward to going to Los Angeles with me, and I was happy to take her and show her off to my parents—as well as my new movie contract! Then Loretta the insurance woman called me, frantically, wanting to know who is the crazy woman demanding all of this stuff from Columbia? Mike Todd or no Mike Todd, Columbia did not want to deal with Miki St. Clair. I remained loyal to Miki, and the deal didn't happen. The world did not get to see a bad B-movie starring P.F. Sloan.

We chilled out in the Village for a couple of weeks, until Sid Bernstein called with news that a recording session had been scheduled—not in New York, where I had expected it to be, but at Sun Studios in Memphis. Sun Studios! Elvis, Jerry Lee, Carl Perkins, Johnny Cash.

After I heard that news I realized, as Paul Newman had once proclaimed, while portraying the fighter Rocky Graziano, *somebody up there likes me*. I felt blessed and fortunate. With all of the trouble that I had gotten into, I was now being rewarded with a great gift—one that was a lot nicer than a gold-painted key. There was life after Dunhill. And a damn good one at that.

Sid explained that Tom Dowd—who had worked with Aretha Franklin and Ray Charles—was going to produce the record, and I should get my songs and act together. He also told me to leave Miki in New York.

SUN STUDIOS

This was a celebration of a full circle—first my meeting Elvis at age twelve, and now recording at Sun Studios.

The plan was for me to fly to Memphis and spend a week recording the songs for the album. The problem was, I didn't have any new complete songs. I had been doing a lot of performing in New York but not a lot of writing—just the opposite of LA. I was playing my music, getting laid, and riding my motorcycle, so everything seemed great— except that everything wasn't great. The civil rights movement was going nowhere, and the Vietnam War was still taking away friends of mine. San Francisco had decayed and collapsed under the weight of the throngs of people who were yearning for truth in their lives, but that truth wasn't coming from a sugar cube or pill. The love revolution had stalled out.

I told Sid that I needed some time extra time to write and Atco agreed to an extra week in a room at the Holiday Inn across from Sun Studios. I started writing, and songs came out.

There were songs about Miki: 'How Can I Be Sure,' 'Country Woman,' and 'One Of A Kind.' 'New Design' was an introspective song that would later be recorded by Kenny Rogers. 'Good Luck' was a bit comedic but further away from the poet beginnings of P.F. Sloan. I was becoming a caricature. 'Star Gazin'' was a remembrance of being at Golden Gate Park on LSD. 'Miss Charlotte' was a sad blues number that I had started back in 1966 about a poor guy working on a song farm. 'Champagne' was a long-winded political mish-mash about things not happening the way I thought they should be. 'The Boundaries In Between,' however, was a beautiful song influenced by a poem by Edna St. Vincent Millay—a song about not knowing where I was going. Finally, 'Above And Beyond The Call Of Duty' was a sardonic look at a superficial slice of life.

I had the best of Memphis's musicians. Steve Cropper—the writer, producer, and guitarist of 'Dock Of The Bay' fame—was there, as were Sam & Dave, Wilson Pickett, and so many others. Duck Dunn played bass. Al Jackson was on drums. On the session for 'What Did She Mean When She Said Good Luck,' Sam Phillips came into the studio. I had been telling Steve that I wanted him to get Scotty Moore's sound but Steve didn't know how to get that. Sam came out of the booth and started telling Steve how to get the right echo.

'You know there's something about you that reminds me of Elvis,' Sam told me.

I told him the story of meeting Elvis when I was twelve. 'This song is helping me to reconnect with my youth, and with Elvis,' I said.

When I finished we both had tears in our eyes. I was twenty-two years old but feeling so much older.

When I initially played Cropper a couple of songs, he just scratched his head and then went into the booth and started complaining to Tom

Dowd about how this was the wrong band for me and he wanted leave. Tom told Steve that I was signed to Atco and that they were the butter on his bread.

Steve then made a call, and an hour later a brown bag of hash arrived at the studio. The band excused themselves and left for the men's room. Upon their re-emergence, they had a newfound interest in the abstract.

'Now, sing me that song about Perry wanting to join the army,' Steve said. 'I think we can turn it into a jazz blues thing.' And he did.

The session lasted four days. I did the vocals after every track. Then, with the tapes completed and ready for mastering, I returned to the Village. Miki heard the tapes and insisted that 'How Can I Be Sure' needed another electric guitar and some vibes. An overdub session was scheduled in New York; Miki played the vibes and I overdubbed fills.

Atco was pleased with the final product, which I called *Measure Of Pleasure*. They told me it was good for a first album but they believed there were greater things to come, and not to be upset if the album wasn't a hit because they knew artists and that it took them time to mature. I had been making records since I was thirteen but that made me feel good as the pressure was off.

The album was released in 1968 and received a 'pick hit' in *Billboard*, so it must have had something going for it. Sid Bernstein oiled the machine with gigs at Colleges in New York, New Jersey, and Pennsylvania. I played a lot at Brooklyn College, Fordham, and Queens College.

I enjoyed these shows. The crowds were receptive and they got my songs. Then came the murders—King and Kennedy. Howard Solomon had closed the Go Go out of deep respect but I made him open it and keep it open all night following both assassinations while I played for brokenhearted souls who wandered in and out in a state of shock, needing a place to congregate and ease the pain.

Maybe it was the funk of the times but things began to go south between Miki and me. She went to live with her mother in Upstate New York for a while, and since she had been the gatekeeper—knowing who and who not to let into my life—the place became overridden with parasites.

I didn't know at the time but Miki had left because she was pregnant and had a miscarriage. She returned to our loft with a deep sense of loss and grief. After that she wanted to go on a pilgrimage to Coconut Grove, Florida, to see her mentor and friend Fred Neil. I didn't want her to go by herself so we made plans to fly there.

We arrived at Fred's house and I saw a ghost of what appeared to be a woman wearing a hat like the one Kathryn Hepburn wore in *The African Queen* riding a bicycle up the street.

'That's Fred,' Miki said.

Fred looked like he weighed 95lbs and could not walk very well, but he could ride his bike. The house was modest, the interior clean but worn. Miki regaled Fred with stories from his past until he fell asleep on the couch. We left and came back the next day. Fred told us a few stories about writing 'Everybody's Talkin'' and 'The Dolphin' and then once again fell quietly into a deep, drug-induced, coma-like sleep.

Fred was thirty-two years old. That was our meeting with the king of folk—the man Miki wanted me to become. We left for the Village the next morning.

I hoped that this was a very low point for Fred. I would soon be experiencing a point as low.

CHAPTER SIXTEEN

THE ANGELS OF GREENWICH VILLAGE

I have a genuine dislike for being called to an office for a meeting, and I was apprehensive when Sid Bernstein called me in.

'The good news is that Atco Records wants to stick with you,' he said. 'The bad news is that Dunhill Records is suing Atco, claiming that they still own you as an artist.'

'Do they?'

'It's dubious. It really depends on how much Atco wants to fight. It could get expensive. And you need to clean your act up.'

'What does that mean?' I asked.

'Get out of the Village, stop using drugs, and get rid of that crazy girlfriend. We'll talk in a couple of months and we'll see where we go from there.'

I had been under the impression that because I had stuck my head in the sands of New York, Dunhill had forgotten about me. How could I have been so naive and stupid? Miki and I had gotten back into using after going to see Fred, and I wasn't happy about it. It led to many arguments that became fights, and eventually she decided she'd had enough and that she had done everything she could do for me. Miki left—and this time for good.

The word in the Village, without me knowing it, was that I had some very expensive guitars—a Gibson J-200, a Martin D-28, and a Guild twelve-string. The Village had been growing steadily darker, just as Bob Dylan had warned. It was almost unrecognizable from just two years earlier. It was a hopeless corpse.

One night, I was attacked in my loft by two robbers. They tied me to a chair and began rummaging for valuables. I had money in my boots that they didn't find, but they stole the guitars and my gold record for 'Secret Agent Man.' I think of them trying to pawn the record and finding out that it was only bronze painted gold, and in fact not for 'Secret Agent Man' but for 'Green Door' by Jim Lowe.

Because I had seen their faces, the robbers decided that it was necessary to kill me. They shot me up with a huge amount of heroin and left me in the chair to die, believing it would be seen as an accidental overdose. I sat there knowing that I was dying yet unable to do anything about it. I desperately tried to hang onto consciousness.

What happened next cannot be explained, unless you believe in divine intervention. But it did happen, so I will relate it here in this narrative for you to discern.

Three beautiful women entered the loft through a door in the wall that did not exist. And yet it seemed natural enough, in the state I was in. They moved close to me and observed my condition. They were beautiful. One was blonde and the other two more Mediterranean-looking. They were extremely fashionable, in an artistic and eclectic way—tastefully flamboyant.

'Look at him,' the first woman said. 'Sad, isn't it?'

'He's dying,' the second woman said.

'Yes,' said the first woman.

'We have to do something,' the third woman said.

'No,' the first woman said. 'It's too late.'

'I don't believe it is,' the second woman said.

'At least we should untie him,' the third woman suggested.

'Fine,' the first woman said.

'I am going to make a large pot of coffee,' the second woman suggested.

'What good could that possibly do? It would take gallons and gallons.'

'If we're going to make coffee, then why not gallons, and why not lift him up and get him walking?' the third woman said.

'We're wasting our time. He's a lost cause,' the first woman said with authority.

'I think there is hope,' the second woman said. 'You'll see.'

They untied me and lifted me up on my rubbery legs and proceeded to walk me back and forth in the L-shaped loft, pouring coffee into me every few moments. This went on I think until dawn.

'We have done everything we can do,' I heard one of the women say. 'Let's put him in bed, cover him with the American flag, and see what happens.'

I awoke to the sound of traffic on West Broadway, trying to comprehend what had happened. I looked for the door in the wall that wasn't there but I kept looking. I checked the actual door, which was unlocked, and I figured that's how the robbers and the angels came in.

I walked out onto the street and headed to The Tin Angel on Bleecker, probably looking like death. The regulars who knew me there were shocked. They told me the word had already gotten out that I had been killed the night before. I ordered a small breakfast of toast and a soft-boiled egg but no coffee—I was saturated with it.

The next night I went on a fool's quest to look for my guitars in every rathole and shooting gallery in the village, and after a couple of days, thank God, I stopped searching and let it go.

I needed to hear a friendly voice, so I decided to call Kim. I went into a drugstore with phone booths in the back.

'Hello, Kim? It's me, Phil. Can you hear me? How are you?'

'I'm just ginger-peachy, Sloaner. Tell me what's wrong. I can hear it in your voice.'

I didn't know what I could tell her without frightening her.

'Oh, nothing wrong. Just wanted to call and say hi.'

'When am I going to see you? You don't belong in that mean old city. For whatever reason you had to be there, I don't know. But I miss you.'

'Kim. I'm so sorry. I don't have any quarters and I'll have to go.'

'Sloan. You come home to me safe and sound, you hear? You're the only one I know who actually likes my poetry.'

I withdrew from heroin alone. It took a focused concentration to fight the egoistic nightmares that begged me to relinquish my hold and give in to my body's desires, but then they disappeared from my mind and I was free of the fight and the drug. It took a couple of days. I was both pleased and distrustful of myself for not knowing better. And it would take time for me to forgive myself as well.

I learned from Sid's secretary that Dunhill had forced Atco to let go of my contract. Sid's attorneys were forced to let go of the lawsuit against Lasker and Dunhill. Atco did not have the time or the money to protect themselves against a madman and a machine with a personal vendetta against me. Sid was fighting a serious illness, she said, and had to let go of his managerial duties, at least for the time being.

I couldn't bear to tell Sid what I had just been through. I felt I had really let him down, but all this was happening for a good reason, and I needed patience and faith.

THE MAGIC DRAGON
It was Noel Paul Stookey of Peter Paul & Mary who came to my rescue as we drank coffee together at the Tin Angel of all places.

'Are you all right?' he asked.

'Honestly, Paul, I don't know. I don't think so.'

'I dig the hell out of "The Sins Of A Family," "For What I'm Worth," "This Mornin'"— I've been listening to you from the very beginning. And I tried to lobby Peter and Mary to record "Sins."'

'That would have been cool.'

'But I'd like to try again because I've got a bit more clout now, and if you're up for it, you could come down to the studio and we could see what happens.'

'How do the others feel about it?' I asked.

'I don't care what they think. I want you to come down to Columbia and we can work on a track for "Sins." How about it?'

I shook my head in agreement, not knowing what to believe.

Paul Stookey came along at the absolute right moment. He was God-sent. Although I did not know it at the time, Paul's plan was to get me working and refocused, and then out of the Village and home to LA. I met him at Columbia Studios twice a week, and for the most part we talked, with a little bit of music thrown in for good measure. Sort of like a therapy session with guitars. It wasn't the nature of his fame but the depth of his being that made me feel worthwhile.

There was never really any intention to record my songs with Peter Paul & Mary. This was Paul's way of getting me to reconnect with my music and self-esteem. He had seen all of this before, and going way out of his way to lift up the spirits of a broken artist was a testament to the heart and soul of the man.

Paul called my parents in Los Angeles and told them that they needed to come to New York and get me back home. I had not been in contact with them for at least a year, if not more. They knew I was in trouble, but this was beyond their experience. I thought they were happy being estranged from me. It gave them a sense of normalcy—being away from the show-business whirlwind I had foisted upon them. I know they enjoyed being Claire and Harry as opposed to the parents of P.F. Sloan. So it was remarkable that Paul could manage to talk them into coming to New York to check out the damage I had wrought. It took a star of the magnitude of Paul to get them on the plane, I am sure. If I had called, I doubt they would have come. But Paul must have used some incredible charm to get them on a plane.

I met Paul at the Carnegie Deli in Manhattan. He was seated at a rear table, away from any public contact, where he became invisible like some celebrities are able to do. When my parents walked in, I pointed them out to him. He stood up and waved them over to the table, shaking their hands and making them feel comfortable and welcomed.

My parents were in shock when they saw my emaciated condition. I was pale and very thin. My skin was the color of the moon.

'You're looking good,' my father lied.

'Are you kidding?' my mother said. 'Look at him.'

'He's alive, Claire.'

'I'm OK, Ma.'

'This is your definition of OK? If it wasn't for Paul we wouldn't know if you were dead or alive.'

'How is my sister?' I asked.

'Your sister?'

'Yeah. Is she OK?'

'Lynn's fine.'

'And the house is good?'

'The house? You care about the *house*? What happened to you? You never even told us why you left, when you did—just if you didn't get out of town there would be hell to pay, and you expect us not to worry?'

'*Your* life was threatened, Mrs. Sloan,' Paul interjected. 'Phil didn't have a choice.'

'Our life?'

'Yes.'

'Good Lord. What did you do? I thought you were writing songs. Since when is writing songs so dangerous?'

'We're talking about the record business, Mrs. Sloan. They can be very dangerous people.'

'We tried to discourage him at every turn,' my father said. 'We wanted him to be a pharmacist.'

'Your son is an extremely gifted songwriter,' Paul said. 'I recognize that, and I am hoping that you will, too.'

The waiter came over to the table and took our orders—coffee and pastry for Paul and my parents and a bowl of chicken soup for me.

How is it possible that I can remember what was ordered that day? I don't know. I think one remembers when one needs to remember. I need to remember because all of it is part of my healing. And for this book, I feel I need to remember it. Every detail, no matter how seemingly trivial, is important to one's overall narrative.

'Phil is not aware of how ill he is. And I am working on getting him to commit to going back to Los Angeles if you will agree to help him back to health. Otherwise, I would strongly suggest someplace like Bellevue.'

'Bellevue?' my father proclaimed. 'My son is going to wind up in Bellevue?'

'Do you want to come home, Phil?' my mother asked.

'I'll try to get home soon,' I said.

'That's not good enough,' Paul said.

'I've got a lot to do. I've got club dates. I've got three months on the loft. I just can't leave like that, can I?'

'Its simple,' Paul said. 'Do you want to live or do you want to die?'

I sat there and wanted to answer but couldn't. Paul then put his hand on mine, and suddenly did not seem to be aware of my parents' presence. He started to recite the lyric from my song 'This Mornin'': *Up every morning, in time to see sun's dawning, your body it is yawning and yearning for more sleep. The problems that have kept you awake all night, I'll bet you, will disappear this morning, and forever they will keep. This morning they will keep.*

'I promise,' I said. 'I will leave shortly.'

'OK then,' Paul said. 'Is that good with you, Mr. and Mrs. Sloan?'

The waiter brought us the food and we all ate with a sense of relief that the hardest part was over. My mother asked Paul about *The Ed Sullivan Show* and what he was like and if he ever met Jackie Mason.

'I know Jackie,' Paul told my mother, impressing her no end.

'What are you going to do while you're in New York?' I asked my parents.

'We're going to visit your relatives, but we came because of you.'

Paul stood up and my mother hugged him. My father shook his hand.

'I love you and you take care of yourself and we'll see you soon,' my mother and father told me.

'I'll see you soon,' I told my father.

Paul left some money on the table and we walked out together, out of the Carni and past the marquee for Carnegie Hall announcing a performance by Judy Garland.

'I think we're going to play here next summer,' Paul told me. 'You get yourself together and maybe you can open for us.'

I went back to the loft and slept for a few days. It's what I needed the most.

I woke up and felt somewhat refreshed. I walked over to the Café Au Go-Go and told Howard Solomon that I was leaving.

'I heard that,' he said, 'and I think it is a good idea. You get well and come back and play. You're welcome anytime.'

I called Sid Bernstein, but he was ill, so I left a message with his secretary. I wanted to tell Miki but I couldn't find her. I left a message with her mother.

I arrived back in Los Angeles on Christmas Eve.

RETURN FROM EGYPT

Within a month of arriving back home I got a call from Jay Lasker, bubbling with joy as if nothing had ever happened.

'I've got some good news for you, P.F.'

'P.F.?'

'That's still your name, isn't it?'

'It is,' I said cautiously.

'That's good, because I just got off the phone with Tokyo.'

'Tokyo?'

'Your record has broken wide open in Japan.'

'Which one?'

'"From A Distance."'

'"From A Distance"?'

'This is going to establish a relationship with Toshiba. Look, they want you to tour Japan, so come into the office and we'll discuss all of this. And let's try to put some of this stuff behind us. I think we can take care of this royalty problem. We've got a lot of positive things to talk about. How about today at about two? We're all excited to see you.'

I hung up the phone and lay back down on my bed. Was this something I could believe? Was all forgiven? The guy who wanted me to cut off one of my testicles was now telling me he was going to set up a tour in Japan and give me back my royalties. I would have to be really naive to believe any of it. Two years in New York had hopefully hardened me and burned out any lingering youthful naiveté. I had looked into the face of death. I could certainly look on his face.

I decided to go meet Lasker. With a healthy dose of skepticism, I walked into Dunhill. Muriel greeted me as though I had left on the day before.

'Jay's waiting for you, Flip. This office hasn't been the same without you. I've missed you. You all right? Go right in.'

I heard Jay's bounding voice as I walked into his unchanged office.

'P.F.,' he said, getting up and patting me on the back. 'Sit down. We have a lot to talk about.'

I sat on the soft chair. Muriel waddled in with a couple of iced Cokes.

'I've been talking to the lawyers,' he said, 'and we think it won't be too much of a problem to get you back on board. You'd like that, right? You'd like your royalties back, right?'

'Of course,' I answered.

'You gave us a few problems with Atco,' he told me. 'It wasn't cheap to threaten to sue them, but in the end we got them to see that your contracts belong to Dunhill. And by the way, speaking of contracts—you realize that you are in breach of your songwriter's contract, dagnabbit? You probably didn't realize this, but you still owe us ten songs a year, and I could be wrong but I think you're a bit behind. The problem is that we're short of songs, and I am sure it's not going to be a problem for you to come up with ten songs by next month and ten songs after that?'

'I thought we were all straight,' I said, starting to get nervous.

Jay's demeanor seemed to be changing by the moment.

'Apparently, the Toshiba people don't want to play by our rules, so I told those bastards to go fuck themselves … what do you think of that?'

'I have no idea, Jay.'

'Then they had the gall to ask me if they could just get you. Do you know what I told them? You're going to love this. I told them P.F. Sloan was killed in a car crash on Mulholland Drive. I sent them a press release stating you were dead. So no tour in Japan, because you're dead. Is that a crack-up or what? Look, Phil. You've got six weeks to come up with ten songs. Call Muriel when you're ready and we'll set up the sessions.'

'What about the royalties?'

'We'll talk about royalties when you finish the songs,' Jay chuckled. 'Fair enough?'

As I passed Muriel on my way out, she looked up at me, beaming.

'Doesn't Jay look good?'

Lured by the hope of getting my royalties back—and even though I knew I was going against the odds—I wrote and demoed a number of songs. Lasker rejected them as not being up to a professional standard. And that was it. I never called them back, and they didn't call me.

That was the last time I saw Jay Lasker alive. He would go on to destroy the lives of virtually everyone who came in contact with him— Steppenwolf, Three Dog Night, The Mamas & The Papas, The Grass Roots—everyone except Steve Barri.

The past two years had been a good for Steve. He had produced Hamilton, Joe Frank & Reynolds, and The Heywoods. He was also producing The Grass Roots—'Midnight Confessions,' 'The River Is Wide,' and 'Temptation Eyes.' He was racking up a wall full of gold records. His dream had come true. He was a successful producer, the executive vice-president of ABC-Dunhill Records, and he had a beautiful home in Encino and a wonderful marriage to Julie. He had come a long way from Norty's Records and auditioning for Screen Gems with Carol Connors back in 1963, and being thrown into a room with a young Phil Sloan. He was living well and enjoying my royalties.

There would come a time for complete forgiveness of all the players in my life. Just not yet. *As he closes his eyes and says with a sigh, Ah, don't things look fine for the man behind the red balloon.*

CHAPTER SEVENTEEN

A TYPICAL DAY

I contemplated a future without music. I thought about my options. I could go back to college and become a pharmacist. My neighborhood rabbi had suggested from an early age that he felt I was suited for rabbinical life. I didn't think so.

I felt free. Unburdened. I felt that there was a possibility of living a normal life. The sun was shining and it was a beautiful day. Why not see a movie?

I hopped on a bus and got off on Hollywood Boulevard. There was a really good hotdog stand attached to the wall of the Vine Street Theatre. I thought I had enough money for a hotdog and a Coke, but when I looked at the menu board, the prices were higher. The dogs were now 35¢.

I got up to leave and the cook asked me why I was leaving. I made up some lame excuse because I was embarrassed. The cook saw through me and told me to sit down and that he was going to give me a hotdog grilled in butter.

I sat back down on the stool. The cook's kindness put me at ease. There was music playing on the radio, and I tried to enjoy it as a normal person would. The disc jockey announced that a new record by The Association would be coming up shortly. I paid no attention, although the group had recorded my song 'On A Quiet Night' a few years back.

Coming from radio, I heard the words

I have been seeking P.F. Sloan
But no one knows where he has gone …

Time stood still. I felt the life force drain from my body. I thought I had to be imagining it. The song played on.

No one ever heard the song that boy set winging …

I came to the conclusion that I had died and that I was listening to Radio Heaven announce that the spirit of P.F. Sloan would be arriving shortly. What else would I think? I wasn't expecting a *Twilight Zone* spin on this beautiful day. I became discombobulated.

'Are you all right, son?' the cook asked.

'Ah … I don't know. I think I have to go home.'

As I was leaving the hotdog stand, I heard another line from the song.

The last time I saw P.F. Sloan
He was summer burned, he was winter blown
He turned the corner all alone …

I felt like a slave who had traveled north to taste freedom across the Mason–Dixon line—only to discover that I had the wrong Mason–Dixon line.

For the next two days I received phone calls from people, congratulating me on my name being used on a Jimmy Webb song, sung by The Association—well-meaning people who thought this would be a boost to my career, when in fact I was about to have a nervous breakdown.

One moment I was fine, the next I couldn't relate to anyone around me. Nothing seemed important, relevant, or real. It didn't matter if there was a world outside or not. I was disconnected from love, caring, reason, compassion, feeling, logic, and sanity. It wasn't the song that put me into this state but rather the combination of the last few years and now this. I had been plugged into the world for so many years that when the plug was pulled I seemed to become lifeless.

My sister had seen an episode of *The Merv Griffin Show* where Merv admitted to the audience that he had been diagnosed with a new disease called hypoglycemia. He explained the symptoms, and my sister began to think that I might be suffering from the same ailment.

Concerned by my mental state, my family got together and decided that I should be admitted to Cedars–Sinai's psychiatric ward. Without putting up a struggle, I told them I would wait in the car.

MY LIFE AS A ZOMBIE

The Cedars–Sinai psychiatric ward was known to have the best Sunday brunch in Los Angeles. They imported their cheesecake and lox from New York. The bagels were delivered daily from Brooklyn Bagel on Beverly Boulevard. Yep. Hollywood Psychiatry. If you're going to have a nervous breakdown in Hollywood, come with a good appetite.

My spirits lifted. I got the impression that this unit was the Four Seasons with nurses, who mentioned to me that many famous stars had passed through these doors. I was checked in as Philip Gary Schlein of Los Angeles. My parents left and the doors locked behind me. All of those orderlies and welcoming nurses with grand smiles on their faces quickly changed into tyrannical, controlling witches and bitches.

I was given blood tests and diagnosed with hypoglycemia. It turns out my sister was right. I was given tens of thousands of units of niacin. Taking that much niacin is like sitting under a sunlamp in the desert. Your skin cooks. I was put on two quarts of desiccated liver a day, since in those days it was thought the disease had something to do with protein deficiency. Where was this famous buffet? The cheesecake was not to be found. Niacin, desiccated liver, and thousands of units of Thorazine, which was thought to cure any mental malady. It was the chemical arrow in every psychiatrist's quiver.

'How are you feeling, Philip?'

'Ahhhhhh.'

'Let's increase your dose and see what we can discover.'

'Ahhhhhh.'

There was a room at the hospital referred to by the nurses as 'the vegetable garden.' It was circular a room where we zombies would walk all day in a circle. Once a week we had a meeting with the staff psychiatrist. My psychiatrist's name was Dr. Bloom. He was a gentle man with an optimistic point of view but perhaps he had spent too much time around people like me.

'Well, Philip,' he began. 'What's exactly the matter with you?'

I couldn't answer. I wanted to but could not.

'What do you do, Philip?'

'I am a singer and songwriter.'

'Oh, you are. Isn't that wonderful? And what songs have you written?'

I reeled off a list of eight or nine songs.

'My, my, you've been busy,' Dr. Bloom said.

'I've worked with The Mamas & The Papas, The Grass Roots, Herman's Hermits, The Rolling Stones—Elvis taught me to play the guitar.'

'Did he, now.'

'Yes. He sang "Love Me Tender" into my ear.'

'Isn't *that* special. I'm a real Elvis fan myself. Do you talk to Elvis often?'

'No.'

'I'm going to be honest with you. Philip Schlein does not ring a bell. I am a fan of popular music and I rather pride myself in how I keep up with the latest sounds. But Philip Schlein?'

'I'm not known as Philip Schlein. Maybe you know my pen name.'

'Oh, what's that?'

'P.F. Sloan.'

'P.F. Sloan. OK,' Dr. Bloom responded excitedly.

'"Secret Agent Man," "Eve Of Destruction," "Let Me Be" …'

'You wrote those.'

'That's right.'

'Who are you really?' Dr. Bloom asked, stuffing a pipe, sticking it in his mouth and lighting it.

'To be honest, Dr. Bloom … I don't know. I don't know who I am.'

'Well,' Dr. Bloom said, 'I met P.F. Sloan at Greenblatt's Delicatessen in 1965. And you don't look anything like him. Do you really think you are P.F. Sloan?'

'No, not really.'

'Do you want to be P.F. Sloan?'

'Sometimes I do and sometimes I don't.'

'Ah. You see, Philip, it's one thing to want to be P.F. Sloan and something else entirely when you think you *are* P.F. Sloan.'

'You're saying I'm not P.F. Sloan?'

'That's exactly right.'

Dr. Bloom became quiet and scribbled something in his notebook.

'OK. I believe you are suffering from delusions of grandeur brought on by hypoglycemia. We'll increase the Thorazine, niacin, and desiccated liver, and see where that will take us. I don't want you to worry. We handle lots of cases like yours. Are you sleeping all right?'

'I can hardly stay awake.'

'Well ... we'll give you something to help you to sleep more soundly.'

Life was a daily routine of walking, taking pills, and drinking liver. Nobody seemed to change. Nobody seemed to be getting any better. I began to think that I would never get out of this warehouse of broken dolls. It gave me a little solace to know that I was a guest at the best psychiatric hospital in the world.

'Dr. Bloom wants to see you immediately,' a nurse told me one day.

'Did I do something wrong?'

'Hurry, hurry!' the nurse, screamed. 'You want to get better, don't you?'

I rushed to Dr. Bloom's office as if I was on fire. And I was, in fact, as the niacin had started to burn me alive. Dr. Bloom was agitated as I walked into the office.

'This is crazy,' he said. 'Absolutely crazy. I am embarrassed to the point of ... well ... crazy.'

'What's going on?'

'I have some good news for you.'

'What?'

'You, my dear boy, are P.F. Sloan.'

'What do you mean, I'm P.F. Sloan?'

'I mean you are really P.F. Sloan.'

'I don't want to be P.F. Sloan.'

'Well, you may not want to be P.F. Sloan, but you are P.F. Sloan.'

'Really? Are you sure?'

'Do they call you P.F. or Phil or what?'

'I don't know what you're talking about.'

'OK. Look. I just got off the phone with Clive Davis. You know Clive Davis, don't you?'

'Yes. Clive Davis is …'

'President of Columbia Records. Mr. Davis told me that he needs to see you, Mr. P.F. Sloan, at the Beverly Hills Hotel at 3pm on Saturday.'

'I really don't want to go.'

'I had a meeting with the head of the unit, and he told me that we can give you a day pass. But you have to be back by 5:30.'

'I don't want to meet with Clive Davis. That's why I'm here … isn't it?'

'Obviously, you're not thinking clearly. You need to consider the opportunity. In my opinion, you'd be crazy not to go.'

'So … if I go to see Clive Davis, I'm not crazy?'

'Nobody said you *were* crazy. I'm just saying, really, you'd be crazy not to go.'

'I see.'

'So you'll go?'

'I don't have anything else planned on Saturday.'

The nurses and orderlies at Cedars were as excited about my meeting with Clive Davis as I would have been not that many years before. I dressed in the clothes in which I had arrived, although the jeans and shirt had been washed and pressed and my boots shined—the handmade boots from Anello & Davide. A cab was called and arrived mid-morning. I was given a small amount of travel cash and hopped in.

'Where to?' the cabbie asked.

'Beverly Hills Hotel.'

The Beverly Hills Hotel on Sunset Boulevard is a pink California-Spanish building nestled into a grove of palm trees. It was a place where important connections happened. An LA icon of pampered repose.

Clive Davis had a private bungalow there, and that is where I was heading. I was under the influence of Thorazine and niacin, and I was a long way from feeling my best, but my spirits were high for being out of the re-circulated air of the hospital.

The cab let me off at the front of the hotel and a doorman greeted me enthusiastically. He pointed me in the direction of the exclusive bungalows.

I found the right one and knocked on the door. Clive Davis greeted me with a warm and hearty handshake.

'Hello, Phil!' he said, immediately putting me at ease. 'Come in. I have been such an admirer of yours for so long … this is just wonderful.'

Clive escorted me into the living room.

'You remember your old Dunhill pal, Bobby Roberts?' I asked. 'I've invited him here because he has an interesting offer for you to consider.'

At the sight of Roberts, a twinge of fear shot through my body.

'We have a lot behind us,' Bobby said to Clive.

'How have you been, Bobby?' I asked.

'I'm out of Dunhill,' he said. 'I'm starting a new label. But we'll get into that.'

Clive invited us out to a little patio where some snacks and soft drinks had been laid out.

'I hope you guys are hungry,' Clive said. 'I've ordered cold lobster and tomatoes. So, Phil, how are you doing?'

'I don't know,' I said. 'I guess I'm all right.'

I must have sounded unsure.

'Are we moving too fast for you, Phil?' Bobby asked.

'No, no,' I said. 'Did the hospital mention that I had to be back by 5:30?'

'We'll get you back in plenty of time, Phil. Nothing to worry about. It's only eleven o'clock.'

'Oh, OK. I just don't know what they will do to me if I'm late.'

At the time, Clive Davis was one of the most important and powerful men in the music business. He had a sense of warmth and affability but exuded power. He was tall and well groomed, his hairless dome was so shiny it could be used as a shaving mirror, and was exquisitely dressed in a Don Loper yellow shirt that looked like it was sewn with money.

'I've asked you here, Phil, because I'm dying to hear any of your new songs.'

'What new songs?' I asked incredulously.

'Certainly you must have new songs. You always have new songs.'

'I don't have any songs. I don't even have a guitar.'

'We can get a guitar.'

'Do you believe in fresh starts, Phil?' Bobby asked.

'Let me ask you, Phil,' Clive said. 'What exactly does Thorazine do to you?'

'Well. It kind of … takes away any concept of yesterday, and any desire for tomorrow.'

'So you're right in the present, huh? That's the perfect place to be, right, Bobby?'

'That's where everyone wants to be, Clive. Phil wrote the song "Live For Today."'

'I didn't write that. The Rokes wrote that song.'

'Who cares about The Rokes? We're talking about a new opportunity, here, Phil.'

Two waiters entered from the garden area with a large platter of cold lobster and tomatoes. They set up the table and Bobby and Clive waited for them to beg their leave. I could have cared less.

'Do you know who loved lobster and tomatoes, boys?' Clive asked us. 'Sherlock Holmes. Dig in.'

Clive and Bobby dug into the food and I sort of watched them, feeling detached. There were enough meds in me to put down an elephant but not a musician.

'So, Bobby. Where do you feel you want to open up shop?'

'Umm … I think maybe … ICM building on Beverly Boulevard.'

'Why there?' Clive asked, cracking open a piece of lobster.

'Centrally located, good lease …'

'I know the owner. I think it's a good idea. How long will it take to be up and running?'

'Tomorrow, if need be. We'll be good to go.'

'And what's going to be your first project? Perhaps another John Bubbles and the tap-dancing Dunhills LP?' Clive asked, playfully ribbing Roberts.

'We're thinking more in line of … P.F. Sloan.'

I could not believe what I had just heard. Certainly, these titans of the entertainment business must have known that I was not up for any of this.

'All kidding aside,' Clive said to me, 'we have a lot of faith and confidence in your abilities to pull this off. And if you do, it is going to turn the past around. All of the bad will be erased, and you will be on top where you belong, and where you will stay. This is a promise.'

'We want to tell you that we love and respect you,' Bobby said, 'and will support you in any way that we can—creatively and financially. It is time to get that nightmare out of your memory for good.'

Bobby turned to Clive.

'Clive? Am I right or am I wrong?'

'You're right, Bobby. And if Phil is good with this, I'm going to make it happen.'

Clive put his hand on my shoulder.

'This is what we're thinking,' he said. 'I trust Bobby and I want him to be your manager. To protect your songs, he's going to begin a new publishing company that your songs are going to go into, and you will be the only artist on our new label, called Mums Records—shh … mum's the word. I know it's not exactly kosher to have Bobby manage you as well as owning the label, but we want to protect you.'

'You can't argue with that, Phil,' Bobby said.

When a pitch is really brought home, and when it hits its mark, you really begin to question whether this time it is for real, like when a trout sees a juicy worm on a hook. *Maybe this time it's not a hook*, he thinks.

Clive got up from the table and returned with a very beautiful Martin guitar and handed it to me.

'I think it's in tune,' he said.

I was holding a guitar for the first time in almost a year and it felt good and natural.

'Play me something,' Clive said. 'Play something new.'

I tried to tell them that I didn't have anything new but they would have none of it. So I made up a song on the spot. It was a song called 'Don't Make A Beggar Out Of Me.' It would eventually wind up on the

Sailover album in 2006, under the title 'Love Is 4-Giving'—just to show that a song never goes to waste.

After I finished the song, I really didn't know what to expect.

'Well,' Clive said, impressed. 'The boy's still got it. You were right. I'm all in. Let's get this show on the road.'

Bobby was happy. He had received what he was looking for.

'Phil? Are you in?' Clive asked.

'Of course he's in,' Bobby answered.

Bobby turned to me.

'This is how it's going to happen, Phil. I've taken the liberty to arrange for your discharge, and I know that's good news for you. I know you'll be wanting to get home and start writing some damn good music and get some money back in the old saddle bag. How does $25,000 by the end of the month sound? And I'm rather sure that I can get Jay Lasker to negate all of that royalty bullshit.'

'And if Bobby can't, I can,' Clive said. 'All we need from you, Phil, is to believe in yourself and get well and record a memorable album for us.'

A limousine arrived to take me back to the hospital. Bobby and Clive walked me to the car. I got into the limo, and as the car pulled away from the hotel I turned to look and saw Bobby and Clive waving goodbye as if I were going to summer camp.

The second I arrived back at the hospital, everything had changed. I was treated more like a special guest than a sick patient. They started referring to me as Mr. Sloan. I was escorted up to Dr. Bloom's office, where he met me with great joy.

'I hope you don't mind, I took the liberty of bringing in some records with songs you wrote and I am wondering if you would sign them before you leave.'

'I'm leaving?'

'Oh, yeah,' Dr. Bloom said. 'Everything has been arranged. And here's the kicker: I didn't tell you because it is just something I don't … share … you know how it is with songwriters … anyway, I'm somewhat of a hobbyist myself and …'

'You want me to listen to your song?'

'Not necessary. Clive Davis has promised to listen to my song, and if he likes it, well … Tony Bennett may be interested.'

'Is that what he told you?' I asked, kind of chuckling.

'You bet he did. And I am to inform you that you, Mr. P.F. Sloan, are now free as a bird. That's got to feel good.'

It felt good to leave that damn mental hospital. Now I would have to find out if I were, in fact, free as a bird.

Bobby Roberts wasted no time in making it clear that he was setting up the star machine. He took out full-page ads in *Variety* announcing my signing, organized gigs at the Santa Monica Civic Center opening for Dave Mason and Cass Elliot, and told me he was trying to secure an appearance on *The Ed Sullivan Show*, as he had done for The Mamas & The Papas, Johnny Rivers, and Ann-Margret. Maybe this would be the comeback they talk about in show business.

IF THE MAILMAN COMES WITH A LETTER FOR ME, JUST FORWARD IT TO MALIBU

Bobby Roberts secured digs for me at the exclusive Malibu Colony, right on the ocean. Since the 20s, Malibu Colony has been a secluded gated and guarded community for celebrities, artists, movie directors, and producers. It is one of the most expensive and exclusive pieces of real estate in the world. Chaplin and Arbuckle lived there!

Malibu Colony was a place to kick back, mellow out, party, and worship the sun. Everyone knows each other and nobody is impressed at how big you are. And the surf was great. It is just north of the famous Surfrider Beach. The swells come in off the underwater canyons and make the waves—not huge but perfect and long-riding. Back in the late 60s, nobody was really talking about the ozone, so people spent hours cooking in the Southern California sun without fear of death—and at the Colony, death wasn't allowed anyway.

I moved into the maid's quarters of a pretty, Nantucket-style home owned by Lesley Ann Warren and her husband Jon Peters, who was still at this time known as 'the hairdresser to the stars' and a man about town. He would later become a successful movie producer and partner of Peter Gruber, and boyfriend of Barbara Streisand, who lived down the beach.

Lesley Ann Warren was a popular, understated beauty and actress—a wonderful woman and caring soul.

On a typical day I would get up early in the morning and go for an exhilarating swim in the ocean. Lesley would make breakfast, and we'd sit at her table and have philosophical conversations. She knew that I was not well, and that must have touched off an instinct in her to watch over me. I could tell that she herself was under some duress, as I believed her marriage was not a happy one.

After breakfast, I would write for three or four hours and then go back into the ocean. I had bought a used 1967 MGB GT and painted it two-tone flat-rat grey with cans of spray paint. The car cost $1,000 but must have had some drag-city mojo as it was in demand at red lights driving on the Pacific Coast Highway, and I was often asked if I would sell it.

I'd drive to Point Dume and watch the sunset, head back south, grab a beer and a burger at the Malibu Inn, and with a little luck, take in Dick Dale & The Del-Tones and his surf guitar. Dick's style was a bridge between what we had done over at Western Recorders and the true root of surf music, which was Hawaiian music, although the harmonies, though sometimes credited to the Mills Brothers, were also influenced by Hawaiian and South Pacific music.

The good news was that I was getting stronger in mind, body, and soul. I had a beautiful place to live, nice wheels, the promise of a lot of money, and a new record deal. Things were looking up.

CHAPTER EIGHTEEN

AFTERNOON TEA AT THE CHATEAU MARMONT

One day, Jimmy Miller—a genius record producer, in my opinion, having recorded seminal albums with groups like Traffic, Spencer Davis, and of course The Rolling Stones—called and asked me to meet him, Mick Jagger, and Keith Richards over at the Chateau Marmont. That sounded good to me. It made me feel like I still belonged. Everyone wants to belong.

Driving fast on the PCH, on a beautiful California afternoon, heading to the Sunset Strip for a meeting with Miller, Jagger, and Richards, I felt pretty fabulous. I took a left on Sunset and headed east into town—up into my old stomp.

The Chateau Marmont was built in 1929 during the stock market crash and decorated with furniture and art from estate sales around Hollywood. It was an eclectic and funky place. Aristocratic hip. A hotel for outlaws. There was an inexplicable magic to the place, which continues to this day. Some people went to the Marmont to live and others to die. And if you died at the Marmont, you were immortally cool.

I went straight up to the Penthouse suite. Mick and Keith were stretched out on chairs. Jimmy opened the door and greeted me warmly.

'Hey, Phil,' Mick chirped.

'Hey, Mick.'

'The Sloan Ranger,' Keith said. 'Where you living?'

'Malibu.'

'Surf's up,' said Keith.

'We may have a role for you to play, Phil,' Jimmy said. 'Have a beer, relax, and listen.'

I grabbed a cold beer and began to nurse it. For the moment my job was to observe and witness.

'Where were we?' Jimmy asked.

'We want to move in a different direction from *Sticky Fingers*,' Mick told him.

'I'm yours, Mick. Whatever you want.'

'No, that's not what we want from you, Jimmy. We want an absolute direction.'

'I'm happy to do that,' he said, 'but I don't know what you need.'

'I'm needing for you to get what I'm feeling.'

'How am I supposed to know what you're feeling? You need to tell me,' Jimmy told Mick.

'I'm interested in the song more than production.'

'Yeah,' Keith said. 'We think you're paying too much attention to the production.'

'Maybe you don't want me as a producer. Maybe you want Phil.'

'Maybe I do,' Mick said.

Jimmy pointed to me.

'You think you could deal with this horseshit?'

'Well …'

'Your job is to listen, Phil. OK?'

'OK.'

'That's why Jimmy's a genius,' Mick said.

'He's our genius,' Keith said.

I was listening to three drunk kings talking about the artistic nature of their work. And when you are listening to artists at this level, there is a sense of timelessness and incongruity. They are expressing their innermost emotions, which may eventually become songs.

'We love you, Jimmy,' Mick said.

A beer bottle flew out of Mick's hand, grazing Jimmy's head.

'Fuck you!' Jimmy yelled.

Jimmy flipped the coffee table over toward Mick.

'Hey, man,' said Keith. 'Let's not do this.'

'Oh, yes. Let's do this!' said Mick.

'All right,' said Keith, as he threw a beer bottle through the television screen.

Mayhem took over the room. Havoc ensued. Mick threw another bottle at Jimmy, missing him but hitting a large, expensive, ornate mirror, which exploded into a thousand pieces. It was *chrystalnach* in the penthouse suite of the Chateau Marmont.

'You're a heartbreaker, Miller!' Mick yelled.

'You're a ball-buster, Jagger,' Miller screamed.

'We're going to give Phil the wrong impression,' Keith laughed. 'It's good for him to see how we work.'

Jimmy picked up a desk chair and hurled it in Mick's direction. As Mick ducked behind the couch, I crawled out the front door. For me, the meeting had concluded. For them, it may have gone on for another week. Just a slice of the rock'n'roll life.

Though Jimmy went on to produce the Stones' next album, *Goat's Head Soup*, the experience at the Chateau opened my eyes again to a lifestyle that was a killer. And I had just signed a contract for another giant spin of the wheel.

I knew at that moment that my heart was no longer into becoming a recording star. It was something I always thought I wanted but really didn't.

The sun was setting at the end of Sunset Boulevard. It was so beautiful.

MALIBU LOST

My health continued to improve. I was swimming every day, taking long walks on the sand, and having breakfast with Lesley Ann. I was falling in love with her. I wouldn't call it platonic and I wouldn't call it agape. I would call it a fantasy.

Jon Peters was waiting for me after I returned one afternoon from having a burger at Patrick's Roadhouse.

'I want to talk to you,' he bellowed.

I'm pretty sure he was high on something, although I couldn't tell what. I started up the stairs and he followed me up to the landing.

'What, man?' I asked.

'I want to talk to you.'

'OK, talk.'

'Stay away from my wife.'

'What are you talking about?'

'Stay away from my fucking wife.'

'I'm not doing anything with your wife.'

'Yeah, well, I think you are.'

'We're just friends. We talk about stuff.'

'And I'm warning you to stay away from her,' he said, his eyes piercing me with a vengeful spirit.

'She's too good for you, Peters.'

Jon took a swing at me and barely missed.

'You're crazy,' he said. 'Get the fuck out of here.'

He took another swing but this time connected with my jaw and sent me against the rail. I answered his punch with a roundhouse right and found my mark right above his eye, sending the hairdresser to the stars down the flight of stairs and into a crumbled ball of confusion. I thought he was dead but miraculously he got up, like a drunk after a car wreck.

'What happened?' he asked, oblivious.

'I don't know, Jon. I wish I knew.'

I knew that after this incident, my stay in this fairytale cottage had come to an abrupt end.

HOME AGAIN, NATURALLY

I didn't know it yet but I was the first of many who were going home. We were a burned-out generation who had lost our direction and were searching for a new north. Nixon had been re-elected. There was a sense of failure of mission, and for some a perceived repression of spirit. Many traded in their tie-dye for pinstripes and their VW busses for Chevrolet Impalas.

My parents were about as happy about my return home as one might be at the reappearance of a rash. My bedroom had been disassembled and turned into a sewing room—bedrooms had been converted to sewing rooms all over the country, and now they were reverting back by the millions. But they understood my dilemma, and like so many other parents in the country they reluctantly bore the burden of the return of the prodigal son.

Bobby Roberts was very angry about what had transpired at the Colony. Jon Peters was the music-industry equivalent to a 'made man' at Columbia. The word on the street had Bobby pegged as the manager of a crazy person. His attitude toward me took a dramatic turn for the worse. He was no longer the jovial Dancing Dunhill but now a man who may have believed that he had bitten off more than he could chew with the likes of P.F. Sloan.

Bobby was running scared, thinking that I may have screwed up his deal with Clive Davis and desperately needing a way to make it work. An album had to be made and it had to be delivered on schedule.

I was sitting by the pool at Del Valle and my mother announced the arrival of Bobby Roberts.

'I'll get some lemonade,' my mother said.

Bobby came out by the pool and seemed cold and aloof. He had learned the art of the business smile that could fool almost everyone into believing he did not have embalming fluid running through his veins. He was a charmer. You had to be skilled to see though it.

'Phil?' he began. 'This is how it's going to be. We're going to make a record. The deal that we had has changed because of your actions, and now I don't trust you. For you to get the money that was promised, you need to show up every day at our offices. We are building a piano room for you. If you want to get paid, you will need to work eight hours a day, five days a week. You'll be on salary, like an employee. But the bonus you were offered is not going to happen until the album is finished. Can you do that?'

'What are you talking about?'

'Your actions at the Colony almost ruined our connections with Columbia. Are you willing to work under these circumstances to redeem yourself?'

'Yes,' I assured Bobby. 'I'll do that.'

I had to say yes. I had to create some money. I couldn't just continue to live off my parents.

My mother set a tray of lemonade at the edge of the pool.

'Lemonade boys?'

'No thank you, Mrs. Sloan,' Bobby said, before leaving abruptly.

'Seems like a nice man,' my mother said. 'I can't understand what you do to these people to make them so angry at you.'

Before I went into the studio, it had been arranged that I was to open for Van Morrison at the Santa Monica Civic Center for two nights and then go up north as part of a three or four city tour. The Santa Monica Civic was packed with 2,500 people.

I decided to do the set without a band—just me and a guitar. I walked out onto the stage, stepped up to the microphone, and my knees started shaking.

I began to sing Eddie Cochran's 'I'm Having A Nervous Breakdown.' By the time I got to the line, *See my knees, how they quiver ... my whole body's in a tither ... I'm having a nervous br-br-breakdown*, the crowd jumped out of their seats, rushed the stage, and tried to pull me into the audience. Two people from backstage came out and grabbed me and pulled me to safety. The house lights went up and the performance stopped.

Van Morrison was livid. Backstage, he accosted Bobby Roberts, who had arrived in time to witness the scene.

'What the fuck?' he said. 'This is an opening act. He's supposed to set them up for me. He gets it straight or he's off the tour.'

'He's a bit distraught,' Bobby replied, 'but I'll take care of it.'

Bobby rushed to me in anger.

'What are you doing?'

'I'm sorry,' I said, thinking that way in the back of his mind, he may consider what he had just seen as amazing rather than threatening.

The next night the same thing happened. I was fired from the show and Roberts told me that he would never put me onstage again.

Four weeks after that, The Moody Blues asked for me to open for them at the Hollywood Bowl. Roberts refused and instead put in a mediocre singer-songwriter who happened to be blind. The Moody Blues were pissed—not that they had an aversion to blind performers, only to mediocre talent.

WHAT IS PAT BOONE DOING IN MY HEAD?

The piano room was completed. It was a small, padded room with an upright piano in the corner. I interpreted the soft walls as a personal insult to my fragile mental condition, though in hindsight I'm sure it was padded for acoustic reasons. A plastic window made it possible for me to be observed from the main office. And believe me, I was. Every so often I would see people peering in at the 'mad genius.'

I wrote songs for eight hours a day, just like I was told to do, in the hopes of winning redemption. A chronic melancholy infected my spirit and had an effect on the songs I was writing.

On *Raised On Records*, I tried to thank my father for buying me a guitar and declared that my true nature was to be nobody's son. The last line describes where I was at—*if it weren't for the music, I would have said goodbye a long time ago*. In 'Springtime,' I wrote, *tell me, am I real or just a song in your imagination?* (Was I writing that line for Jimmy Webb?)

The recording sessions were set up at Wally Heider Studios in Hollywood, the most advanced studio in Los Angeles. The album was produced by Don Altfeld, Jan Berry's best friend and producer and writer of so many of the Jan & Dean songs. I had been with Don on many sessions for Jan & Dean. He had become a doctor, and who better to keep an eye on me? Roberts figured Don would be able to communicate with me, since he was incapable of doing so. Since Jan's accident, Don had been making inroads in the recording industry and had been producing many artists since that accident.

My old friend Hal Blaine and Johny Barbata from The Turtles were brought in for drums. Joe Osborne was on bass, and you don't get any better than that. Ben Benay—who would later join Tom Petty & The Heartbreakers—wrote out the charts and played guitar, as did Rick Nelson's guitarist James Burton, who would later be with Elvis for his Vegas shows. James was one of the greatest guitar players of all time. Wayne Perkins, Elvis's session guitarist played on the album as well. Larry Knechtel played electric piano, and Michael Omartian was on organ— Mike worked later on with many greats, including John Lennon and Eric Clapton, but this was his first recording session, and he was grateful and thrilled. I had heard him play and wanted him on the session. Táta Vega and Phyliss Brown sang backup. Jim Horn played flute.

The record had been mixed and mastered but not yet released. It was probably not possible to fit more talent into a recording studio.

The melancholy affected my vocals. From the delusionary artist's point of view, the album was real, it was hurting, and it was hauntingly sad. From the record company's point of view, it was flat and without energy.

Raised On Records was autobiographical—as autobiographical as anything I had written. I was exposing my pain. Even though Phil Sloan was an obvious wreck, the poetic nature P.F. Sloan drew inspiration from his seeming demise. The album cover was a shot of me with long hair and a thick beard, an original painting by David Larkham. Catatonia was starting to show in my eyes.

As we were waiting for the release date, Albert Hammond showed up at Mums Records, looking to peddle some songs. Like Jimmy Webb, Albert had been turned down by every publisher in town—including Steve Barri, who had given him my name and told him where he could find me.

Albert had a European vibe to him. It was hard to see him in any other light but that. He asked if I would listen to his songs and I agreed.

'I have been rejected by everyone,' he said, 'including your ex-partner, who gave me your name.'

'You've got no monopoly on rejection,' I told him.

The first song he played was 'It Never Rains In Southern California.'

'That's a hit song,' I told him.

Albert was stunned at my response to the song.

'Really? You think it's a hit song?'

'That's definitely a hit. A No. 1 hit!'

I told Albert that I'd talk to Bobby Roberts on his behalf, and I did. Roberts decided to sign Hammond on my recommendation. The only hint I had of foul play—or business as usual, depending on your perspective—at this point was that Roberts told me to tell the arranger to make sure the song was put into my key. The session was set up and

Albert was ecstatic. The tracks came off beautifully and Albert put his vocals on. Albert left happily and Bobby told me to go into the studio, remove Albert's vocal, and put mine on in its place, and we would release it on my album.

I couldn't say no. This guy had my balls in his hand. My plan was to go through the motions of singing it but to explain in the end that the song was not working for me. I put the earphones on and began to sing to the track when the strangest thing happened. I heard Pat Boone's voice in my headphones!

'Philip. You cannot do this.'

I know how this sounds. I was no fan of Pat Boone. Sure, I might have liked 'Friendly Persuasion' and 'Love Letters In The Sand,' but that's because they were great 'make-out' songs. When he did 'Tutti Frutti,' I was done with him. So what was Pat Boone doing in my head now?

I really thought I had gone completely batty—and in fact, I was, but I listened and believed for a moment, because it was so crazy and extraordinary.

'Philip,' he said again. 'You cannot do this. It's wrong.'

After a few more tries of pretending to sing the song, I simply threw my hands up and told Bobby that I couldn't sing the song because it was in the wrong key.

Had 'It Never Rains In Southern California' been put on the album, it is possible that the album would have been very successful.

'I'm sorry, Bobby. I can't sing it.'

'You are a sorry son of a bitch, Phil,' he said. 'You can kiss that bonus goodbye. And that Lasker deal? Gone.'

The album was released with a two-page spread in *Variety*. He's back! And Mums/Columbia has got him! Albert's record went to No. 1, and Mums had its star. The truth was, I was gone, and I wasn't coming back.

CHAPTER NINETEEN

SLEEPTIME

I walked out of the studio, got into my MGB GT, drove home, got into bed, and collapsed. I could not walk or talk. And the hypoglycemia kicked in full throttle. The lack of physical energy kept me in the bedroom, where I had written many of my memorable songs only seven years prior. I was virtually helpless and dependent on my parents for survival, as I had been when I was a child. I was diagnosed with severe catatonia. Maybe I should have taken that coconut instead of the ukulele.

Being in a catatonic state is like this: you walk into the room and say hello to me and you tell me your name but I can't remember it a second later. I can't even remember my own name. I can feel your presence, your love or your worries, and I can hear what you are saying, but I can't hold on to it. It's not like being in a vegetative state. You can feel, understand, hear, see, and think; there's just no energy to process it. I was forced into being in the now. I might feel sad for myself for a second but I would forget about that sadness a moment later. And so it was with happiness as well. You can discern that people feel sad for you but you don't really know why. Nothing matters. The lack of memory makes people feel uncomfortable.

'Did you hear that Elvis died?' No.

'Do you remember I met you at a party a number of years ago?' No.

People felt hurt because they thought that they didn't matter to me. Everyone matters. All you can muster are simple one- or two-word answers.

'Are you hungry?' No.

'Are you feeling all right?' Yes.

'Can I get you anything?' No.

'Did you hear that John Lennon was shot?' No.

And so it was with me for years.

While I was in sleeptime, people began to take credit for the work I did, thinking that I wasn't coming back and advancing their own egos. *What's the harm? Phil Sloan is never coming back.* Johnny Rivers took credit for my guitar riff on 'Secret Agent.' Steve Barri started to stake claim to my songs. Lou Adler insisted that my 'people' music was the result of him sending me home with a Bob Dylan album and telling me to write songs like that.

People were picking my creating bones clean.

E.T.'S IN THE FRONT YARD

In 1979, I started regaining the ability to process. I began getting stronger. Though my world was four blocks, I did my best to get my body moving again. After a walk I would rest at the feet of the forty-niner, who seemed to remain optimistic and loyal throughout my ordeal.

During my sleeptime, P.F. Sloan faded away. Though I had written many hundreds of songs, it doesn't take long for most people to forget. There was a blessing, I suppose. I slept through the entire cocaine and disco haze that enveloped Los Angeles during the 70s. I don't remember a single moment of any of that.

Most importantly, I started feeling alive. Every now and then I would pick up my guitar and strum a few songs. My father had begun to paint in oils, and he was quite good. It relaxed him. He generally had his easel set up by the pool. One afternoon, I heard music that sounded vaguely familiar. It was *Raised On Records*.

I walked out to the pool.

'What's that you're listening to?'

'It's your album.'

'Why are you listening to it?'

'Because it's good and it helps me to relax while I'm painting.'

That moment is one that I cherish. It was the first time he had ever complimented my music. He had never looked at my music with anything but suspicion, never giving me the impression that he liked any of my music.

The father I had was probably like many fathers. He wasn't the kind of guy who would openly show affection or pay compliments. But there was an osmosis. The connection between father and son was on a deep subliminal level. I knew he loved me, but it was never said.

On the night my father died, my mother and sister were in deep grief. I didn't feel anything. I felt sorry for myself that I wouldn't get to work out with him the walls and blocks that prevented us from having a real relationship.

I walked outside to have a cigarette. It was dark—perhaps 9pm. I looked up at the moon and was surprised at that moment to see seven discs of light, hovering high and still, in the night sky. I was transfixed. A truck, like those used in film production, pulled up in front of the house. Smallish men started getting out of the cab, opening the back of the truck, and setting up equipment. I figured they were making a movie. But at 9pm on a small, sleepy bedroom street? Wouldn't they have given some word to the neighborhood?

The men started setting up really bright lights. In this state of fascination, I noticed that there was no power source attached to these lights. I sensed there was a connection between the discs in the sky and these strange trucks and smallish men, wearing industrial like uniforms.

Aside from the truck, everything was quiet outside. Disturbingly quiet. I had had a number of experiences of witnessing unexplained phenomena but nothing like this. I noticed within myself that there was no sense of trepidation, just quiet excitement.

When you think you are seeing something out of the ordinary, you immediately question what you are experiencing. This could not possibly be. There had to be another explanation. Maybe this really was a movie company, and soon there would be Kraft services and actors I recognize.

I walked calmly into the house, hoping that when I went back to take a look this scene would have vanished and I could chalk it up to the shock of my father's passing playing havoc on my imagination.

My mother and sister were grieving in the living room.

'There's something outside I need you to see,' I told them.

'What's the matter with you?' my sister said. 'We're not interested in anything. Leave us alone.'

'Please, Philip. Leave us alone.'

I walked out of the door again and the creatures were still there. I closed the door, fell into a chair, and held my head in my hands.

BOMBAY ALLEY

My sister found a one-bedroom apartment for me in a quad on Cloverdale Ave off of Sixth Street, near La Brea. It was a working neighborhood with low rent and a Jewish landlady who said she would be happy to take care of me. My apartment was on the ground floor with the bedroom next to the garage, which meant it was noisy in the morning, with people leaving, and at night, with people returning from work. The place was by no means beautiful but would allow me to regain my independence.

I was receiving ASCAP checks but the amounts were so small I couldn't live on them. I had to find work. At night I took a telemarketing job, calling people on the phone, preferably during dinner hours when I was told they would be at home so I could ask them hundreds of deeply personal questions, hoping they would freely give this private information to a total stranger over the phone. It was amazing how nice so many people were to me, giving of their time so freely. And I was grateful for their kindness.

One particular job that stands out was getting people to buy cases of beer without labels for a large discount. I would then be given a van to deliver the beer to customers, return the next week to pick up the empties, and ask them to rate the beer. I couldn't allow myself to think about my old life. My new life was far away from music—as far as I could imagine.

After a period of time I felt secure enough to rent a piano for fun and amuse myself. A new song emerged spontaneously, and I enjoyed pounding it out on the piano keys—much to my neighbors' dismay.

A song can come from past, present, or future experience. 'Living In

A Bombay Alley' was a song about something that had not yet happened but was connected to my past, written in the present, and about my future.

I had always been intrigued by the line in Secret Agent: *you're swingin' on the Riviera one day, then bleeding in a Bombay alley next day.* I used the same duality in 'That's Cool, That's Trash.' With that strange image from the past capturing my imagination I wrote a little song called 'Bombay Alley.' The first verse went something like, *I'm living in a Bombay alley … Oh, how I miss the warm sunshine … but tonight in the Bombay alley, I believe it is going to glitter and shine.*

Maybe, through this lyric, I could admit to myself that being out of the music business was the right choice but not what I really wanted, and *oh, how I miss the warm sunshine* was me saying that I was subconsciously missing the spotlight. *But tonight in the Bombay alley, I believe it is going to glitter and shine*—maybe that meant there was the possibility of return. Perhaps someday, in this nightmare, the tragic hero would leave, and I could enjoy my creativity without paying a drastic price for it.

I had no idea I would soon be coming into contact with a God-Man from India who would change my life for the better, and that I would be actually walking in a Bombay alley where I was to experience an enlightenment of sorts.

I booked a little studio on Fairfax called Hitman Studios and recorded the song on a tiny early Casio electric piano. It was really a toy. But at $10 an hour and lots of gravy (echo), I was satisfied. I enjoyed being in a studio again—recording and experimenting and creating, and all outside the purview of business. I was anonymous—I had signed into the studio as Vince Vangoughberg.

The engineer was impressed with the song and told me that the studio also had a publishing arm as well as a little record label, and that he thought they would sign me for sure and on the spot. I had to pass on the idea. I was only in there to have fun, and I did not want to be drawn back into the maelstrom, though I missed the connection I had with my muse, who I had been working with day and night for years and who was my constant companion. And I had always received a sense of inner fulfillment. P.F. Sloan, my muse, had probably moved on to some other songwriter by now. Or that is what I was told when someone heard a Billy Joel song that reminded them of me.

What I found difficult was telling people what I had been—having to go into so much personal explanation that always evoked in them, *Oh, what a pity*, or, *Oh, how sad*. I didn't want the sympathy. I needed to live a Secret Agent's life. I no longer wanted to tell people about my other identity.

'Hi. Nice to meet you. What do you do for a living?' *I sell life insurance. I am a contractor for an irrigation company; I work in a delicatessen.*

I needed to become an ordinary man, but I didn't have the skillset. I found out that there was a position in a local insurance agency for a bright, young man who had a way with people and a gift for the gab. Now I could tell people the truth. I really did sell insurance. I decided to apply for an interview.

A very attractive and well-heeled woman in her forties asked the questions.

'So, Phil, have you ever sold insurance?'

'No. Never.'

'And what makes you think you can?'

'I am a fast learner,' I told the woman.

'It says you were … in the music business?'

'Yes. I was. I am no longer in the music business.'

'And what did you do in the music business?'

'I … wrote songs. I produced songs. I arranged songs. I found songs. I played songs. And I sang songs.'

'So your interest was in songs primarily?'

'Yes.'

'And were you successful?'

'Depends.'

'Would I know any of them?'

'It's hard to say, really.'

'Well. It's not an easy road, I'm sure. May I ask you, Mr. Sloan, if you are currently under any medication?'

'Yes, too much television.'

'I meant … doctors' prescriptions. The reason I ask is that it says that you have been in a mental institution.'

'Just for the cheesecake, really. But I think I can sell life insurance.'

'So. You've written a lot of songs and you are currently delivering beer. Well. I would like to encourage you to be patient. We will go over your application very carefully. We are always interested in eager young men who are not afraid of a challenge.'

I waited for a week or two, knowing full well there wasn't a chance in hell that the woman at the insurance office would call. It's funny, though, how I jumped every time the phone rang. I was living off of what my sister and mother were giving me, and they helped me get food stamps. One banner day it was announced on the local news that President Reagan had arranged to give away 5lbs of American cheese to anyone who showed up at the government cheese warehouse. I showed up with my sister and we waited in line for six hours to get that cheese. It lasted about a month and it was delicious. It wasn't processed cheese but real cheese. And good cheese. Real American cheese.

I was bound and determined to do the things that I would never have thought of doing in a million years. Maybe I proved to my sister that I wasn't the swelled-headed, showoff celebrity that she took me for. We bonded for a moment during that cheese experience. It hurts to think that my great fall from grace was giving my sister a sense of satisfaction.

I recall when we first moved to Los Angeles and were living in the apartment on Crescent Heights, I'd see Marge and Gower Champion arrive in a limousine and everyone on the street was abuzz about it. And now, every once in a while, a limo or hot car would pull up in front of the apartment and Jan Berry or Peter Noone or Gene Clark would get out and come in for a visit. The buzz in the neighborhood was that I was somebody, but nobody was sure exactly who or what. It's harder to be nobody than somebody it seems.

Jan Berry would stop by occasionally and we'd sit and talk about music that was on his mind to do. I enjoyed Jan's company. It had been more than a decade since his accident and he was still very much recovering. We both were, and we could relate to each other on that level. But Jan didn't have any money, and he wasn't able to pay me for any work I might do, so I'd be back where I was with the puppet master!

Peter Noone stopped by and held out hope when he asked me to write some songs for him. But I knew that was make-believe. I know he was just trying to make me feel better, and I appreciated it. Peter had a wonderfully kind heart.

If I gave in to the hope of getting back into the scene I would lose my commitment to ordinariness. That put me back on top of the fence. On one side of the fence was ordinariness, where nobody expected anything from you. They took you for what you were worth. For me, that life seemed good enough, although it was unrealistically romantic in and of itself. On the other side of the fence was the slightest hope of being back in music. I knew it wasn't going to happen and I didn't really want it to, and yet I was holding onto that hope for life. I had an overly romantic notion of both sides.

The apartment upstairs from me had been vacant for a while and now someone was living there. I went upstairs and introduced myself. We sat down and talked about nothing in particular when I asked if I could use his bathroom. I went inside, and there on the commode was a Grammy!

I asked him about it when I returned and he told me that he had been the producer of the *Annie* soundtrack from Broadway, and it had sold so many millions of records that he was promoted to head of A&R at Columbia. That was his downfall, he said. He started drinking and doing cocaine big time, and in no time he was fired. He showed me a tattoo that he put on his arm of a bottle with a red slash going through it, to constantly remind himself to remain sober.

I really don't remember the guy's name, and maybe it's better I don't. Suddenly, this out-of-the-way apartment building had turned into a halfway house for recovering musicians. *OK*, I thought, *this is how God had planned it, who am I to disagree?* The dream of happiness would come from not jumping off the fence to one side or the other but from flying above it.

CHAPTER TWENTY

THE BOTTOM LINE

In 1986, I got a completely unexpected call from fate in the guise of Brian Gari, the grandson of the great vaudevillian and movie star Eddie Canter.

'I want to do a show with you at the Bottom Line in New York,' he told me.

'That's sounds great,' I replied, 'and I thank you for thinking of me, but to be honest, I don't know you, and I don't think I can do that right now.'

'Of course you can. I will walk you through it. I have been a fan of your music all of my life. We'll rehearse for a week in Union City with a really great band and I'll be there every step of the way. I am doing this out of my love for you and your music. You must do this. I think the folks in New York will love it, and I think you will love it. So think about it and call me back.'

I agreed to think about it. I bandied the idea around for a month or more, taking Brian's phone calls while he shot me full of encouragement. The band would include Dennis Diken, who would go on to become the drummer for The Smithereens; Don Ciccone from the hit pop group The Critters; Brian on guitar; and Ray Van Stratton, a notable studio keyboardist.

I took the chance and flew out for a week of rehearsals in New Jersey. It was serious work, and running though all of my songs I began to realize the heft of what I had done in a few short years at Dunhill. After many long hours and great patience from all the musicians concerned we headed out to opening night at the Bottom Line and my voice disappeared. I tried to relax but I was nervous as hell. Brian knew that my voice was shot. He was freaking out but trying his best to stay cool. I went into the bathroom, locked the door, and prayed to God for my voice to return.

God answered in the voice of Elvis Presley. I heard it as clearly as if he were standing next to me.

'Don't worry, Phil,' he said. 'I'll sing through you until you get your sea legs.'

The audience was packed in. Jimmy Webb was there, as were Eric Anderson, Leonard Melfi, Lou Reed, and Howard Solomon from the Café Au Go Go, plus press people from all over the country, I was told.

As I ran through the first two songs, 'From A Distance' and a bluesy arrangement of 'You Baby,' my voice had so much power, depth, and flexibility, I thought I was *hearing* Elvis, so I stopped in the middle of a song.

'Am I the only one who's hearing Elvis?' I asked.

'No, Phil, we hear it too. Don't stop. Just keep singing.'

I received a validation from the audience that I was not hallucinating. The spirit of this great artist was protecting me. And everybody accepted it. I was the one who was skeptical. What was the matter with me? What seemed perfectly natural to the audience was seemingly impossible for me to believe.

'Don't worry about it, Phil,' somebody called out. 'It's all sounding good.'

A few songs in, my voice got stronger. Elvis's voice left and mine took over.

There were four shows over two nights. Each one became more relaxed and casual than the last. Everyone was having a good time. I began to kibitz with the audience. It was the first time I had ever told stories between songs and people seemed to enjoy it. That's how Will Rogers started telling stories—between rope tricks in vaudeville shows. I felt the audience wanted to know things about the person they came to see, not just the songs—and, more importantly, these stories were their stories. They had lived through them as I had. We were all part of the same play.

What people initially expected was a sentimental journey. What it turned out to be was a professional, fun show with new arrangements of songs and storytelling, and it was refreshing for the audience. I enjoyed doing it, as well as getting paid in hundred-dollar bills. But I had completely exhausted myself in this endeavor, and Brian had trepidations as he saw me in a nearly lifeless state after the gig. We decided it would be best for me to leave right away for Los Angeles to recover. I had put out so much energy for the first time in so many years that I was physically and mentally drained. But it was worth it.

ER INDIA

In a lifetime of wonderful, wholly unexpected turn of events, this one stands out as the most wonderful to me.

When I was ten years old, my uncle Jerry had given me a book of saints that he had purchased when he was in India at the end of World War II. While leafing through the hundreds of photographs of hold men and enlightened beings, I stopped at the picture of someone named Shirdi Sai Baba. I was transfixed by the black-and-white photograph of a man sitting in a mud hut with torn clothes. Underneath the photo was the caption, 'A great Faquir died in 1918.'

I showed the picture to my mother and told her that I wanted to be like him.

'But honey, he's a faker,' she laughed. 'Do you want to be a faker?'

'Yes that's what I want to be.'

My mother had a good laugh at that. I kept the book, but after a time it got put away into a closet and forgotten about.

One night as I lay sleeping in bed, only a few weeks after I had done the Bottom Line, I had a dream. In this dream, a man in an orange robe with a very large Afro told me, 'I know you are suffering. Come to me and I will heal.'

'I don't who you are or where you're from,' I replied, 'and I have no money!'

'It will be given.'

The dream ended, but I had a deep feeling about it and I yearned to know more. The answer would come from my old friend Bob Burchman many, many months later.

I had not been in touch with Bob for many years when I ran into him serendipitously at a local music store. He seemed to be glowing and very happy. At first he pushed me away, and I didn't blame him. I wasn't healthy at all, and I understood that some people think mental illness is contagious. I persisted in asking him how was that he seemed to be glowing? He finally relented and told me he had just come back from a trip to India to see Sai Baba.

Bob showed me a photograph, which I instantly recognized as being of the man from my dreams, and I told him about that. He listened somewhat skeptically but gave me the names of some people who could tell me more about Him. Now I had learned his name and where he came from. However, I also remembered that Shirdi Sai Baba had died in 1918.

MCA Music called me out of the blue one afternoon, and that was a banner phone call, as I had had no dealings whatsoever with MCA, even though they had bought the rights to Dunhill Records many years before. They told me that they had a check for me for $2,500, and they were going to deliver it by messenger. And they did. So the money was provided!

I called the numbers Bob had given me and spoke to some people who had been to see Sai Baba, and they told me he was the reincarnation of Shirdi. *The reincarnation of Shirdi?* I went to the passport office, renewed my passport, and bought a round-trip ticket to His residence in India, which was called Prashanti Nilyam (Abode of the Highest Peace) and was in a little tiny village in the South of India called Puttaparthi. *Put a party in your life*, I thought.

I landed in Bombay—oh, Lord, Bombay!—and then took a plane to Bangalore, and from there rode on an old tin bus for eight hours to the ashram. I never even considered my fragile state. I felt energetic and excited to be on a physical and spiritual adventure, a bit like Herman Hesse's Siddhartha on his journey for meaning.

I spent the first month in a hot, prefabricated shelter with 150 fellow pilgrims from all over the world. We slept on a concrete floor and ate only vegetarian food, for which we were not charged any money. Any time anyone needed medical treatment—I was treated for a mild, intestinal infection at one point—the care was provided without cost.

If we cared to participate, we would awake at 3am for prayers. Then we sat in a line with 500 or so men and women until 7am, when we would enter an outdoor hall where Sai Baba would walk around and take letters from some, talk to others, or manifest ash for healing. It was rather like a voluntary spiritual boot camp—we weren't forced to do anything. We could sleep all day or tour around town.

I was getting fit and strong. On my first day there I was sitting in the front row with as many as 3,000 people when Sai Baba walked up to me and asked where I had come from.

'Los Angeles,' I said.

Then he said something in Japanese to two men sitting next to me and walked on. I called him back. He stopped what he was doing and walked back to me and gave me a smile and asked me what I needed. I blurted out to him that I was not from Los Angeles but from Hollywood. He laughed, and in a sweet voice he said, 'I know.'

After Darshan (which means 'breathing the same air as a holy person') was over and Baba retreated to his little room, the Japanese gentlemen told me that Baba had informed them that I was a brave soul for traveling there alone in poor health and that they should look after me for a time, which they did.

Sai Baba challenged me to test him and not accept anything on blind faith.

'Anyone can become a parrot and say their lines as if they mean it,' he said, 'but I want you to draw your own conclusions.'

I took Sai Baba's advice and tested him daily. I was the skeptic who wasn't going to buy anything until I had satisfied myself. I had doubts about being a Jew in a Hindu temple, but Baba would say, 'There is only one religion: the religion of love. Don't leave your chosen religion after seeing me, use what you have experienced to make your mother religion more meaningful for yourself.'

I was experiencing something I thought had been lost to me forever. I was happy inside—truly happy—and almost every time I saw Sai Baba I was filled with bliss. It was a state of absolute knowingness, without thoughts of any kind filling up my mind. I could do whatever I felt like doing in that state for hours. When it left and I felt my mind well up with thoughts of doubt and other worldly fears, I realized that it was better being without them. This bliss was impossibly better than a full measure of Oreo cookies.

When it was time to leave, I bid Baba farewell, caught a cab to Bangalore, and splurged on a high-class hotel. I sat in a hot shower for an hour, ordered a beer and a sandwich, and watched the moon rise from my balcony, overcome with the sensuous smells of dung and urine and trash that burns twenty-four hours a day on the streets and smells like burnt chocolate.

My airline reservation was not for another two days, and I wondered what I was going to do with the time. I decided to get a taxi and explore. We must have driven for an hour—the city streets faded from sight and the scenery gave way to back roads. The driver maneuvered along dusty back roads and didn't respond to my demand to take me back to my hotel until he stopped in front of a small building in the proverbial middle of nowhere.

The driver got out of the cab and opened my door like I was getting out of a limo in Hollywood.

'This is my cousin's hotel, sir,' he said. 'I will get you a good rate, don't worry!'

You fool! I told myself. *This guy picked you out as a sucker and you bought it! What the hell did I get myself into?*

I looked around the landscape, which was deserted as far as I could see—dirt roads, a bridge that seemed to lead to nowhere, and this little white stucco hotel. I walked in. The hotel felt empty. The owner welcomed me like I had been staying there for thirty years and showed me to a room upstairs.

'Don't worry,' he said. 'I'll give you a good rate, sir!'

I stepped inside a small twelve-by-fifteen room with a bed and a tiny black-and-white TV with one working channel that showed reruns of old soccer games.

'We have grape Nesbitt here,' he said proudly, 'but no orange. Orange next week. The demand has been very high for the orange. I hope that is all right with you, sir!'

'Yeah,' I said. 'The orange is pretty good.'

'Yes. Excellent taste.'

'But I really don't know what I'm doing here,' I added, not really knowing why I wasn't going downstairs and demanding that I be returned to Bombay at once.

I watched the cab drive off and stared out the window at emptiness and dust. I must have been asleep for an hour or more when bells started ringing outside in the street. I looked out of the window and the alley was lit up like some saints day in Little Italy. Hindu priests were stepping off a large truck, ringing bells and waving incense sticks. Many people with animals were suddenly crowding into the alley. The priests were blessing the animals.

I watched with pleasure and thought, *OK, this is something people don't see every day.* Maybe I was there to witness this. As suddenly as it began, however, it ended, and the truck with the priests left the dusty street empty again. I sat on the bed and fell into a deep, contemplative sleep.

I had hoped to give up the nicotine habit while I was in India, and had promised myself not to buy a pack, but I found while I was there that they sold individual cigarettes, and I wanted one. I fought the feeling for ten or fifteen minutes. I walked out of the door of my room, went up to the manager's desk, and asked where I could buy a cigarette. He smiled and pointed. I watched where he was pointing to and followed into the street where the priests had done the animal blessings. There was nothing there!

I walked around and discovered a land bridge over a marsh and crossed it. It was a quarter-mile or so long, and there were a few shops but no smoke shops. I had a small bite to eat at a little stand and walked back to the hotel. It was around 5pm. The sun was beginning to set and I was still on the search for a smoke shop. I went into a small alley and found one, and I thought to myself, man, here you are in a Bombay alley!

The line I had written was *bleeding in a Bombay alley,* and I began to scare myself. And then something caught my attention. It was how the alleyway seemed to go on and on into an ever-widening and curling labyrinth. I felt an urge to explore it. The sun was still going down, as I began to walk into unexplored territory. There were no more familiar shops ahead of me, but I could see a lot of people in what looked like a small village community.

Suddenly I heard a voice exclaim, 'He's here! Baba is here!'

I felt a great sense of exhilaration and began looking all around for Sai Baba, although I couldn't see him. As I walked further into the alley, people were sitting on the roadway as if waiting for a parade. A strange feeling overcame me, and I felt these were all my dear relatives. In my mind, I heard, *Oh, there's Narayana and his two children. He just got over a severe cold, and he's been grateful that he's feeling better.* I saw an old man, and I heard myself say, *Just a hundred hairs left on his head and missing one tooth in his back pocket comb!*

Windows flew open and people cried 'Baba, baba!' I felt myself gliding above the street, blessing each and every one from a heart filled with a universe of abundant love! The sun had gone down and lights came on in the alleyway, like a miniature Las Vegas. Music began playing and there was joyous noise everywhere.

It was dark as I reached the place where I had first entered into the alley. I didn't know what had just happened, but my mind was telling me that I had just gone way over the edge.

I walked into the hotel and asked for my room key.

'Did you see Him?' the manager asked.

'See who?'

'Sai Baba was here tonight! Did you see him?'

'No, I didn't.'

'Such a pity.'

Every seven years, the people of this little town save up enough money to celebrate a religious holiday. They wrote to Sai Baba asking him if he would attend, and he sent a letter saying that he would. The same cab driver returned the next morning and took me back into the city of Bombay, where I stayed uneventfully for another day before returning home.

CHAPTER TWENTY-ONE

CAN YOU WRITE ANOTHER ONE JUST AS GOOD?

One day in 1990, I was having dinner at my sister's house. She had been having a very rough time of late as her husband had died of alcoholism and her adopted son needed a father. Her then boyfriend had contracted MS, and she had become his caregiver, as well as raising her son who, at twenty-three, was living at home with his girlfriend in a bedroom he had painted black, passing the time using heroin and ecstasy. I wanted desperately to be the loving uncle, as I had plenty of experience to share with him.

The phone rang and my sister answered.

'It's somebody named Clive Davis. He's calling from Germany.'

I took the phone from my sister and pulled the cord behind a hallway door for privacy.

'Phil? Clive Davis. I'm calling from Germany. I'm working on an exciting project. Do you have a moment to talk? How are you, by the way?'

'Thank you, Clive. I'm fine. What kind of project?'

'Well. Here's the thing. I'm putting together a charity album for the World Wildlife Fund. And I'm thinking … what songs do I want on the album? And it occurred to me that I want a new "Eve Of Destruction." Can you write it?'

'That's impossible, Clive! That song was given to me as a gift. I really didn't write it. It wasn't a song for hire, Clive!'

'Gift? What do you mean, a gift? Who gave it to you?'

'What I mean is, Clive … my muse. God. A gift from God.'

'Oh, I see. Well. That's great. Can you write another "Eve" in a couple of days? The World Wildlife Fund is in dire need of money. The wildlife parks are being poached. The animals are being slaughtered, and there's no money to pay for protection. I have guaranteed that the album will make a lot of money. We're having 150 children singing in choir, but it all hinges on your song. We need a monster record.'

The thought going through my mind was, *My God, I'm living on vapors and handouts. Writing this song could be a real blessing.*

'I wish I could, Clive. I really wish I could.'

As I got done saying that, I picked up a pen and began to write. *The western world it is in danger, we the people have become like strangers … taking polls and opinions, while the fabric decays, for the greed of a few how much the innocent pay. And my fear for you America is never far away …*

'Look. I can get Barry McGuire over here, and you, too, if you'd like to come. All we need is the song, Phil. All we need is the song.'

As Clive continued to talk, I continued to write.

'Uh huh,' I mumbled, as I was writing.

'Again, I can't tell you how near and dear this is to my heart. My wife and children are deeply concerned about the wellbeing of the planet, as am I. Is there anything that I can do to help you write this song? Do you want to use my bungalow at the Beverly Hills Hotel?'

'Clive?' I said, putting down the pen. 'You won't believe this. I just finished your song.'

'God, Phil, I knew you could do it. I'm going to call Barry McGuire and set up a recording studio, I'll bring in some studio musicians and you'll come out and teach them the song. I'll call you tomorrow.'

I hung up the phone.

'What was that all about,' my sister asked. 'Nothing. I just wrote "Eve Of Destruction 2."'

'"Eve Of Destruction 1" wasn't painful enough for you?'

'I'll never write another one,' I said.

'Ha,' she blurted, mockingly.

I submitted the new lyric to MCA/Universal, who own my copyrights, but they refused to publish the song. It was the second time a publisher had refused to publish "Eve." They claimed it was a derivative work of the original, and that Steve Barri might object.

He might object? He might object?

The reason he would object, I learned, was that his share would go down to 25 percent (instead of his 50 percent) of a song he never wrote, didn't like, and didn't want anything to do with. And now he was going to object to the song because he would get less money for it—a song with a new lyric for The World Wildlife Fund?

I started getting phone calls from young, caring executives at MCA. The new young turks were disgusted that the song was not going to be allowed to be published. These guys started researching my contracts and were horrified at the barbarism of how things were done in the past. Everything bad about the record business was summed up in my contract. It was so bad that they felt that it could destroy the reputation of MCA/Universal if word ever got out.

Though it would take another twelve years before the contracts were changed, this was the beginning. Even though the new crowd at MCA knew that Barri didn't have anything to do with the song, he had a contract—orchestrated by Jay Lasker—that gave him 50 percent of everything I wrote, and they couldn't do anything about that. But Barri eventually relented, and 'Eve Of Destruction '90' was eventually released on the WWF-affiliated album *El Dorado*. The album was marketed primarily in Europe and did very well for the WWF.

THE BIG LIE

Eugene Landy was the therapist who had gotten his claws into Brian Wilson's life and wouldn't let go. He was involved in Wilson's writing, his producing, his financial affairs, and his personal life. Brian couldn't do anything without him. Brian mistakenly trusted Landy as he thought it was the only way he could get well.

I had heard about Brian's nightmare from his ex-wife Marilyn, but there was little I could do but pray for him. That prayer was answered in 1991 when Tim White, who at the time was an editor at *Billboard*, called me on the phone. He explained to me that a reporter had asked Landy what gave him the right to create music with Brian Wilson, and Landy had replied by claiming to have written and produced 'Eve Of Destruction.'

Tim asked me nervously if I could prove in a court of law that I was in fact P.F. Sloan. I was a bit anxious about that because of what Lasker had told me about owning my name. But since Lasker had recently died, I felt there shouldn't be a problem in claiming that I was legally P.F. Sloan.

Tim sounded relieved and asked if I would write a rebuttal to Landy's claim, which he would then print in *Billboard*. I did. I called it 'The Big Lie.'

As the composer and co-producer of the Barry McGuire record 'Eve Of Destruction,' I wish to make it clear to the record buying public that Dr. Eugene Landy's claim to have written or co-produced the record is a big lie and a fabrication of his ego.

I have never worked with Dr. Landy. Who could possibly be fooled or impressed by his phony claims to having any real talent. I hope this will set the record straight and that it in some way helps Brian Wilson.

P.F. Sloan
Los Angeles

Shortly after the letter was published in November of 1991, Landy lost all of his credibility, and with it his hold on Brian Wilson.

Shortly after Lasker's death, I was asked to record the Bobby Darin song 'Sing A Simple Song Of Freedom' for a compilation CD called *True Voices*, produced by Sol Davis for Capitol Records. It was my first recording since 1972.

SEVEN SISTERS

I was now living in a one-bedroom apartment in Venice, California, that my sister and mother helped me pay for. Venice was good for me. I could walk along the beach—hopefully avoiding stepping on syringes—and breathe clean air, which was no small feat in Los Angeles.

Barry Gruber and Bruce Paskow, transplanted New Yorkers living in Seattle, had tracked me down and came knocking on my door one morning. Barry told me that he had unlimited studio time and some great musicians in Seattle, and he wanted me to make an album with him. After a number of meetings, I agreed to give it a shot. Barry and Bruce seemed like decent people; they were sincere, and they promised that it was all about the music. I liked Barry. He seemed to be a guy who was doing his best, and I appreciated that.

The early Romans called the hills surrounding the city of Rome the Seven Sisters. The Pleiades Constellation goes by this name as well, and there are references to the mythology of the Seven Sisters in almost every culture. They were considered to be the seven muses of humanity, and I wanted to reconnect with them with this album.

Barry Gruber was the son of a very wealthy man, and he paid a stipend to a group of exceptional musicians to hold them for any recording that he may want to do. Bruce Paskow, his partner, was a thirty-year-old folky from the well-known group The Washington Squares.

When we were recording the tracks for 'Still On The Eve Of Destruction' (the third version of 'Eve') Barry interrupted the take and told me that I was not keeping up with the band and not playing well enough. He suggested we let Bruce play the part instead.

This was a very fascinating turn of events, and a scene I recognized from my years at Dunhill. I had so often tried to get musicians on their own records, and so many were disappointed that they couldn't be. And here I was, being asked not play because I was not good enough to be on my own record.

This time it was different. The band didn't feel too great about it. We had become a cohesive unit. We had spent weeks rehearsing for this album. Barry felt that he had these guys under control and hadn't expected them to disagree—but they did. The band walked out of the session, and that was it. For all practical purposes, the project was dead.

I returned to my hotel and packed my bags to go back to Los Angeles. Barry came over to the hotel and begged me to try again one more time. He said he would allow me to play the guitar. He called the musicians back to the studio and we went to work. The guys in the band told Barry that it was not my job to keep up with *them* but rather their job to keep up with *me*. They understood that my slowing down at specific places was not due to a lack of timing but for emphasis and musical expression.

In an interview that Bob Dylan gave to *Rolling Stone* around 2000, he proclaimed that he had found his dream band—a band that followed him, rather than him following them. I think Barry finally understood that line of thinking.

'Beethoven's Delight' was the birth of my interest in Beethoven the man. This first superficial song served merely as an introduction to what would later become a much richer and deeper connection to the composer—one that would result in the making and writing of a popera called *Louie! Louie!*

Barry did not want me to play piano on the song, however, so he hired one of the world's leading session pianists, David Lanz, to play on it instead. No matter how hard I tried, though, I could not get David to feel the warmth of the music. He insisted that his interpretation was correct, but for me his playing was closer to Bach than Beethoven, and more mathematical than spirited. He played the notes perfectly but without any deep emotion.

Lanz's interpretation was a blessing, however, as it caused me to delve deeper into the song. I discovered that Beethoven himself worked for eight years on his only opera, *Fidelio*. It was performed once or twice and considered to be wanting. But instead of discarding it as a failure, Beethoven spent another number of years rewriting it, and the work became a masterpiece. I would try to do the same with my collection of songs on the life of Beethoven, which became known to my friends as 'Philip's Folly.'

Bruce Paskow did not care too much for P.F. Sloan. His wife, however, was a P.F. Sloan aficionado. Bruce and I sat down for a cup of coffee one morning before a session.

'My wife had a dream,' he said. 'She told me that I was going to be working with P.F. Sloan, and the experience would be very important for me. I told my wife that I didn't like P.F. Sloan and really didn't care about P.F. Sloan. I told her she was crazy, but here I am, producing this album, and it has been one of the most joyous experiences I have had in my life.'

For me, there were two artistically wonderful songs on *Serenade Of The Seven Sisters*, 'Spiritual Eyes' and 'Help Me Remember To Remember,' that proved to me that P.F. Sloan was alive and well. True, he was not writing twelve great songs on an album, but then nobody was anymore. It certainly was not what people expected or wanted from me. The vibe of the album was less blues and folk and more modern jazz. Folk-jazz? We completed the album and Gruber immediately sold it for a nominal fee to Pioneer Records in Japan, where I had had a cult following since the early 70s thanks to 'From A Distance' and the *Here's Where You Belong* album. Gruber was ecstatic. He had produced and sold an album, and now he was expecting great things. The album was selling for $35 in Japan and sold 10,000 copies in its first month.

In the year 2000 I went into a small studio and reworked every song, redoing vocals and echo mixes, adding instruments deleting others. I called it *Seven Sisters Redux*. It was just something I had to do to see if there were any hidden gems that were smothered in too much gravy. But for me it remains uneven at best, though again the renditions of 'Spiritual Eyes' and 'Help Me Remember To Remember' came out far better than they had originally and are well worth a listen.

DR. Z AND THE RELUCTANT ROCK STAR

A prominent Hassidic rabbi pal of mine and I went to a Bob Dylan concert together. We had backstage passes, and after the show we were put into a holding pen for people going back to see Bob. The rabbi, David Cohen, was an interesting character. He was sweet, loving, and playful. The odd thing about him was that he had, through a genetic quirk, naturally purple hair. It was quite astounding.

A huge bear of a man with a barrel chest, shock of beard, wild hair, and arms like an LA cop leaned his face against the pen.

'Hey, you,' he said. 'Are you free inside the fence or am I free outside the fence?'

I dismissed the man almost immediately as a crazed fan, and then David came over and pulled me back from the conversation with him.

'Hey,' the man said to David. 'I've got something you've been looking for your whole life.'

'Oh yeah? What's that?'

'A mystical letter from a rabbi, written in 1732,' the man said, opening a leather case.

He showed the letter to us through the chain-link fence and David gasped, visibly shaken.

'Come outside and be free,' the man told us. 'There are more important things than being backstage at a Bob Dylan concert.'

David grabbed me and we went outside to where the man was standing. He gave the letter to David, and David became mesmerized by it. Then the stranger then turned to me.

'I've been waiting to meet you all of your life,' he said.

'You've been waiting to meet me all of my life?'

We followed this creature to a patch of grass and sat down.

'I don't understand how you ... I mean ... how could you have possibly ...'

'We'll get to that, David.'

'David? Wait this is too much. I never ...'

The man opened up a leather-like bag and showed us what looked like the largest raw crystal either of us had ever seen. He said it was a memory chip for his ship.

'You're not going to believe what I have to tell you,' he said. 'I happen to be a time traveler, and I am making a very good living singing your songs on other planets in the galaxy and other dimensions, I might add. And let me tell you, playing in other dimensions is one tough room.'

At this point in my life, I was drug-free, psychosis-free, and feeling pretty darned good about myself. Naturally, I assumed I was speaking to a psychotic lunatic classmate from Cedars. But what was I to think when David declared this mysterious letter to be authentic? I decided to keep an open mind.

'My name is Dr. Z. I'm here to help you disconnect from all of the negativity in your life.'

'Can't argue with that,' David said.

'When you were seven years old, you had a magic arm,' Dr. Z told me. 'You could throw a ball so high that it looked like it jumped over the moon. Am I right?'

'How did you know that?'

'Everyone knows that where I come from.'

'Where do you come from?'

'A different time and a different place.'

'What do you want?' David asked.

'Nothing,' he said, and then he turned to me. 'On every planet you are known as P.K. Sloan.'

'Oh yeah?' I asked. 'What does P.K. Stand for?'

'The Preacher's Kid.'

You may believe this or you may not. I am simply recounting my experience as it happened. I trust you as a confidant and friend. I am not trying to pull your leg or to create humor fantasy for the sake of interest. I have been reticent since this happened ever to mention it. Please take it for what it is worth.

Thus began my three-month relationship with one Dr. Z, and my journey into the unknown every time he opened his mouth. This character became the subject of my song 'P.K. And The Evil Dr. Z,' which P.F. Sloan wrote with joy and relish as I looked on in dread, the lyrics pouring out in fifteen minutes, and which I reluctantly recorded for my *Sailover* CD.

About a month after selling *Serenade Of Seven Sisters* to Pioneer in Japan, Barry Gruber decided he wanted to make an impact in Los Angeles, so he devised a promotional idea to take over the Troubadour and put on a tribute show to me. And so he did, and he spent a good deal of time and money to make it happen. He took over the top two floors of the Continental Hotel on Sunset, where I had once listened to *Highway 61* with Bob Dylan. The Continental had long since lost its luster as a hip hotel, but it was still two floors. But Barry didn't expect to have to contend with someone like Dr. Z, who told him that all his plans had to be run by him for approval or there would be no show. I witnessed all this and decided to be an observer rather than a participant. Besides, Barry and I were not really getting along since his selling of the album to Pioneer in Japan and then re-selling it to a small American label without me seeing any money from all of it.

Terry Black was flown in from Canada for the show, and Gruber provided limos for Terry, Jan Berry, Johnny Rivers, Howard Kaylan, and Noel Harrison. Even Steve Barri showed up. Bruce Paskow was there to play electric guitar and steal the show if he could; Neil Rosengarten was on bass, with Paul Goldberg on drums, three background singers, and me on electric piano and guitar.

The evening was a red-carpet affair and the place was packed. Anybody who has ever been to a Troubadour special show knows that everyone in town is aware of it.

Jan Berry did 'I Found A Girl.' He explained to the audience that the reason we were used as harmony for Jan & Dean was that Steve and I could deliver the sound that he and Dean couldn't. Jan was very close to the end. He was suffering from paralysis. His wife Gertie and his friends didn't think he should perform but he did, and he pulled it off flawlessly, singing and joking with the audience. He got a standing ovation, and the love poured out to him.

Johnny Rivers showed up wearing his customary black and made a point of letting everyone know that J.R. was in the room. He did a great version of 'Secret Agent Man,' and the audience loved him. I was grateful to Johnny. We had had our tensions over the years but it was all washed away on that night.

Howard Kaylan of The Turtles sang 'Let Me Be' and 'You Baby,' and the audience went nuts as Howard regaled them with personal horror stories that made everyone howl with laughter. I felt like I was on Dick Clark's Caravan of Stars.

Noel Harrison did a flawless version of 'The Man Behind The Red Balloon.' I hadn't seen Noel in years. I think he was in town doing *My Fair Lady*.

Terry Black was humble and wonderful. The crowed felt it and gave him a tremendous ovation after he sang 'Unless You Care' and 'Say It Again.' I came out and opened with 'Love Go Easy On Me' from *Seven Sisters*.

At the end of the show I was presented with two-dozen red roses. I crushed all of the roses and threw them out onto the audience, showering them with the petals. The *LA Times* reviewer wrote that he loved the new songs and my vocals but considered the rose-throwing to be strange an erratic behavior.

After the show, Dr. Z hustled me out the back door, disappointing everyone who had wanted to hang out. He had set up a press conference in the Continental's hospitality suite with wine and cheese. The room was filled with reporters. They all loved the album and were very taken with Dr. Z, who they perceived to be my new manager. He fielded the questions with remarkable skill and with an infectious and likeable personality. The press loved him.

Dr. Z moved into my apartment in Venice for two weeks. He then causally told me that he had business to attend to and would be in touch with me in the future and left as mysteriously as he appeared.

Rabbi David was disappointed when Dr. Z left. David had been hoping to reconnect with him and was interested in acquiring more Jewish artifacts.

When Dr. Z left, I received a bill for more than $10,000 containing thousands of area codes from all around the world. I called Pacific Bell and tried to explain but they wanted their money.

'How can I pay a phone bill of $10,000?' I asked.

'You should have thought of that before you started making calls to Liberia and Tonga and Bolivia.'

'But my phone bill has only been $11 for the past two years.'

'Has someone been using your phone without your permission?' they asked.

'Yes, that's possible.'

'Unfortunately, you are still responsible for the bill. Unless of course, someone broke into your house and used your phone.'

I could have lied and told them that was the case but I didn't feel right with that. Over the next month, I spoke to a number of supervisors, and they agreed to lower the bill to $2,500, and then, after a series of conversations, they agreed to lower it to $1,000. In the end, they lowered the bill to zero. And then, in a complete reversal of events, I was given to one free year of service and an updated phone.

That took the sting away from the negativity and grief I was getting from friends who kept telling me that Dr. Z had just been manipulating and using me. Shortly after he left, my mother passed away. We had achieved a loving and mutually respectful relationship, though she never understood my role in music. More importantly, though, she loved the person that I had become as result of my spiritual journey. That was a great gift.

TOKYO PHIL

About a month after the Troubadour show, Bruce Paskow, whose wife had had the dream that he would be playing with me, died suddenly from an aneurism. We were just beginning to become friends.

Shortly after that, I received an unexpected phone call from a small independent record company in Tokyo. They had met someone I knew who was traveling there and told them how to contact me. I was told that there was a strong interest in me and they wanted me to come for a visit to discuss business. I had planned a trip to India that summer, so I decided to stop in Japan on the way.

On my arrival in Tokyo, these same businessmen picked me up, put me up in a penthouse, and drove me around the city, showing me all of the great sites. A famous Japanese disc jockey arranged for me to meet with the heads of all the major Japanese labels—RCA, Sony, Warners, Toshiba—the following evening. The reason these executives wanted to meet me, they said, was because they had learned to speak English by listening to *From A Distance*. I was told by one of the executives at MM Records that if it were all possible, the greatest gift I could bring would be anything autographed by the great Hideo Nomo, the Japanese pitcher for the Los Angeles Dodgers. So, before leaving for Tokyo, I went to Dodger Stadium and purchased a number of baseballs signed by him.

I received a grand tour of the Ginza, explored record stores filled with bootlegs that blew me away, and was given dozens of CDs of outtakes by The Beatles, the Stones, and Dylan. My interpreter was a transplanted Englishman from Liverpool by the name of David Ridges, and he was doing this for a living at the time. He is now a movie and TV star in Japan. He and I had noodles for dinner. I met many of his friends and the evening ended pleasantly.

The next morning I was moved to another hotel near the ocean, away from the noise of the city, and I felt at peace. The cherry blossoms were in bloom and Tokyo was celebrating. That night we were to meet the big execs at a tiny sushi restaurant where they would apparently meet and get ripped together once a year. They had been doing this since they first started in the mailrooms of their respective companies, and by now they had all risen to the top. The guest of honor this year was to be P.F. Sloan.

A limo picked me up around 7pm and dropped me off in front of a small door in a seedy back alley. I was shown in to a private room that was decorated in typical Japanese style. I was introduced to the executives by the DJ, who served as the interpreter for the night. I presented the signed baseballs to the executives, who were all deeply moved by the gesture. And then the party began.

Bottles and bottles of Saki, plum wine, and champagne plus dozens of platters of food were brought into the room by very slim women in white silk kimonos. The executives were laughing rowdily, asking me questions about the lyrics to my songs. They were interested in my tales of Hollywood, and I tried to answer the best I could. After an hour or two of drinking, their coats came off, and from there it seemed like they hardly noticed that I was there. One of the executives stood up and began singing 'From A Distance' to me in his broken English. They all began to join in, and then I was asked to sing it for them with a guitar that was brought in, which I did.

I watched these grown men with tears rolling down their eyes, celebrating their success in life. The song had helped them in some way. I was blown away. I signed autographs for them all, and then after a few more hours of partying I was ushered out as they had private business to discuss.

I was treated with more respect that night than I could ever remember. I love Japan. The next morning, I bid farewell to David and did an interview for the *Japan Times* at the airport before boarding my flight to India.

CHAPTER TWENTY-TWO

THE REVIEW

In 1973, Lester Bangs reviewed Bruce Springsteen's first album, Asbury Park, in *Rolling Stone* magazine.

> *Remember P.F. Sloan? Sure you do. It was back when every folk-rocker worth his harmonica holder was flushed with Dylan fever and seeing how many syllables he could cram into every involuted couplet. There was Tandyn Almer of 'Along Comes Mary' fame ('The psychodramas and the traumas hung on the scars of the stars in the bars and cars'—something like that), and David Blue had his own Highway 61 too, but absolutely none of 'em could beat ol' P.F. He started out writing surf songs but shook the world by the throat with his masterpieces 'Eve Of Destruction' and 'The Sins Of A Family,' and all his best material was just brimming with hate. Boy howdy, the first thing the world needs is a P.F. Sloan for 1973, and you can start revving up yer adrenaline, kids, because he's here in the person of Bruce Springsteen.*

The review came and went; Bruce Springsteen became 'The Boss' and rocked the world to its foundation with intelligent, working-class grit. During the early days of the internet, the reviews of my albums were often negative and dismissive. But after Lester Bangs's review of Springsteen started to spread around, sometime around 2004, things changed dramatically. Artists like Fiona Apple, Alanis Morissette, and Hootie & The Blowfish were talking about how they were influenced by my songs in a very positive way. And suddenly the reviews for my albums became five stars and must-haves. Now, instead of being dismissed as someone floating in the backwaters of 60s-ville, I was being referred to as a seminal artist of the times. *Rolling Stone* had given absolution to those who were influenced by my music, and they were now free to admit it. That little review changed everything. I could hold my head high.

I first met Jon Tiven when I was in New York around 1992–93 to appear on *Geraldo Live*. He had suggested me to the talent coordinator for the show, whom he knew, and assured her I was fully capable and in my right mind, contrary to what she might have heard around the rumor mill. Jon had seen me on a local TV show that was filmed in Los Angeles and then rebroadcast in New York. He got my telephone number from the host of the show, Art Fine, and Jon and I began talking to each other.

The theme of Geraldo's show that day was to be 'songwriters who wrote controversial songs.' Lee Greenwood and Pete Seeger were set to feature, but out of the blue Seeger declared he would not be on the same stage as P.F. Sloan and pulled out. Geraldo talked him back into doing it and Pete agreed, but only if he could be filmed in his own living room. Twenty-five years after 'Eve,' Seeger was still treating me like an outcast—not an authentic folksinger. Go figure.

Geraldo and I had never met before, and all he knew about me was from the songs I had written and the rumors of me being out of my mind. Naturally, he was apprehensive. He interviewed me extensively in his office, and eventually I managed to allay his fears. He asked if I would do him the favor of singing 'Eve' to the studio audience before the show began, and I agreed. As I began the second verse, all the lights in the studio began to pop and fizzle, and everything went dark. I continued to sing, though, and finished the song. The audience gave me a standing ovation, and Geraldo agreed to have me on his show.

Jon Tiven had a reputation as a brilliant producer. He had produced records for Wilson Picket, B.B. King, Don Covay, and many others, and now he wanted me to do an album with him. The experience of recording *Seven Sisters* had left me feeling a little gun-shy, however. Jon would call once a month, and I would always tell him that I wasn't ready.

Jon continued to call me every now and again for many years. Then on one particular night when he called, in 2005, there happened to be a piece of paper and pencil on the table in front of me. While I was giving him the reasons why I didn't want to do an album, I started writing, as I had done with Clive Davis a few years earlier. This time, however, lyrics began pouring out of me.

'I think P.F. Sloan wants to do an album,' I told Jon. And in four days I had written eleven songs.

Jon's studio was in his house in Nashville, so I took over a spare bedroom and we began cutting tracks for the album. Craig Krampf, drummer for The Robbs and now a successful record producer in his own right, volunteered his time to do whatever was needed. Buddy Miller, the great guitarist and producer for Emmy Lou Harris, played on a number of tracks. Felix Cavaliere from The Rascals, who was now living in Nashville, played organ and piano. Garry Tallent from Bruce Springsteen's E Street band and Tom Peterson from Cheap Trick shared bass duties. And Lucinda Williams and I did a duet on 'The Sins Of A Family.'

I remembered meeting a woman called Lucinda years back in the alley behind Raji's, the much-loved dive east of Vine on Hollywood Boulevard where I used to hang out with Bryan MacLean and Kim Canoe. She wore a beat-up cowboy hat and tight jeans. She was just starting out then.

Lucinda didn't really want to do a duet with me. She was being worked hard by various record producers as a background singer or singer of duets and I felt she was she was being mistreated by them. But she would give these unappreciative record types her absolute all, and she wowed them every time. So, in her mind, she figured my record was just another gun-for-hire session, although she knew Jon Tiven and knew he wasn't like the others.

The night before the session, Jon and I had dinner with Lucinda and her husband. I got her laughing—really laughing. Her husband told me that she hadn't had such a good laugh in years and that she had been suffering from depression. But that evening clinched it, and the next day she was in the studio with Jon and me. She nailed the song and had a good time as well. I could sense I was in the presence of royalty when she began to sing.

Jon was also producing an album by the great Frank Black, aka Black Francis of the Pixies, around the same time. Frank told Jon that he loved 'Halloween Mary' and wanted to sing on it. We of course were thrilled with that idea, and Frank also did a couple of verses on 'Eve Of Destruction' as well. Frank is a divine artist—the way he is able to deconstruct pop songs into something new and malleable with heart and intellect and soul is incredible. That's why the Pixies were the best, and the inspiration to all the great groups like the Smashing Pumpkins and Soundgarden.

Stephen Kalinich had co-written a few cuts for The Beach Boys like 'Little Bird' and 'Be Still.' But he was more of a poet than a lyricist, and had published a number of books of poetry. He told me that he had gone up to Dunhill to meet and hopefully write with me after he first heard 'Eve' but was tossed out the door like an unwanted encyclopedia salesman. Instead he got a contract from Brian Wilson to work at Brother Records. I put Stephen's small epic poem 'If You Knew' to music, and then we wrote 'Soul Of A Woman' together after seeing a moving van emblazoned with a portrait of the Virgin of Guadalupe.

The album, *Sailover*, was released by Hightone Records and distributed by Warner Bros, and I was finally able to fulfill my dream of going out on the road on tour. I traveled to thirty cities in the United States, performing in concert to people who had only ever known my name and never seen me perform before. The tour continued into Canada and then Europe, with a run of shows at hip clubs in England, Holland, Denmark, and Spain. The Sloan Rangers turned out in their droves, and it was standing room only. I would even break into Baggys numbers like 'Tell 'Em I'm Surfin'' for the encores.

I felt most at home in England, but then a funny thing happened in London. I was to play at the Luminaire, with Procol Harem backing me up, but only thirty people showed up. There had evidently been a promotion mix-up. But we gave them the best show you ever saw, and that's what it's about. It doesn't matter if there's one person or one thousand—you play to who is digging it. The funny thing was when the manager gave me a £5 note for my trouble and said I was being overpaid! But I enjoyed playing my songs for people, and I had no problem performing for two hours or more if they wanted me to. I had been given the gift of a tremendous amount of energy and stamina, perhaps following my boot camp in India.

I include the following review of one of the shows, written by Keith Baumert for the-grassroots.com, not to boast but rather to show the power of redemption. I have had some mighty low points in my life, but by God's grace I have managed to come back from each one.

P.F. used a silent pause when he wanted to emphasize a song or what he was saying about them. He used this effect on his next introduction for the intro riff and his production techniques on The Mamas & The Papas' signature tune, 'California Dreamin'.' Through his story behind the song, the audience was able to understand the elements that P.F. brought to the table as producer and performer. He explained that John Phillips had a simple folk song (which he demonstrated in his initial presentation). The song sounded similar to any other folk song. He explained that he thought of a twist in another popular song at the time to combine with Phillips' song to give it an edge. P.F. felt that if they incorporated the tempo of The Ventures' 'Walk Don't Run' into it, they would end up with a whole different presentation. He then added the famous intro riff that he composed to start it. He then demonstrated the brilliance of the idea to the astonished audience.

For his next song, P.F. reeled back in time and played something that made Johnny Rivers more famous than ever. His rendition of 'Secret Agent Man' was a crowning moment of the show. Duane Jarvis had the lead guitar licks perfect for the classic riff on electric guitar that everyone knows so well. How many millions of listeners can pick that tune out with little effort? Since the start of the show, the performance was nonstop. When P.F. said there would be a short break to put on a new string, most of the audience rushed to the rest room or walked around, sharing their praise of the performance. He returned to the stage after a few short minutes and was again ready with all the energy that he started the concert with—truly amazing. He launched into the song that started The Grass Roots, 'Where Were You When I Needed You,' and played it like no one else can. Again, after a long applause, you could feel that he appreciated every individual handclap. He started into a long silent pause. Suddenly, the audience started requesting their favorite tunes. I think it was music to his ears to hear those requests. He started humming 'I Can't Help But Wonder Elizabeth' when it was requested. He then picked the audience request for 'Let Me Be' and 'Here's Where You Belong.' Duane Jarvis respectfully left the stage. It was the master himself creating all the sounds on these emotional requests from his friends. He was master of his craft with this outstanding end to a long tour and his show that night.

After the tour, *Sailover* was still being pushed by Warner Bros, and I headlined a concert for record executives around the country at their annual marketing and distribution summit in Kissimmee, Florida. I performed under a huge banner of the lyrics to 'Eve Of Destruction.' I was playing music and working the room with the president of Hightone. The support I received from those folks made me feel accepted and loved. The *Sailover* tour was a wonderful experience in my life.

A PICNIC AT THE GREEK

In 2007, Kim Canoe came down from Oregon to kidnap me and to take me on a mystical adventure, which she was quite sure I needed. She had a lot of good memories of LA.

I hadn't seen Kim since Raji's, ten or so years before—back around 1995. Back then, Bryan MacLean, Eric Burden, Kim, and I were hanging out and talking about the possibility of putting a little group together and doing some shows. The group never materialized, but I always liked being with Bryan and Eric. Eric was an artist—smart and abstract. Bryan had become a friend through Kim, who was his closest confidant in the world.

In those days, Bryan was in need of healing, and Kim kept him stitched together. Kim knew that Bryan was starting to really break down. He would spend six months drinking himself into oblivion and six months going to his church and writing extraordinary hymns. Kim saved his life so many times. She would go over to his apartment to make sure he was eating and writing. I would go over there with her, often with cookies and cold milk.

'I am going to leave now so you can work,' she would always say. 'I will leave, and you will write beautiful songs that will mesmerize everyone in the midst of earth-shaking, twinkling chaos.'

Bryan wrestled his whole life with his demons. When you are dealing with a creative genius, it is difficult to interfere with any of those experiences. You want the genius to be healthy and be happy, but their self-destructive nature may be part of their way of investigating the depths of darkness so that they can then communicate those experiences to other people—to be able to pull *us* out of that darkness. If I had any weight at all with Bryan, it would be that he recognized a kindred spirit. And though we were both in love with Kim, it was clear to me that Bryan was extra special to her, and he needed her more than I did.

Bryan took the label of genius and star all too seriously and allowed himself to carry the burden of it. This burden killed many of my friends and contemporaries, in my opinion—Janis Joplin, Jimi Hendrix, Tim Buckley, Phil Ochs, Tim Hardin, Fred Neil, and Lenny Bruce to name but a few. They all seemed to drown trying to live up to this great expectation. You are much more than what people think or say you are.

One day, Kim told me that she needed my help. Bryan had been invited to play at a major concert at the Glen Helen Amphitheater. Kim asked me to be with Bryan onstage as he hadn't performed in ten years. She was concerned that he would back out and be too nervous. The headliners of the show were Buffalo Springfield Revisited, The Mamas & The Papas, and John Sebastian.

By 1995, my hypoglycemia had been healed. The so-called schizophrenia with which I had been diagnosed had disappeared. I was mentally and physically healthy. I was happy and I was doing OK. I was doing OK because I had learned to forgive and to love. If you carry anger and it turns to bitterness, it doesn't hurt the person with whom you are angry—it hurts you. Anger and bitterness will eat you alive.

P.F. Sloan is not a victim. He is a creative spirit. People were always trying to tell me that it was unrealistic not to be bitter: *You must really be angry. You must really be hurt. How do you get through the day?* I get through the day because I have forgiven. I have forgiven Lou Adler. I have forgiven

Steve Barri. I have forgiven Jay Lasker and Bobby Roberts. I've forgiven them all from the bottom of my heart and can even say I love them—not their behaviors or decisions but their life force, which comes from God.

Bryan took the stage at Glen Ellen and begged me to come out with him, which I did. Bryan got his confidence back right after the first song. Five thousand people poured their love out to Bryan, and he responded by coming alive. Nothing makes you feel more alive than 5,000 people loving you in the same moment. I was accompanying Bryan on the guitar, but I was really there for support—a friendly face there so he could turn and look at me and see that everything was all right. Bryan was fragile. This show gave him a new lease on life, although the lease was short term as Bryan died of a heart attack in 1998.

Something miraculous happened after the show: the spirit of healing and forgiveness seemed to take over the entire event. John Phillips walked up to me. The last time I was with John, he was waving a knife in front of me. John walked up to me and apologized for treating me the way he did and asked for my forgiveness, which I gave him. John Sebastian, who had been badmouthing me for years, also apologized. This was indeed a concert of healing and forgiveness. Dewey Martin—who I had been financially taking care of for years after Neil Young left him to own devices of drinking and drugs—had hurt me as well, and now here he was apologizing for it. Jim McGuinn apologized for all the years he had spoken unkindly about me. The rift with David Crosby was healed. And Barry McGuire apologized for the years he had spent believing I was the devil, during which time his church had forced him to stop singing 'Eve.'

A month later, Kim showed up at my apartment unexpectedly at about five in the evening and told me she was going to take me someplace I would not regret. It was always good to see Kim. She had left Bryan a few days after the concert in high spirits. Now she had driven her 1986 Toyota pickup truck back from Oregon, where she was living with her kids, and here she was at my place. She had a picnic basket in the front seat.

'Where are we going?' I asked.

'You'll see. You'll love it. I guarantee it, Sloaner,' she giggled as we headed up Sunset, past RCA Studios, which had since been converted into a Mercedes dealership.

'Do you remember where we first met?' she asked.

'I had just come back from the "Paint It Black" session. It was about four o'clock in the morning and raining. And I thought to myself, *what kind of crazy person is hitchhiking at four o'clock in the morning in the rain?*'

'And I was thinking, *what kind of crazy person is going to pick me up hitchhiking at four o'clock in the morning in the rain?* And it just happened to be you, Sloan.'

'Yeah, it just happened to be me.'

We drove up Vermont Canyon Road and onto Vista Del Valle. We parked and started to walk up the hillside.

'We're going on a climb, Sloan.'

'What kind of climb?'

'You'll see.'

We parked the truck on a dirt road and started hiking up into the hills. We were on a well-worn path at first but it soon gave way to brambles and thickets.

'Keep up, Sloan. You're falling behind.'

'Where are we going?'

'You'll love it. Have I ever disappointed you?'

We made it up to a grove of evergreen trees. I followed Kim over to the side of a hill and we looked down, and there was the Greek Theater, filled to capacity and lit for a show.

'Who's playing tonight?' I asked.

Kim spread out a blanket and opened the picnic basket.

'Cold chicken?'

She laid out chicken, cheese, crackers, wine, and cookies.

'I was thinking about something on my way down here,' she said.

'What?'

'I would have given anything to be a fly on the wall when you were creating some of your songs. But I would have flown out the window when you were working on "Summer In New York."'

The first group onstage was The Grass Roots, who began their set with 'Mr. Jones' and followed it with 'Where Were You When I Needed You?' and 'Live For Today.' Next came Herman's Hermits, who did, among others, 'A Must To Avoid,' 'Hold On,' and 'All The Things I Do For You Baby.' The Kingsmen did 'Louie, Louie' followed by 'That's Cool, That's Trash.' Paul Revere & The Raiders did a set, as did The Buckinghams.

And then The Turtles took the stage. They started with 'It Ain't Me Babe' and went through 'Let Me Be,' 'You Baby,' 'Can I Get To Know You Better,' and all their other great hits. When they got to 'Is It Any Wonder,' Howard Kaylan paused. He spoke quietly, taking the audience into his confidence, as if speaking to old friends.

'I wonder where Phil Sloan is tonight?'

I had climbed the mountain, by His grace, after falling off it more times than I can count, and I got to watch the show from that unique and marvelous vantage point. May God bless us all with an unselfish heart and mind so that we may make each day better than the one before for each and every one of us.

Lokah Samastah Sukhino Bhavantu. May all beings in all the worlds know peace and happiness.

P.F. Sloan

AFTERWORD
BY CREED BRATTON

"I want to be alone"
—Greta Garbo (or, as you know him ... P.F.)

Phil is a harbinger of the Aquarian Age. He can't be anything else. His songs will stand the test of time. Enough said.

Phil shows you light and returns later to see how you've reacted to it. He worries less now than he used to, and I think he's at ease with his gifts.

God, I hope so. He deserves some peace.

There's a big plan going on, and he takes it personally if he feels he's not doing his bit. He is a patient man, just waiting for the world to catch up. *Come on world ... help this mensch out.*

I've been lucky enough to call him a friend. As an Aquarius, I don't have a lot of Virgos in my immediate circle, but Phil's in my cards.

I can expect every few months or years to hear from him after he's done musing. We might play a gig together or just laugh about the state of it all.

It's the Eternal Stuff we gravitate to. It doesn't matter how long it's been—we get each other and take up the conversation right where it left off . . . or so it seems.

Now, understand this could be true or not ... it's just my take on it. But I do know this etherized plan we created for ourselves is better with him in it.

Creed Bratton
Los Angeles
February 12 2014

THE P.F. SLOAN SONGBOOK

'A Girl Never Knows'
Sloan–Barri
Steve's forte was songs about girls: girls who wanted rings or marriage proposals before they would let anything happen. This was one of the first songs 'for hire' written with Steve in 1963. Connie Stevens was a huge star at the time—a teen idol from the television show *77 Sunset Strip*. She recorded the song as a single, and it meant a great deal to me. Steve wrote almost all of the lyric and I the music.

'A Melody For You'
P.F. Sloan
This was written in the Hollywood Hills at a friend's house, for a lady with whom I was infatuated. She was a sculptress, and she was married, so I had to keep it to myself. I sang to her in my mind—*If my thoughts could be played just like notes then I'd play you a melody so fine … to wish you love all of the time*. The lyric came first, and then I set to music—the majority of my best work was done in this manner. I got to record it as a single.

'A Must To Avoid'
*Sloan–Barri**
The music for this song was written on Donovan's guitar while he was performing onstage at the Trip on the Sunset Strip. His manager and producer, Mickie Most, said he needed a song for the upcoming Herman's Hermits movie, and that he was leaving for England the next day. The line about a 'complete impossibility' came from the thought that what he was asking for was impossible. But it got done, and it became a hit.

'Above And Beyond The Call Of Duty'
P.F. Sloan
This is one of my favorite songs from *Measure*

Of Pleasure. *Perry wants to join the army, cos he's all mixed up inside* was a line I wrote after talking to a guy who wanted to go to Vietnam. *Well-knit Roger looks almost blameless in a room of Mickey Rooney fans* … I was at a party with cool operators and smooth talkers, and I saw that it was hard to tell what they're trying to sell. I enjoyed the dark and wry insight of the song.

'Ain't No Way I'm Gonna Change My Mind'
*Sloan–Barri**
There is a grit and simple spirit in this song. It flows. The lyrics were written first. Whimsical. Glen Yarborough recorded it, as did Barry McGuire. Glen was considered to be the pope of folk music at the time. If he gave his approval to something, it must have been good. Perhaps this song is evidence of my folkster authenticity that the 'tall man with the banjo' had somehow overlooked, despite his wrath for P.F. Sloan. It was one of the magical five songs that came out the evening I wrote 'Eve.'

'All I Want Is Loving'
Flip Sloan
At thirteen, I was in love with a girl named Judy, and this song was meant to get her to notice me. It was recorded at RCA Studios in Los Angeles and produced by Bumps Blackwell for Aladdin Records. The number of minor chords in this song is interesting to me. Until The Beatles, most pop songs did not have a lot minors, but this one goes from E-minor to an A-minor. The fact that love wasn't going to happen is emphasized by the use of a minor chord. When love *was* going to happen, I switch to a major. The chord reflects how the songwriter is feeling, and how the story is developing, but the frequency of the minor subdues the spirit. Trying to control the emotions of the listener

with major and minor chords was fascinating to me, and it still is. Eugene O'Neill attempted to control the tension of the audience by the use of tom-tom drums in his play *The Emperor Jones*. That always intrigued me.

'All That Time Allows'
P.F. Sloan

It took me twenty years to let the tears flow for John Winston Lennon. This was the song that helped me do it. When I was writing this song, I cried the whole day. This song was inspired by the love of John Lennon. *I watched it on the TV. I learned to cry again today. The newsman said how someone took their life away. What can I say now, all that love allows.* From *Sailover*.

'All The Things I Do For You Baby'
Sloan–Barri

This song, written almost entirely by me, was about Steve's relationship with his wife. He was having a very rough time at home. Interestingly, he left his wife and wound up with my girlfriend. *I leave the house every morning at eight, and I work plenty hard for the money I make, but you don't seem to appreciate all the things I do for you baby …*

'Alone On The Beach'
Sloan–Barri

Loneliness. With Brian Wilson and Jan Berry, it was always about two girls for every guy. I wasn't experiencing that. I wanted to write what I was feeling, but instead I wrote about walking on the beach with a fantasy girl. Jered Cargman, Steve Barri, and I sang this on the Fantastic Baggys' album in 1964.

'And The Boundaries In Between'
P.F. Sloan

My heart is warm with friends I make, better friends I'll not be knowing, but there isn't a plane I wouldn't take, no matter where it's going. The first lines are from Edna St. Vincent Millay's poem 'Travel.' It continues with my own thoughts: *Something is driving me to where I have no idea, just the boundaries in between.* I was under pressure to make a deadline, and I wasn't aware that I was drawing upon something that I had read that inspired me. Later, a fan let me know that the first four lines were lifted from the poem. That's the reason why many songwriters don't want to listen to other peoples' songs. George Harrison did not maliciously steal 'One Fine Day' for his 'My Sweet Lord.' He had been hearing that song for years and years, and it was ingrained in his consciousness. The guitar riffs of The Beatles' 'I Feel Fine' came from Bobby Parker's 'Watch Your Step.' I don't think Lennon and McCartney did that intentionally, but I believe if one doesn't own up to the either conscious or unconscious plagiarism, then your work is suspect.

'Another Day, Another Heartache'
Sloan–Barri

A country-style song with a Mamas & Papas vibe. The Fifth Dimension recorded it as the follow-up to John Phillips's 'Go Where You Want To Go.' Right from the beginning, the Fifth Dimension were able to crossover into pop radio. Arranged by Jimmy Webb for Johnny Rivers' Soul City Records, the song managed to reach the *Billboard* Top 30. It was the forerunner of all the great Webb hits for the group that would follow. Steve Barri contributed a couple of lines, and that's Hal Blaine counting off at the beginning of the song.

'Anywhere The Girls Are'
Sloan–Barri

Yeah. I had so much fun doing this! The Fantastic Baggys and a broken Gibson tube amp that produced a fuzz tone. I played all the guitars on the Fantastic Baggys songs—a 1963 Fender Jazzmaster. The opening riff, of course, is a takeoff of Barrett Strong's 'Money.'

'Autumn'
Sloan–Barri

I wanted to create a Vogues-style sound for Steve, as he loved The Vogues. I had some riffs that I wanted to fit into the tune as well. The song was introduced on *The Ed Sullivan Show*, as performed by The Thomas Group. It was ultimately recorded by The Vogues themselves, as well as by Gary Lewis & The Playboys.

'Baby I Can't Stop Myself'
Sloan–Barri

One of the few songs written at the piano during the early Screen Gems years. You wouldn't normally expect a seventeen-year-old to be writing this kind of mature music, but I had been soaking up the influence of hundreds and hundreds of records.

'Baby You Do It So Well'
Sloan–Barri

This cut seems to have been left off of the Grass Roots compilations, but it has kind of a Detroit feel to it that I dug. I put some congas and bongos in there, and Steve added his usual two lines.

'Beethoven's Delight'
P.F. Sloan

A primitive exploration of my love and obsession for Ludvig van Beethoven and his life, this song would become fully realized after thousands of hours of writing. *My Beethoven (Canto)* would emerge from the wreckage. From *Serenade Of The Seven Sisters*.

'Big Gun Board'
Sloan–Barri

Great inside-surf lyrics. Fun to do. I think our version (as The Fantastic Baggys) is good, because it is less produced and raw. My favorite sound is really un-produced, but with surprises of creativity. Steve and Jered were doing background vocals.

'Bitter Sweet'
Sloan–Barri

The Robbs were a group from Oconomowoc, Wisconsin, who wanted a P.F. Sloan song, so they came to Dunhill, picked this song, and Steve and I produced them. I experimented with musical form in this song, adding an a capella break in the middle. It was a nice hit for the band, but it didn't break all over the country at the same time. It hit the Top 10 in the Midwest in January, and by April it was hitting in New York—and then, three months later, in the South. Timing is everything.

'The Black Robed Spaniard'
P.F. Sloan

The opening song from *Louis! Louis!*, my musical (I call it a popera) co-written with Steve Feinberg. Beethoven shows up in Vienna as a twenty-two-year-old composer, dressed in a velvet jacket and pants, well-heeled boots, pointed sideburns and Spanish haircut, looking very much like a pop star of today. People referred to Beethoven as the Black Robed Spaniard—a derogatory dig. From *My Beethoven*.

'Blue Lipstick'
Phil Sloan

I was really young when I wrote this—fifteen, maybe—but I was already infatuated with the so-called Bohemian lifestyle. I was reading transcendental poetry and prose from Emerson, Thoreau, and Hawthorne. This song is about a girl who loses her boyfriend and decides to wear blue lipstick to tell the world how sad she is. Patrician Anne recorded it, and it was a No. 1 hit for her in Canada. It was thematically hip, I thought.

'Brothers In The Wind'
P.F. Sloan

This song was written from a visual idea. I saw the way the tall pine trees were bending together in the wind while looking out from a window in Seattle, and they seemed to be telling me that they were all brothers. From *Serenade Of The Seven Sisters*.

'Can I Get To Know You Better'
Sloan–Barri

This was originally written as a blues song, sung by Betty Everett in 1963. It was a slow-dance favorite in all of the Chicago clubs. Later, after I reworked it, it became a hit for The Turtles, as the follow-up to 'You Baby.'

'Can't We Go Somewhere'
Sloan–Barri

This was different, musically, to anything I had done up to that time, and certainly influenced by Leonard Bernstein's 'There's A Place'—familiar phrasing to Beethoven fans. It was a double-sided hit for Terry Black with 'Unless You Care' in November 1964.

'Champagne'
P.F. Sloan

I wrote this in a hotel for the Atco sessions at Sun Studios in Memphis. It's not a fully realized song from a songwriter who was driving break-neck speed toward the edge of a cliff.

'Child Of Our Times'
P.F. Sloan

This was written as a poem of hope; I added the music later. *Child of our times, product of our society, what will you grow up to reject, what will you grow up to protect? In your burnin', turnin' mind, you are your own worst enemy.* This was the A-side follow-up to 'Eve Of Destruction.' It made the charts but died quickly.

'City Women'
P.F. Sloan

A folk-blues story song. I listened to a lot of folk blues when I was fifteen or sixteen—Brownie McGhee, Josh White, Odetta, Doc Watson, Leadbelly. I turned the song into a folk-rock kind of thing, based on the idea of a guy who doesn't have any money, robs a store to make his girlfriend happy, kills a guy, gets caught, and then the girl skips town with the money and the guy is hung. John Phillips was a fan of this song, and we built 'Monday, Monday' from it.

'Cling To Me'
P.F. Sloan

Johnny Tillotson was one of my favorite teenage idols. He wrote 'Poetry In Motion' and 'Send Me The Pillow You Dream On.' He was a gentleman and a great songwriter, but his career had started to wane. He asked me for a song to record, but Dunhill didn't think Johnny was worth saving and told me not to respond. I sent him 'Cling To Me.' Johnny proved Adler wrong, and he turned 'Cling To Me' into a country hit for himself. He expressed his gratitude to me many times, and I got the chance to express mine to him. That was one of the big kicks—getting a song with someone you idolized.

'Como'
P.F. Sloan

I was living in the Malibu Colony, above Leslie Ann Warrens and Jon Peters' house. Her housekeeper was from Mexico, and I kept asking her how to say this or that in Spanish, and she would always respond with, 'Como?' From *Raised On Records*.

'Country Woman (Can You Dig It All Night?)'
P.F. Sloan

I was in love with a country-blues woman at the time, and this was written for her. The girl was Miki St. Clair, Mike Todd's stepdaughter. Duck Dunn was playing his electric bass, but I wanted stand-up bass. They had one in the studio—Sun Studios—and that bass had been on a lot of records. I wanted that fifties sound from Elvis's 'My Baby Left Me.' Maybe that accounts for the enthusiasm in the song and the wry laughter in the vocal. Perhaps I was trying to convince myself I was where I was supposed to be.

'Crazy As A Daisy (Times Three)'
P.F. Sloan

Written for a certain lady. Done in a Ray Charles/ Harry Connick Jr. kind of way. I'm playing the piano fairly well on the record. From *Serenade Of The Seven Sisters*.

'Cross The Night (Across The Night)'
P.F. Sloan

Kim Canoe and I drove over the county line into Ventura, where the lights of Los Angeles don't block out the stars. We were excited to see Haley's comet that night, but we were amazed that it wasn't moving. It looked more like a cotton swab standing still in the night sky. From *Sailover*.

'Day In The Country'
P.F. Sloan

Beethoven gets to escape the pollution in Vienna and marvels at how happy he feels, until he has an unexpected brush with his personal demons. From *My Beethoven*.

'Debbie Be True'
Sloan–Barri

This was written with Jan & Dean in mind, but they never recorded it. It was a natural for them, I thought. It has rich harmonies and a lot going on in it. The Baggys released it as a single.

'Do What You Did'
Sloan–Barri

This was by Willie & The Wheels—one of many groups invented by Adler to make money for his production company. This one was particularly ridiculous, as we sounded like we had just stepped off the set of *Pygmalion*. I was Willie.

'Don't Come Running To Me'
Sloan–Barri

The Iguanas recorded this—a Beatles-esque song written with them in mind. The Iguanas were a great Mexican band from Ensenada with a good deal of heart. This hit the charts in Mexico and Spain, not to mention East LA. Long live The Iguanas!

'Don't Start Me Talking About My Baby'
Sloan–Barri

This song was written around the time of Screen Gems and Carole King and The Cookies—one of those follow-up songs written to prove to Screen Gems that I was a real songwriter.

'Don't You Wonder Where It's At'
P.F. Sloan–B. McGuire

Barry McGuire recorded this great musical hippie manifesto. *Why can't we sit at one table, we're one family, the family of man. We could use more of how we are alike rather than how we are different songs.* But what do I know? I added a few lines, that's all. He insisted on giving me a writing credit.

'Dragon Lady'
Sloan–Barri–Alfeld–Bruce–Gorman

This was written with several of Steve's writer friends. He really wasn't happy about being teamed up with me and figured he'd better keep his options open. Don Altfeld, the writer on many of the Jan & Dean songs, worked on this song as well.

'Drums A-Go-Go'
*Sloan–Barri**

This was a small hit for Hal Blaine, one of the greatest drummers in rock history. The guitar work is in homage to The Kinks' 'All Day And All of The Night.' I was over at Reprise Records with Jimmy Bowen, the label's A&R man. Jimmy played me this demo by The Kinks and wanted to know my opinion, because Reprise was thinking about passing on them.

'That's a No. 1 record,' I assured him.

'You're out of your mind, Phil,' he replied.

That afternoon, I had a session with Hal Blaine to do an album so I just wrote the song on the spot, to signal that The Kinks were coming.

'Where that's riff from?' Hal asked.

'England,' I answered.

'I dig it,' Hal replied.

Dave Davies of The Kinks said he appreciated this gesture of welcoming in The Kinks. Since it was an instrumental, Steve didn't write anything for it, despite what the credits might suggest.

'Eve Of Destruction'
P.F. Sloan

Written as a prayer to God in the form of a poem, begging for clarity and understanding about the state of the world, teetering on the edge. I didn't want to live in this world where hatred and hypocrisy overruled love and beauty. The music came as an afterthought.

I loved and appreciated Tiny Tim's version of 'Eve.' People laughed at him but the man was an artist, and his eighteen-minute version was revolutionary. What he did was turn it into a piece of theater, and because of that he opened the door to new ways to express the song. Hot Tuna did an elongated 'Eve' ten years later, and it was received well at their concerts. I remember, after putting the pencil down on this song, the feeling that I had received 'something wonderful.' It's been called everything you can imagine and more. As have I. If you believe we are on the eve then we must find a way to prevent it. If you don't believe, then sit back and watch it being destroyed by greed and selfishness. Steve didn't have anything to do with this song, but he still gets a writing credit on many websites.

'Eve Of Destruction (The Environment)'
P.F. Sloan

Written spontaneously while on the phone with Clive Davis for The World Wildlife Fund. This was the second—unbeknownst to me at the time—of a trilogy of 'Eves.'

'Everyone Can Tell'
Sloan–Barri

I wanted to move Terry Black away from the Elvis comparisons that came from 'Unless You Care.' The natural place to move him into was a Canadian-British style. This song is all pretty little melody and strictly adolescent fun, like two straws in a Coca-Cola.

'From A Distance'
P.F. Sloan

A heartfelt exploration of my spirituality, and how difficult it can be to maintain faith when things seem to be going wrong in your life. The lyric again came first. Ricky Nelson was one of my favorite idols. I learned to get rid of a very thick New York accent by studying his manner of speech on the *Ozzie & Harriet* television show. On Ricky's *Album Seven* (the one where he has his hair parted in the center, and is wearing a green sweater) there was a song called 'From A Distance.' I thought that something was missing with the song, and that they had somehow missed the point, so I wrote a new song using the title, not expecting for anyone to ever hear it. The record bubbled under the Hot 100 but was a big hit in Japan in 1970 and elsewhere in England and Europe. It was a great thrill to meet Rick and Dave Nelson one night in the early 70s after a show with The Ventures at the famous Palomino Club in North Hollywood. It took all the strength I had not to imitate Ricky's speaking voice in front of him.

'Garbage City'
*Sloan–Barri**

The flipside of 'That's Cool, That's Trash.' A lot of people considered these two sides to be the beginning of punk rock, but it was really garage-punk. Somewhat different. It was a way to get away from over-produced Pablum. There was no money for a B-side when the demo was sold as a record, so I dropped chairs and broke things for the instrumental track.

'Goes To Show (Just How Wrong You Can Be)'
Sloan–Barri
My take on dreams of love a-fleeing. I had high hopes concerning my career and my love life. I was young, and I thought that everything good would last forever. Goes to show just how wrong you can be.

'Halloween Mary'
P.F. Sloan
This is a Picasso-style like song about a number of mystical women that I have known, all woven into one. These extraordinary women were my teachers and shamans. I learned so much about myself from them.

'Help Me Remember (To Remember)'
P.F. Sloan
Have you ever met someone for the first time but felt that you already know him or her somehow? This is a folk-style ballad about the reincarnation theory, and how I need to remember who I am, where I came from, and where I am going. From *Serenade of the Seven Sisters*.

'Here They Come From All Over The World'
Sloan–Barri
This is the theme for *The T.A.M.I. Show*, as sung by Jan & Dean. I was given a list of all the performers and asked to put it into a song. I believe it also was a competition with other writers working on the same project, but I knew when I came up with the title it would win. The song had so much energy! I did all of the background harmonies and falsettos on the recording, as well as the lead guitar. *The T.A.M.I. Show* is considered today to be one of the greatest filmed rock shows of all time, not to mention James Brown's greatest taped performance.

The only grief I received from this song was for saying the Rolling Stones were from Liverpool, rather than from London. But that's the way it was written on the performers' bio I was given, and it shows how early it was in their career, for that sort of mistake to have been made.

'He's My Man'
Sloan–Barri
Ann-Margret recorded this R&B number. I love the way she sings it. There's a woman who has so much soul. I worked with Ann on this record in the studio as writer-arranger-producer, as well as playing all of the guitars. Ann was sweet and humble, happy to take direction from a sixteen-year-old year kid.

'Phil, do you think I should be doing it this way?' she'd ask.

'Yes, Annie. Let's turn off the lights and enjoy the music.'

Of course, Lou Adler was in the booth, acting as executive producer, and he was actually in charge.

'Hey There Mary Mae'
Sloan–Barri
Don & The Goodtimes recorded this. For me, it was a follow-up to the 'Kick That Little Foot, Sally Ann' genre, and an homage to the great Harry Belafonte. It was a hit for The Goodtimes in a regional way, and a goodtime fun song to write.

'Hold On!'
Sloan–Barri
This was the title song for the Herman Hermit's movie. It was written on guitar at the same time as the lyrics. The song is jumping and great fun, and it represents a time and place that was full of optimism like 'She Loves You.'

'Hollywood Moon'
P.F. Sloan
I read they were experimenting with technology for realistically putting advertisements on the moon. If it's a full moon tonight, Toyota, say, would light up the moon with its name, all

around the world. Advertising madness is way out of control, as we all know. From *Sailover*.

'Horace The Swinging School Bus Driver'
Sloan–Barri-Altfeld

This is the first song I co-wrote that was recorded by Jan & Dean. It may have come about because Don Altfeld was Jan's best friend. Any time you wrote with Don, you might get it on a Jan & Dean record. Glen Campbell and I are on the guitars. Leon Russel on piano and Hal Blaine on drums—that's Hal shouting 'move that thing, lady!' at the end of the song.

'How Can I Be Sure'
P.F. Sloan

This one stands up for me still as a poem, not so much as a recording. The lines *You've got me flyin' way too high and I'm still afraid of falling.* Or how about *candy colored Christmas eyes that taste the sun like lemon Jell-O*? To be honest, I was on a candy-store binge of drugs, but I still like the meter and images of it. Recorded for the *Measure Of Pleasure* album in Memphis, 1968.

'How Many Guys'
Sloan–Barri

Terry Black, 1964–65. The idea that if you asked a girl how many guys they had had was absurd, but if you turned it around to 'who loves you as much as I do?' hey, you might have a song.

'I Can't Help But Wonder, Elizabeth'
P.F. Sloan

The Kinks' PR manager, Ray, flew over to meet me with a lady named Elizabeth. She had skin like a porcelain doll and long thin brown hair with sad brown eyes. I fell in love with her. It broke my heart when it didn't work. A young Bernie Taupin, whom I met at a party with Ray and Elizabeth, seemed to fall for her as well. I wrote the string arrangements with a friend, which was a first. I called in all of the favors

with the Wrecking Crew, who did it without pay because it was an unsanctioned session. 'Karma' was recorded that day, too, but Dunhill refused to release it. Steve Barri wound up doing it with the Grass Roots. It was the last thing I ever recorded at Dunhill.

'I Don't Want To Say Goodnight'
Sloan–Barri

A nice upbeat, good-times song in the Cookies (Dimension Records/Screen Gems/Goffin-King) genre. This was a song for hire, with lyrics mostly by Steve, and was recorded by Gary Lewis & The Playboys, with the great Snuff Garrett producing.

'I Found A Girl'
Sloan–Barri*

I wrote this in the throes of love with the young, pretty receptionist at Dunhill. We had been dating, and everyone thought it was only a matter of time, but she wanted security more than anything else, and my sudden emergence as a star came as a threat to her. Steve then started going out with her while I toured England. Eventually they would marry. So the song could have been called 'I Lost A Girl,' later on. It was written as a poem, and the simple rhyme pattern—*coincidentally, just happens to be, in love with me*—caught John Phillips's attention. He was so impressed by the use of the word 'coincidentally' that he began writing using three-syllable words. It really broke the syllable ceiling wide open, and there was no turning back.

'I Get Out Of Breath'
P.F. Sloan

An interesting remark came from Harlan Ellison, the renowned science fiction writer. In a magazine interview, he was asked how is it possible that a twenty-year-old writer could believe that a third of his life is shot, referring to a line in one of his stories. The line *our morals have decayed, and this I cant abide* makes me think this song has an Irish spirit to it. The beauty of my Gibson ES-175 had a rich mellow sound that, for me, made the recording of the song more personal and warm. I used it on most all the songs on the *Songs Of Our Times* album.

'I Know You'll Be There'
Sloan–Barri
Another song for hire, recorded by Shelley Fabares and The Turtles. Shelley was America's sweetheart—a true beauty, inside and out. There was nothing phony in her, or about her. She lit up the room. And she was a big star. She was on *The Donna Reed Show* and in many of the Elvis Presley movies. 'Johnny Angel' was her big hit. And every song commissioned by Lou Adler was an attempt to get her back on the charts. The Turtles later chose this song as a cut on their *It Ain't Me Babe* album.

'I Love You When You're Mad'
Sloan–Barri
Another song written for Steve Barri's first wife. Enough said.

'I Wonder Who The Lucky Guy Will Be'
Sloan–Barri*
This was written when I was aware that Steve was falling in love with my then girlfriend. I mused in front of him, *I wonder who the lucky guy will be ... I wonder who will take the place of me.* Freddy & The Dreamers asked Dick James Publishing for an original P.F. Sloan song to record. They wanted to get away from being a cute novelty act and get more into straight performing. The song did well for them in England and across Europe.

'I'd Have To Be Out Of My Mind'
P.F. Sloan
For me, this was Woody Guthrie-like humor. A very early P.F. Sloan song. *You can tell your lies to the next guy waiting in line, if I stayed with you, I'd have to be out of my mind. The way I let you*

hurt me, it was just a crying shame, I don't know how I fell for you, I must have been insane ... but I don't need glasses to show me where I've been blind ... Hey Hey! I can actually be heard chuckling on the recording. I recorded it for the *Songs Of Our Times* album, and it was also done by Barry McGuire.

'If You Believe In Me'
Phil Sloan
I was fifteen. Joe Lubin, who did so many songs for the Doris Day movies, produced this for A-side for Arwin Records. I was trying to sing like Ricky Nelson, whose TV show I watched religiously. Sandy Nelson was on drums, with Steve Douglas on sax. Bill Pittman was on Dano electric bass. I did my first electric guitar overdub on this date. I thought that maybe made me a musician.

'If You Knew'
P.F. Sloan–S. Kalinich
Steve Kalinich had written a book of poetry with this title and asked me to write a song from it. The problem was it was sixty pages of continuous two-liners, and there were no rhymes. But I figured out how to do it, and this little gem was made. The president of Warner Bros Records, who was distributing the *Sailover* album, told me that it was one of his 100 favorite songs ever recorded when I performed for the Warners Distributers Convention in Kissimmee, Florida.

'In Celebration Of P.F. Sloan'
K. Reid
I met Keith Reid—the brilliant writer of all the Procol Harem hits, and a wonderful poet—in London on the *Sailover* album tour. I told him I was working on an under-the-radar project called *Louis! Louis!* and he handed me a page of poem-lyrics, which I was able to use and intertwine for this beautiful song. From *My Beethoven*.

'Is It Any Wonder'
Sloan–Barri
*You see things in me that nobody else can see
... or had looked quite deep enough to find ...
you passed over all my faults and you came
through it all ... when no one else would have
taken the time.* Steve Barri added a bridge to
this song when he cut it with The Grass Roots,
but I never approved of it or thought it fit. A
chart record for The Turtles.

'It's The Thought That Counts'
Sloan–Barri
This was an early Screen Gems tune—a nicely
crafted and well thought out piano song.
It was recorded by the female duo Jackie &
Gayle, who were making local hits in LA, and
also by The Honeys.

'It's Too Late Baby'
P.F. Sloan
This song has a cocky point of view, and I liked
it. You listen to it once and you go, *man, there's
something to it, I want to hear it again.* It might
have been sardonic but it felt good.

'I've Got Better Things To Do'
Sloan–Barri*
A sweet song with a very moody, bluesy feel to
it, written when I was seventeen and recorded
by Sandy & The Accents. I took the train to
San Diego, met the group, and produced the
song that became a record. San Diego was
way, way out of the loop of the Los Angeles
pop scene, and Adler really wasn't interested
in them, but I was. Buddy came from Lubbock,
after all. And they had a really cool sax player. It
turned out there were some future members of
the Wondermints—Brian Wilson's backup and
recording band—there.

'I've Got Faith In Him'
Sloan–Barri
Steve and I would drive into Watts, the West
Coast Harlem of sorts, and knock on people's
doors, saying, 'We're looking for someone who
wants to make a record.' Can you imagine?
We found someone who wanted to make a
record, and the label signed her to a contract.
They gave her the name Dandy Dawson. She
didn't get anything for all her hard work and
trouble, and after they were through with her
she just disappeared. I used to often think of
what became of her, and whether I did her more
harm than good.

'I've Got No More To Say'
Sloan–Barri*
A Lennon-esque song. What can I tell you? I was
getting worn out from the constant work, and this
song said it for me in some way. Tony Thomas
and his group recorded it. Tony became one the
most successful television producers in America
with Thomas-Witt Productions, and came to my
rescue when I was down and almost out.

'Jilly's Flip Side'
Sloan–Barri*
Jilly was Jan Berry's girlfriend, Jill Gibson, who
replaced Michelle Phillips in The Mamas & The
Papas as punishment to Michelle for not going
along with John and Lou's program. Today,
she's a famous sculptor and painter living in the
Southwest. An instrumental throwaway.

'The Joke's On Me'
Jerry Riopelle–Phil Sloan
This was the follow-up song to Terry Stafford's
big hit 'Suspicion.' Terry Stafford was a Ral
Donner/Conway Twitty/Elvis kind of singer that
I loved. Jerry Riopelle had a connection with
Stafford, and me being a big Elvis fan, he asked
me to co-write it with him. Steve Barri was
writing with his friends at the time.

'Joy Of The Ninth'
P.F. Sloan
A song that comes to grips with Beethoven's

feelings about his abusive father—and, coincidentally, my abusive mother. From *My Beethoven*.

'Karma (A Study of Divinations)'
P.F. Sloan

This one was considered unpublishable. What else was new? It was memorable for me because I was able to get a master Japanese kyoto player on the recording, and nobody had done that before, to my knowledge. I used a couple of lines from the Old Testament, from King Solomon: 'There is nothing new, just what you've forgotten.' That seems to make the point that there is nothing new under the sun. The singing was somewhat influenced in part by Donovan—it crept in unconsciously.

It was a time when kids stopped dancing and just started to tune in. It was the time when you went out and bought a good pair of headphones and became transported, and you could repeat that experience over and over again—you always got more than what you expected. You always heard the little things that were buried in the mix—things that nobody else heard. That was the joy of music then. Out of your ordinary daily mind and consciousness, into the mind of a composer and artist. And you had to trust that composer and artist, if they are to take you on a journey, hopefully into a higher state of awareness. *The Buddha was knowledge, and the Christ was beloved, and it sounded to be holy, so I kept my ears uncovered.*

'Kick That Little Foot, Sally Ann'
*Sloan–Barri**

I wrote this song when I was sixteen. I had Harry Belafonte in mind, but I never got it to him. There is something happy and gospel-like about this song. It probably came from Freddy taking me to her church in Watts when I was fourteen or so. Round Robin may not have been as good a singer as Chubby Checker was, but he caught your full attention.

'Where did you come up with the name "Round"?' I asked my pals at Domain.

'Chubby is taken and Fats is taken. So we called him Round.'

This song was the first of many Slauson dance records.

'Kisses For My Baby'
Sloan–Barri

A smooth teenage song, recorded by Terry Black for his *Black Plague* album.

'Let Me Be'
P.F. Sloan

It was what I was feeling, and what everyone else in my generation was thinking: let me be to be like I want to. 'Another dangerous song by P.F. Sloan!' the press decried. Good for human rights, though. The Turtles, Barry McGuire, and also Dino Desi & Billy all recorded it. There was definitely an edge to Dino Desi & Billy—they were living the life of privilege but still felt like outsiders.

'Let's Make The Most Of Summer'
Sloan–Barri

Steve's other favorite group was The Lettermen, so I wrote this it in that style, and we recorded it as The Fantastic Baggys. From *Tell 'Em I'm Surfin'* by The Grass Roots.

'Limitless'
P.F. Sloan

Recorded by Garnett Mimms—the celebrated soul singer who did 'Cry Baby'—in 2009, and written about our potential, and how love is limitless. I wrote some of the lyric with a Philadelphia rapper who was working as a plumber's apprentice at my house but he asked me not to give him a credit. He was known as Brother Nelson. He had heard me working on some chords in my cottage and began a stream-of-consciousness rap. When I caught hold of some of the phrases—like *I rest my case in your sweet embrace*—I wanted to write them down, but he didn't think anything of it. Garnett, then a Pastor in St. Louis, heard the song and recorded it with a 100-voice choir from his church. He told me that he loved my phrasing so much that he wanted to do it as I envisioned it.

'Little Girl In The Cabin'
Flip Sloan

That's me trying to imitate Elvis at thirteen years old. This was recorded at RCA Studios in Los Angeles for Aladdin Records; Bumps Blackwell produced it. I have thought about it for years, and I have no memory of any girl in a cabin! I didn't know where that came from. It's a mystery to me.

'Little Liar'
Sloan–Barri

This was a No. 1 record in Canada for Terry Black. A throwback to the early sounds of Dion & The Belmonts' 'Runaround Sue.'

'Lollipop Train (You Never Had It So Good)'
P.F. Sloan

Another song to Steve's wife at the time, with a few of my own problems thrown in for good measure. The Grass Roots, P.F. Sloan, Barry McGuire, and The Elementary School Band all recorded this song. It was also very popular in Sweden, where it was recorded by Firebeats, Inc., Thorstein Bergman, and Harri Haka.

'Look Out Girl'
Sloan–Barri*

I dug this song a lot because it had a Buddy Holly feel to it. Buddy was a big favorite of mine and obviously a phenomenal singer-songwriter, because he wrote about what was happening in his life. There was very little fiction. I wanted to do that! I wanted to get away from nice little songs, or songs for hire with which I had very little personal or meaningful connection. Interestingly, aside from The Grass Roots, this song was recorded by the singer-songwriter Tommy Roe,

who started out doing Buddy Holly material.

'Love Go Easy'
P.F. Sloan

A semi-realized, breezy jazzy cut. It sounded better in my head. But the opening line—*Say you've suffered enough*—said a lot to me. From *Serenade Of The Seven Sisters*.

'Love Is 4 Giving'
P.F. Sloan–Jon Tiven

Written initially after the LA riots and updated when 'driving while black' was the outrage of the day. *Judgment day is still coming my friend*. Jon Tiven plays a soulful guitar solo. This was the song I made up on the spot for Clive Davis at the Beverly Hills Hotel, and it later became 'Don't Make A Beggar Out Of Me.' A good riff never goes to waste. From *Sailover*.

'The Man Behind The Red Balloon'
P.F. Sloan

I couldn't tell anyone the truth of how I was feeling, so I hid it in metaphors in this song. Steve Barri and his little black case; Lou Adler walking up the street, looking great; me in a batman cape, pretending to be a spy; and Barry McGuire slipping into a manhole. It became a hit for Noel Harrison in Europe. My version was also a minor hit in many Spanish-speaking countries around the globe.

'Meet Me Tonight Little Girl'
Sloan–Barri

Steve and I were sold again as an English duo, Phillip & Stephen, and there's a very early Beatles influence to the song. It was also recorded by The Iguanas, who did a splendid job.

'Michele's Melody'
Sloan–Barri*

Just another Trousdale publishing song, this one being an instrumental, as recorded by Sheridan Hollenbeck. Who was Sheridan Hollenbeck?

'Midnight At Pink's'
Sloan–Barri*
Every city has its favorite hotdog place. We all used to eat at Pink's on La Brea and Melrose after sessions, so I gave a shout out to them on this instrumental number. Hal Blaine recorded this song for his *Drums! Drums! A Go-Go*.

'Midnight Girl'
P.F. Sloan
I was romancing a young journalist from Oklahoma. She was busy all day, and I could only see her occasionally at night. I was hoping she could keep me stitched together like the leather coat she wore. From *Raised On Records*.

'Miss Charlotte'
P.F. Sloan
This was initially an experimental demo, featuring changes in tempo and new-weird guitar sounds that I had never done before. It was about working on a song farm and needing to escape, and was recorded by The Epics. Later I rewrote it as a blues song for the Atco album, influenced by 'Baby Let Me Follow You Down.' I tried to do it like Sir Percy Sledge.

'Mr. Man On the Street—Act One'
P.F. Sloan
After hearing this for the first time, Barry McGuire said to me, 'What the fuck is this?' He told me he had worked for a while as an elevator operator and had taken a nasty fall. So I turned into a six-minute fun and fantasy song. 'Act Two' was not to follow.

'The Moon Is Stone'
P.F. Sloan
This is experimental, for me, and oh so melancholy. I was reaching out for someone, but again no one is there for me. I was living at home again. I was twenty-four and basically had been stripped of everything I loved. I had been through so much already. I got a small

ukulele and wrote this song for the *Raised on Records* album.

Everybody loves a dreamer, a schemer, a football player, a ballerina, but what I am is what you'll see me to be … I felt destroyed when I wrote this song. Dylan Thomas once wrote that there are 'writers who *want* to write and writers who *need* to write.' Perhaps I was the latter.

'My Beethoven (Canto)'
P.F. Sloan
Beethoven realizes that he is doing God a favor if he commits suicide and his reasons are logical and natural. Taken from his letter of intent to commit suicide, written to his brother. From the unrealized early song 'Beethoven's Delight' on the *Seven Sisters* album came this highly evolved lyric, music, and orchestral arrangement, which took thousands of hours. It became known to my friends as 'Philip's Folly,' as there were hundreds of revisions. But this song was the lynchpin to all the rest of the songs that and to the eventual and natural evolution of the writing of the musical. From *My Beethoven*.

'My First Day Alone'
Sloan–Barri
This was an early Screen Gems Music song. I was working in a piano room every day after school. I was asked to write something for Steve Alaimo, a big star on ABC Records and a regular on Dick Clark's TV show *Where The Action Is*.

When Peter & Gordon recorded it, I felt a great sense of appreciation. These guys only do the best songs, and they were saying this early song was really good. I recently ran into Peter at a party, and we reminisced a bit about Gordon and his recording of the song.

'Myths Unbuttoned'
P.F. Sloan
Beethoven's latest effort is panned in the *Vienna Times*, so he takes out a full-page ad in

response to his critics. True story! And it shows his great sense of humor. From *My Beethoven*.

'New Design'
P.F. Sloan
I didn't realize how good a song it was until Kenny Rogers recorded it. I've been singing it that way ever since. Steve Cropper did a really nice arrangement, though, for my Atco album. The first verse is written to the girlfriend of a soldier who is going overseas. My sentiment was that I hoped she didn't have to find another.

When I was asked about my feelings on the Vietnam War, the line that I used to express it was, *some say these things will never change others say its getting better and that there will always be war*. I was against the war that caused the loss of friends mainly because it wasn't righteous. I'm not a pacifist. I believe there is such a thing as a righteous war. I just haven't seen one. From *Measure Of Pleasure*.

'The Night The Train Broke Down'
P.F. Sloan
I was the train, and the song breaks down as well in spots. I wanted to do my best under hard circumstances. From *Raised On Records*.

'Oh Loving Lord (Of All The Worlds)'
P.F. Sloan
A spiritual song I wrote after one of my many visits to see Sathya Sai Baba in India. It was performed for Sai Baba in India in 2001 by a large choral group to an audience of 25,000 people, and was also recorded with my vocal for an album of spiritual songs, becoming a favorite at many spiritual centers around the world.

'On A Quiet Night'
P.F. Sloan
The Association recorded this sultry and introspective song, which Bones Howe produced. I had worked with Bones when he was a second engineer on all of the Jan & Dean albums I sang

on. He became a star producer in his own right, recording The Turtles, The Association, The Fifth Dimension, and so many more. The Association would also record Jimmy Webb's 'P.F. Sloan' as a single. During the Songwriter's Association Awards show, where I was slated to perform, I had the dressing room next to The Association's. When I spoke to Jerry Yester and the others, and introduced myself as P.F. Sloan—the subject of the song they were about to perform—they were flabbergasted at my actual existence. They thought I was just a made up person. Well, that's what they told me!

'On Top Of A Fence'
P.F. Sloan
This is an important song for me. Deeply introspective. I was alone and trying to get my bearings. I couldn't conform to the nonconformists, or, likewise, to the conformists. Where is the middle ground? There isn't any. You had to choose which side you were going to be on, and I was on the fence. Then I realized: *why should I jump when I can't see the ground?* I would find out much later the answer was not to jump but to fly. It isn't easy to find yourself, but it's worth the effort.

'One Of A Kind'
P.F. Sloan
This song is downright Southern bluesy. Steve Cropper and Duck Dunn played on it at the *Measure Of Pleasure* sessions in 1968, with Tom Dowd producing. It was written for Miki St. Clair—she was one of a kind.

'One-Piece Topless Bathing Suit'
Sloan–Barri–Altfeld
You've got to come see … there's a chick wearing a one-piece topless bathing suit. Originally, the punch line was that she was six-years-old and supposed to be cute but Jan & Dean turned it into a little old lady in a bathing suit. And the reaction was *oh no!* This was a

Screen Gems song written for Jan Berry, but Bruce Johnston and Terry Melcher recorded it and had a chart record with it.

'Only When You're Lonely'
Sloan–Barri
Kay Starr was like the male Frankie Laine. They belonged to a generation of singers in the 50s who belted it out, club style. My parents were fans of hers, so having a recording of her doing my song almost meant I'd made it in their eyes. Almost. The original Bill Fulton Group left due to mistreatment by the label, and so again I became the lead singer of The Grass Roots on this cut. It hit the national charts and died a natural death.

'Ordinary Girl'
Sloan–Barri
A No. 1 record for Terry Black, this song had a sweet melody, with lyrics written mostly by Steve Barri, and was heavily influenced by The Everly Brothers.

'Out Of Touch'
Sloan–Barri
My take on Leiber & Stoller's 'Little Egypt': *She looks so good on the outside, but inside she's out somewhere.* This is the song that Creed Bratton of The Grass Roots first played lead guitar on, which almost got me fired from Dunhill … again.

'Patterns (Segment Four)'
P.F. Sloan
This song still gives me a laugh. *Two old ladies sitting in the sand, each one wishing the other was a man.* Very highbrow. *They're throwing a rock and roll party at a nudist camp. I saw Paul Revere drive up as an electric amp. Everybody famous is gonna to be there. I wonder what Sonny & Cher are going to wear? More hair! … I bought the greatest watch last week. It does everything but eat and sleep. It's dustproof, it's waterproof, it's guaranteed, it cannot be destroyed. It was stolen.* I thought it was like Woody Guthrie, homespun humor, and I loved it!

'Paula's Percussion'
Sloan–Barri
A discarded instrumental for a discarded musician's wife.

'Pied Piper Man'
Sloan–Barri
This was a song for hire for Lloyd Thaxton, who was signed to Domain Records after the success of 'Kick That Little Foot, Sally Ann.' He was a famous DJ, and he was funny, like a Soupy Sales slapstick comedian who loved pop music. He was our West Coast Dick Clark. Lloyd was authentically hip, and it was an honor to have him record one of my songs.

'P.K. & The Evil Dr. Z'
P.F. Sloan
Rabbis with purple hair, time travelers, midnight baseball with 300lb Samoans in Hawaii … what more do you want? The truth is, I never wanted to even talk about this experience, I just wanted to bury it in my memory and then forget it, but then P.F. Sloan wrote the lyric in twenty-five minutes, all in perfect synch and rhyme. I had to give in and played it for my friend and producer, Jon Tiven, who laughed aloud upon hearing it and suggested we include it on *Sailover*.

'Please Don't Go Now'
Sloan–Barri
A well-produced record with Yvonne Carol, lost in time it seems. But it was a good song, written in the Screen Gems apprenticeship days. It runs through my mind every now and then. The lyric was mainly by Steve.

'Pretty Please'
Sloan–Barri
A Supremes-style song for hire—and another attempt by Lou Adler to get a hit for his sweet, beautiful wife, Shelley Fabares.

'Raised On Records'
P.F. Sloan

I needed to explain why I am the way I am and what I am doing here. *I was raised on records, rock'n'roll radio, and if it wasn't for the music I might have said goodbye a long time ago.* I thanked my father for buying me a guitar when I was thirteen. I tried to explain that even though I was destroyed, I was still looking for the truth in my heart and mind. James Burton, Jim Horn, Hal Blaine, Ry Cooder. Larry Knechtel, and Joe Osborne are all on this record. At the same time the album was released, Elvis released *Raised On Rock* and Joni Mitchell *Raised On Robbery*. It's hard to hold onto what seems like an original idea when the universe wants to share it with others.

'Sailover'
P.F. Sloan–Jon Tiven

I was asking a lady friend to drop by and see me. 'Just sail over,' I said. But then I realized it's also Secret Agent talk: 'Sai' is the name of my Guru, and combined with 'lover,' voila, you get 'Sailover'! It must have been the secret decoder ring I got in a box of crackerjacks that made me this way.

'Save Your Sundays (For Surfin')'
Sloan–Barri

A rediscovered gem of Baggy music found in the vaults of Imperial records, and released with pleasure by Bob Irwin of Sundazed Records. I play drums and guitar on the recording.

'Say It Again'
Sloan–Barri

Tollie Records was just starting out, and Terry Black was the label's first major artist. A few months later, it would put out several early Beatles releases as well. It was one hit after another for Terry and The Beatles. This was a No. 1 record for Terry in Canada. His signature was an electric twelve-string, as used by Glen Campbell on the 'Unless You Care' session, and I used it

through all his recordings, generally playing it myself, as Glen was becoming a hit artist.

'Secret Agent' and 'Secret Agent Man'
Sloan–Barri*

There was a worldwide contest to write the US theme tune for the hit British TV show *Danger Man*. The lead character, Drake (played by Patrick McGoohan), was a thinking man's James Bond, and the show was more psychological thriller than action adventure. Steve and I worked on the one verse of lyrics needed for 'Danger Man' together, but when the show's title was changed to *Secret Agent*, I rewrote the lyrics on my own. I was a fan of the Bond movies, and that feeling inspired the opening guitar riff.

I made an instrumental demo of the song, which The Ventures—who were awe-inspiring guitarists to me, on a par with James Burton, Duane Eddy, and Link Wray—recorded as 'Secret Agent Man.' It became their fastest-selling record ever. I then made another demo with a verse and chorus worth of lyrics, which Johnny Rivers recorded for the TV show. When Johnny was finally convinced to record the song as a single—probably because of the success The Ventures were having—he released it under the title 'Secret Agent,' which I personally prefer.

'See Ya 'Round On The Rebound'
P.F. Sloan

This was a new-style folk song, about me, a guy who had been smacked around a bit too much by love lately. Sandy Posey did a sincere job with her version of the song. Shelley Fabares—who was attempting to break into the folk-rock scene with the blessing of her husband Lou Adler, who produced all of her records—cut a version, too, but Sandy beat her to the charts.

'The Sh-Down Down Song (You Better Leave Him Alone)'
Sloan–Barri

This was Steve Barri's lyric. The connection was

to Betty Everett's 'The Shoop Shoop Song.' It was recorded on Dunhill by Dandee Dawson—a made-up name for an African American singer who got very little support from the label after the record came out and didn't do well.

'She's My Girl'
Phil Sloan
I loved Richie Valens, and this song was patterned on his style. It was released by Mart Records—that was the second record company contract I secured. I was barely fifteen, but I had no fear of rejection. Steve Douglas played sax on the record, which got a 'pick hit' in *Cashbox* and *Billboard*. And I went back to class the next day.

'The Sins Of A Family (Fall On The Daughter)'
P.F. Sloan
The words to this song were written on the same night as 'Eve Of Destruction.' I wrote the melody later. This is a song about my very young first cousin Barbara who sometime resorted to giving sexual favors to men to get money for her schoolbooks. She was was both angry and pleased with me about it. Issac Asimov referred to the sins of a family in one of his stories: Martians are coming to Earth to study the culture of the planet, and Asimov says you'll need to listen to the sins of a family to learn what you need to know about earth. Strange! Murray The K—the No. 1 disc jockey in New York, and the man known as the 'Fifth Beatle'—recorded the song himself as his only single and played it constantly on his show.

'Skateboard Craze'
Sloan–Barri
Another one by Willie & The Wheels—that's Steve and me being sold as a group again.

'Slauson Town'
Sloan–Barri
Round Robin was from Slauson Avenue, the primarily black LA neighborhood where the Slauson dance craze began. This was the natural follow-up to 'Kick That Little Foot, Sally Ann.'

'Somebody's Watching You'
P.F. Sloan
This one features Jim Horn on flute and Sid Sharp on violin. It's very melancholy, baby, as I was burning out fast. From *Raised On Records*.

'Someday Soon'
Sloan–Barri
A typical writing session with Steve would involve me writing the music to a few lines that we would come up with together, but because Steve was working two jobs, I would finish many of them myself. Ann-Margret recorded this song first, and later Betty Everett.

'Soul Of A Woman'
P.F. Sloan–S. Kalinich
Another song written with Steve Kalinich, the LA-based songwriter and poet originally from Binghamton, New York. Steve wrote 'Little Bird' and 'Be Still' with Dennis and Brian Wilson. I met him at a party thrown by Marilyn, Brian's ex-wife, whom I had known since the early days. He told me that in 1965, he had gone to Dunhill Records wanting to write with me, but was not allowed to meet me. He signed with The Beach Boys instead. Years later, we connected, and we wrote a few songs together for *Sailover*.

'Spiritual Eyes'
P.F. Sloan
I was happy to be P.F. Sloan again after writing this. It was a looking-back-at-what-it-must-have-been-like-for-my-parents-to   raise-this-child-up kind of song.

'Springtime'
P.F. Sloan
Oh I once knew a girl, her name it was Springtime. I told her that I loved her; she said she loved me too. She said I'd built a wall all

around my heart, without ever knowing I had built a wall at all! I was burned out by the events in my life circa 1972, and then this gem is given to me. From *Raised On Records*.

'Star Gazin''
PF. Sloan
Remembrances of Golden Gate Park in San Francisco, back when psychedelic days were fun. From *Measure Of Pleasure*.

'Still On The Eve (Of Destruction)'
PF. Sloan
The last part of the 'Eve' trilogy of. The first two verses, after I re-listened to it today, didn't draw me in, but the last two verses are filled with passion and energy and truth. So I give it a thumbs up. It's not as great as the original, obviously, but I can't dismiss it completely. From *Serenade Of The Seven Sisters*.

'Summer Means Fun'
Sloan–Barri
Jan Berry was not into recording my songs. There was more money in doing his own. But then Terry Melcher made a hit out of it, and Jan cut his version. The original version by The Fantastic Baggys is still the best, in my opinion. I talked Steve Barri into doing the lead vocal, New York accent and all. Bruce & Terry, Jan & Dean, The Legendary Masked Surfers (Mike Love and Dean Torrance)—they all loved and recorded this song.

'Sunflower, Sunflower'
PF. Sloan
This was a song I hoped would help me find my life mate. I was thinking I might not need to travel too far to find her, and that she would find me and was somewhere nearby.

'Surfer Boy's Dream Come True'
Sloan–Barri
The first time I heard a falsetto was on Elvis Presley's first album for RCA—the one where he sings 'Blue Moon.' My teenage sister's girlfriends heard him doing that and thought it was weird. 'Why is he singing like a girl?' they asked. They didn't know the rich country tradition of yodeling. But then along came Lou Christie, The Skyliners, Franki Valli, Brian Wilson, Dean Torrance—and don't forget Slim Whitman.

'Surfin' Craze'
Sloan–Barri
James Darren, the teen idol, sang this song on *The Flintstones* as James Darrock. They said it was one of the highest-rated episodes of the show ever. Cool for school, man. From *Tell 'Em I'm Surfin'* by The Grass Roots.

'Surfin's Back Again'
Sloan–Barri
Surfing, as a popular culture, was dying at the time. Surf songs turned into car songs. I was saying that surfing was back because many of the kids in my school are starting to wear Pendelton clothes again. Teenage fun.

'The Swim'
Sloan–Barri
A simple song for hire. Lou Adler sold Barri and me as The Wildcats for this record. Bobby Freeman wrote and recorded a song called 'Lets Do The Swim' that started a national dance craze, and Lou hoped his new production company could cash in on it. Bobby also wrote two of my personal favorites, 'Betty Lou's Got A New Pair Of Shoes' and 'Do You Wanna Dance.'

'Swim Time U.S.A.'
Sloan–Barri
Same story as above. On this record, Steve and I were The Life Guards. The recording was arranged by Jack Nitzsche.

'Take Me For What I'm Worth'
PF. Sloan
A very early P.F. Sloan song. I was trying to

describe the turmoil I was experiencing, and how difficult I knew it was going to be for many to understand me. *Don't try to understand me you, never could do that ... And in the end you'll wind up being hurt ... I'm a man with too many problems that keep pounding on my brain, so if you want me you'll take me for what I'm worth.* The Searchers had dropped off the charts for two years. This song would put them back on the charts. I loved their version. It had a fabulous opening guitar riff.

'Tell 'Em I'm Surfin''
Sloan–Barri
I was given a recording studio in which to work and a contract with Imperial to write and sing surf songs. This is raw, energetic, teenage energy. I loved it. *And if that pretty little girl from across the street, who's been bothering me for days, asks me to go swimmin' in her pool, well, her pool's real cool, but it hasn't got ten-foot waves.* Yes, there really was a pretty girl across the street with a cool pool.

'That's Cool, That's Trash'
*Sloan–Barri**
For me, in 1963, this was a beginning of garage-punk. My uncle would often call me a punk. 'You're a punk and you'll always be a punk, Phil,' he'd say. Why not own it and turn it into a badge of honor, I thought. So the punk in me is singing this song. *Hey, there's gonna be great big party at my house ... Na na na na na. That's Cool. But I'm charging two dollars to get into my house ... Na na na na na. That's Trash.* This was recorded by The Kingsmen on their hit album *Louie, Louie*. Adler also sold the demo to a label on the East Coast as a recording by The Street Cleaners.

'Then It Begins'
Sloan–Barri
This was sort of a Billy Joe Royal, down in the boondocks, *Where The Action Is* kind of song. The pop side of my personality, readymade for

a teenage group with a world-famous father—The Thomas Group.

'There He Goes'
Sloan–Barri–Bruce
Steve's best friend Harvey sat in on the writing session, and Steve demanded he get credit. Harvey was a good guy, so why not? This is an R&B type song, sung by Yvonne Carol and produced beautifully.

'There's Something About You'
Sloan–Barri
Another hit for Terry Black in Canada, and another Beatles-esque tune. The label, Tollie, put my demo version on Terry's album by mistake.

'(These Are) Bad Times'
Sloan–Barri
An early take on The Rolling Stones' blues side, cut in early 1963 and done nicely by Mark Lindsey of Paul Revere & The Raiders, with Terry Melcher producing them. Bill Fulton and The Grass Roots did it as well.

'Things I Should Have Said'
Sloan–Barri
The hit follow-up to 'Where Were You When I Needed You.' Good production. Good harmonies. As far as the pop side of my personality was concerned, this was exciting.

'This Is What I Was Made For'
*Sloan–Barri**
People enjoyed playing this at weddings for a lot of years, which gave me great joy. For me, there's an Irish lilt at work here, and I love it. From *Songs Of Our Times*.

'This Little Woody'
Sloan–Barri
An ode to a car that carried a surfboard to the beach. Steve added a lot to this song. I liked the way I used minor chords in it. I loved the

ocean, and I did a lot of bodysurfing but not much board-surfing. Dennis Wilson and Terry Melcher surfed. But the dirty, little secret of surf music is that a lot of the ideas for lyrics came from surf magazines. I got cool little nuggets of inside terminology from them. The Rip Chords and The Fantastic Baggys recorded this song.

'This Love'
P.F. Sloan
A song about Beethoven's true love, written in his own words. From *My Beethoven*.

'This Mornin''
P.F. Sloan
Written on the same night as 'Eve'—the fourth song that evening. It has, for me, a beautifully rich, Irish-poetic spirit. *This Morning I am no more* … I was declaring that 'I' was dead. Phil Sloan died the night P.F. Sloan was born. I was realizing I was going to take on this life, and I didn't know if I could bear or bare the insights of this new awareness, but I believed it would be worth it.

'This Precious Time'
P.F. Sloan
A realization that time is too precious to waste on a relationship that has lost its heart. Terry Knight and The Pack (the precursor to Grand Funk) did this song, as did Paul Anka, The Grass Roots, and Barry McGuire. It was one of Barry McGuire's last chart singles for Dunhill.

'Tip Of My Tongue'
Sloan–Barri
A tip of the hat to Mick Jagger and the Stones. The arrangement is Stones-ish, but my vocal is surprisingly Paul McCartney-ish. We were once again without an actual Grass Roots group, so I filled in the gap as lead singer.

'Turn On The Light'
P.F. Sloan
Man, did I love Eddie Cochran! What songs, and what a guitar sound! 'Turn On The Light' was an ode to his song 'Nervous Breakdown,' which I sang at Santa Monica Civic Center while having a nervous breakdown. From *Raised On Records*.

'Unless You Care'
*Sloan–Barri**
For me, this song was special. I wrote it when I was sixteen, for Elvis. It's very simple, but that in itself is not as easy as it may sound. It spent weeks at No. 1 in Canada for Terry Black, and punched into the US charts after Terry appeared on *American Bandstand* and *Shindig!*

'Upon A Painted Ocean'
P.F. Sloan
The follow-up to 'Eve Of Destruction,' this was originally to be the B-side of 'Child Of Our Times,' but it became the A-side. I was imagining what the new age might be like, and I fantasized that those who placed tradition ahead of love would be chained to the dock and ridiculed as the rest of us sailed into the new age of enlightenment.

'Violence'
P.F. Sloan
An exploration of the psychology behind the amount of violence I was watching and couldn't seem to get enough of, and the 'numbing' effects it might have on society. From *Sailover*.

'Wah Wahini'
Sloan–Barri
Recorded by Bruce & Terry—Bruce Johnston and Terry Melcher. The chord changes in this song are somewhat different to those used by Brian Wilson or Jan Berry, and the song stands out for me because of that. It is simply a fun song, but it made the charts as well.

'Wake Up, Wake Up'
Sloan–Barri
This was the follow-up to 'Things I Should Have Said'—a Beatles-esque psychedelic cut.

Interesting new chord changes for me. Like George Harrison said, any day you can learn a new chord is a good day. The Grass Roots had Top 40 hit with this song.

'Wax Up Your Board'
Sloan–Barri
For me this was just a filler song for the Fantastic Baggys album, but we were still learning and having fun doing it.

'The Way You Want It To Be'
P.F. Sloan
A sad and melancholy breakup song, and a song that was musically experimental for me at the time. *If that's the way you want it to be, well all right, I can take it.* From *Raised On Records*.

'Welcome Home Baby'
Keith Colley–Phil Sloan
Keith Colley had a Spanish-language hit, 'Enamarado,' in 1963. He asked if I would help write his follow-up, as he had a songwriting contract with Screen Gems Publishing.

'What Am I Doing Here With You'
Sloan–Barri*
I only stopped in this town for a hot cup of coffee and a few hours of sleep, but your pretty face looked so sweet, and I was so tired and weak. A country lyric and feel, written in early 1965. I wrote this for myself, but I was hoping to get it to Johnny Rivers, who eventually cut it. It then became a hit for Dev Douglas and Twinkle in England, and for Bev Harrelson in Australia.

'(What Did She Mean) When She Said Good Luck?'
P.F. Sloan
I loved Elvis's cut of 'My Baby Left Me.' I wanted to get that type sound for my Atco record. Steve Cropper did the Scotty Moore part, and I did Elvis. Duck Dunn was on bass. The legendary

Sam Phillips was at that session. At that time, he almost never attended any of the sessions at his studio, but we had an Elvis connection. He felt it and I felt it. From *Measure Of Pleasure*.

'Whatever God Wants'
P.F. Sloan
A good song that didn't make the *Sailover* CD, but was subsequently included on an EP put out by Hightone Records.

'What's Exactly The Matter With Me?'
P.F. Sloan
The big question of my life. Parents, teachers, girlfriends, lovers, record companies—they all wondered. Why didn't I fit in? This was one of the first songs I wrote as P.F. Sloan, and it was the A-side of the 'Eve Of Destruction' single.

'When Surfer's Rule'
Sloan–Barri
The waves are up, and for now they're more important than math class. From *Tell 'Em I'm Surfin'* by The Grass Roots.

'When The Wind Changes (How Quick We Forget)'
P.F. Sloan
The first verse of this song was an open letter to the Soviet Union, recounting the days in the 1920s when the Western World sent them millions of tons of food to fight the famine they were going through. Funny how wisdom changes to suit the convenience of those needing a new lie. From *Twelve More Times*.

'When You're Near You're So Far Away'
Sloan–Barri
This was written with Bob B. Soxx & The Blue Jeans in mind. Darlene Love sang a duo with me for the demo (she only charged $15 for a demo session, even though she was the star of The Crystals). Dunhill again sold us as an English duo, Phillip & Stephen. Crazy!

'Where Sleeping Dogs Lie'
P.F. Sloan

Written about the wild dogs I saw roaming in India. For me, this wasn't a well-conceived song. I redid it in a small studio in 2000 and tried to fix it by letting the musicians play long, sweeping instrumental sections under my harmonica. From *Serenade Of The Seven Sisters* and *Seven Redux*.

'Where Were You When I Needed You'
Sloan–Barri

Steve came up with the title for this song; I wrote the lyrics and melody. It has a very unique opening—one that to my (limited) knowledge had never been done before: a 'walk down' riff that begins in the key of C and ends in D, the key in which the song is played. (The 'walk down' riff later became the signature to Led Zeppelin's 'Stairway To Heaven.')

The other interesting aspect of the song is that the drumming is offbeat, and consciously so. It was played by Bones Howe, who wasn't a professional drummer—in fact, this was the only time he ever played drums on a record. The musicians who had been in the studio beforehand had left a harpsichord, which was due to be picked up in an hour, so I used it for the solo. Serendipitous.

The demo was mistakenly released to local radio with my vocals on lead. Because of the great reaction it received, and because Dunhill wanted me as a songwriter only, the label eventually had Bill Fulton and then Rob Grill sing it. After The Grass Roots had a hit with the song, it was subsequently recorded by Del Shannon, Nelson Riddle, Lacy J. Dalton, and The Bangles.

'Wild Strawberries'
P.F. Sloan

A true story folk-blues song about a friend of mine, John Moore. This song came out on an EP released alongside the *Sailover* album.

'Working'
P.F. Sloan

Beethoven passes through a typical day, composing at his piano with little human contact, until a woman passes by his window, hears him playing, knocks on the door, and tells him that she likes his tune. And it means the world to him! From *My Beethoven*.

'You Baby (Nobody But You)'
Sloan–Barri

There was an old blues song that I heard as a kid called 'Nobody.' It alluded to the happiness of love, but in fact the singer had nobody. 'You Baby' asks *Who makes me feel like smiling when the weary day is through?* For me, the answer was nobody. But when I thought of others who were in relationships, I wanted to connect them, so I made it *nobody but you, baby.* I was able to catch the joyous feeling of love for some and yet remain true to my own experience at the same time. This song was recorded by the Turtles—and was a big record for them—as well as by The Mamas & The Papas and The Vogues.

'You Say Pretty Words'
Sloan–Barri

This was an early Screen Gems Music song for hire, recorded by the very talented Warner Bros soul singer Ramona King, with Joe Saraceno set to produce. I wasn't at the session, and I was disappointed with the final arrangement, which was nothing like what I'd heard in my head. The lyric was mostly by Steve. His themes were marriage, rings on fingers, and why don't you love me? We must have written twenty-five songs on those same themes. The thing was, I learned something new after every effort, so it was all all right with me.

*Titles marked * listed on record as Sloan–Barri compositions but written by P.F. Sloan.*

SELECT DISCOGRAPHY

Albums
Song Of Our Times (Dunhill, 1965)
12 More Times (Dunhill, 1966)
Measure Of Pleasure (Atco, 1968)
Raised On Records (Mums, 1972)
Serenade Of The Seven Sisters (Pioneer, 1994)
Child Of Our Times: The Trousdale Sessions,
1965–1967 (Varese Sarabande, 2001)
Sailover (Hightone, 2006)

Singles
'All I Want Is Loving' / 'Little Girl In The Cabin'
(Aladdin, 1959, as Flip Sloan)
'If You Believe In Me' / 'She's My Girl' (Mart,
1960, as Phil Sloan)
'The Sins Of A Family' / 'This Mornin'' (Dunhill,
1965)

'Halloween Mary' / 'I'd Have To Be Out Of My
Mind' (Dunhill, 1965)
'From A Distance' / 'Patterns (Seg 4)' (Dunhill,
1966)
'City Women' / 'On Top Of A Fence' (Dunhill,
1966)
'A Melody For You' / 'I Found A Girl' (Dunhill,
1966)
'Sunflower Sunflower' / 'The Man Behind The
Red Balloon' (Dunhill, 1967)
'Karma (A Study Of Divinations' / 'I Can't Help
But Wonder Elizabeth' (Dunhill, 1967, as
Philip Sloan)
'New Design' / 'And The Boundaries In Between'
/ 'Above And Beyond The Call Of Duty'
(Atco, 1969)
'Let Me Be' / 'Springtime' (Mums, 1972)

ACKNOWLEDGMENTS

From P.F. Sloan
Sangeeta Haindl has been the Godsend and
instrument for getting this book on the boards.
We are so grateful. Sairam!

Sarah Joyce is an astounding singer and
songwriter. Her personal encouragement to
proceed with the writing of the book, when it
felt too much for me to deal with, was much
appreciated. Thank you, Sarah!

Guy Webster is a rock-photographer
legend and we are so grateful to have his
photo on the cover. He was the original rock
photographer at a time when no one imagined
the worth of photographs of young musicians
at the beginning of their careers. He was the
inspiration for all the greats that would come.

We love and thank you, Guy, and your family
and team!

Tim Forster had purchased a photographic
archive of my photographs and generously
made it available for our book. I thank him and
his lovely wife Maggie!

Larry Sloven was a true pioneer as an
indie record label owner. He took a chance
on signing me to his label and gave me the
best experiences that I have had with label
executives. Thank you, Larry, for making a
teenage boy's dream come true—no matter
how old he gets.

Alan Adler has set up a website for fans to get
memorabilia that I am able to part with and have
others enjoy: museumofmomandpopculture.com

Andrew Sandoval is an artist-songwriter—a staple and influence on the LA music scene. He is the go-to guy for the liner notes on many of the great CD boxed sets and compilations. When we needed to double-check facts or had questions about my own music, we called Andrew.

David Ridges showed up at my doorstep from Japan at a very low period in my life and reminded me that I had not been forgotten. He set up an early website for fans to get info and news. Thank you, David.

Most of all, I need to give my love and heartfelt thanks to fans, who in all honesty I never expected I would ever have. They never gave up on me and forced me out of my seclusion. Without their kind notes of appreciation and active lobbying, I do not believe this could have ever happened.

From S.E. Feinberg

I would not have been able to write this book without the love and support of my dear wife, **Alice**. Alice has always supported me with a passion that I truly do not deserve. I love you, Alice.

James Stephens encouraged me to continue to pursue this challenging project—listening to stories about Phil with patience and curiosity. **Jay Lynch, Pat Lynch, Andrew Lynch, Marie Moreshead**, and **Carrie Lenard**—friends who inspired me to keep moving forward. **Bob Badway, Joaquin Montalvan, Randy Barnes**, and **Eunice Font** always raised my spirits. Special thanks to **Robert Morse**, who was the first person to teach me that music helps to cure an anxious heart, and to **Eric Lilljequist**, who brought the name P.F. Sloan back into my consciousness.

INDEX

Unless otherwise noted, words in *italics* are album titles; words in 'quotes' are song titles. Numbers in **bold** refer to illustrations.

Abbey Road, 105
ABC-Dunhill Records, 9, 160, 187–8, 229
'Above And Beyond The Call Of Duty,' 217, 219
Adam Productions, 70
Adler, Lou, **10**, 48, 53, 55–60, 63–4, 66, 68–9, 71–2, 77–80, 89, 90–1, 95–6, 98–9, 100–1, 108–12, 121–3, 127–9, 133–4, 142–3, 152–4, 160–1, 180, 183, 187–9, 194, 194, 196, 252, 286
'Ain't No Way I'm Gonna Change My Mind,' 81, 87, 96, 133
Aladdin Records, 7, 45, 37, 51
Album Seven, 296
Aldon Music, 52–3
'All I Want Is Loving,' 7, 47
Alpert, Herb, 48, 59
Altfeld, Don, 63, 248

American Bandstand (TV show), 25, 61, 159, 163
Anello & Davide, 102, 235
Animals, The, 134, 201
Anka, Paul, 91
Ann-Margret, 54, 77, 172, 240
Annie (soundtrack), 258
'Another Day, Another Heartache,' 180
Apple, Fiona, 281
Around The World In Eighty Days (film), 38, 215
Asbury Park (album), 280
Association, The, 17, 74, 230–1
Atco Records, 68, 214–15, 217–18, 220, 223, 228
Atlantic Records, 68, 137
Auden, W.H., 213
Axton, Hoyt, 130

Babaji, 141
'Baby Blues,' 61
'Baby Talk,' 59
Baez, Joan, 104
Balin, Marty, 118
'Ballad Of A Thin Man,' 111–13, 117
Bangs, Lester, 280
Bar Mitzvah, 39
Barbarians, The, 71
Barri, Steve, 8, **9**, 48, 53–4, 91, 96–7,

100, 109, 121, 123, 127, 132–3, 135, 140, 147, 154, 160, 185, 187–8, 196, 205, 229, 249, 252, 268–9, 276, 287
Bay, Mel, 43, 45
BBC, the, 99
Beach Boys, The, 52, 63, 66–7, 71, 74, 92, 120, 283
Beatles, The, 57–8, 76, 79, 80, 91, 101–2, 107, 114, 120, 149, 154, 161, 165, 178, 182–3, 194, 197, 201–2, 214, 278
Beau Brummels, The, 118
Bedouins, The, 119–120
Beefheart, Captain, 197
Beery, Wallace, 36
'Beethoven's Delight,' 272
Beethoven, Ludwig Van, 18, 21, 23, 198, 272
Belafonte, Harry, 49, 60
Benay, Ben, 248
Bennett, Tony, 65, 101, 240
Benton, Brook, 40
Bergman, Thorstein, 302
Bernstein, Sid, 214, 216, 218, 220, 226
Berry, Chuck, 29, 55, 71
Berry, Jan, 50, 62, 71, 78, 157, 248, 257, 276

Big Brother & The Holding Company, 118, 199
'Big Gun Board,' 65
'Big Lie, The,' 270
Bill Hailey & The Comets, 29
Billboard (magazine), 47, 51, 121, 147, 218, 269–70
Billy J. Kramer & The Dakotas, 71
Binder, Steve, 71
Bitter End (club), 213
Black, Frank, 76, 283
Black Plague, The, 156–7
'Black Robed Spaniard, The,' 293
Black, Terry, 48, 79–80, 156–7, 276
Blackwell, Bumps, 46–7
Blaine, Hal, 54, 66, 72, 74, 76, 79, 94, 96, 140, 143, 149, 182, 248
Blob, The (film), 79
'Blue Lipstick,' 54, 158
Blue Thumb Records, 61
Blues Project, The, 213
Bob B. Soxx & The Blue Jeans, 55
Bono, Sonny, 135–6
Boone, Pat, 42, 50, 178, 248, 250
'Boundaries In Between, The,' 217
Boys Don't Cry, 17
Bratton, Creed, **9**, 162, 183–4, 198, 290
Bread (band), 50
'Bridge Over Troubled Water,' 76
Bringing It All Back Home, 89, 111
British Invasion, The, 58, 173
Britz, Chuck, 64, 73–4, 89, 96
Brooks, Martin, 58, 61
Brown, James, 71
Brown, Phyliss, 249
Brownie & McGee, 49
Bruce & Terry, 50, 65–6, 91–2, 276
Bruce, Lenny, 212–13, 215, 286
Bubbles, John, 78, 237
Buckley, Tim, 197, 286
Bunyan, John, 24
Burchman, Bob, 63, 261
Burden, Eric, 285
Burns, George, 34
Burton, James, 76, 248
Butch Engle & The Styx, 118
Byrds, The, 91–2, 94–5, 113–15, 120, 133, 136, 149, 173, 197
'By The Time I Get To Phoenix,' 179, 181

Café Au Go Go, the, 213–14, 218, 226
'California Dreamin',' 127–9, 153–5, 284
California State University, 58
Campbell, Glen, 66, 72, 75, 79, 181
'Can I Get To Know You Better,' 55–6
Canned Heat, 140, 213
'Can't We Go Somewhere,' 79, 294
Canoe, Kim, 168, 204, 222, 282, 285–8
Cantinflas, 39

Capital Records, 52
Capote, Truman, 213
Cardinale, Claudia, 109
Cargman, Jerry, 64, 66, 70
Carnaby Street, 102, 105
Carter, Mel, 50
Cashbox (magazine), 10, 121
Cassidy, Hopalong, 30, 36
'Cattle Call,' 31
Cavaliere, Felix, 282
Central Music, 19
'Champagne,' 217
Champion, Marge and Gower, 34, 257
Charren, Barbara, 63
Chateau Marmont, the, 242, 244
Cheap Trick, 282
Chess, Leonard, 45
'Chi-hua-hua,' 50
'Child Of Our Times,' 129, 156
Christian, Roger, 63
Christie, Lou, 308
Ciccone, Don, 259
Ciro's (club), 95, 114
City Lights Bookstore, 119
City Without Walls, 213
'City Women,' 154
Clanton, Jimmy, 66
Clapton, Eric, 201, 248
Clark, Dick, 61, 276
Clark, Gene, 114, 257
Clarke, Arthur C., 210
Clarke, Michael, 114
Cliff Richard & The Shadows, 56
'Cling To Me,' 294
Clooney, Rosemary, 65
Clovers, The, 40
Clyde, Buddy, 79, 156
Cochran, Eddie, 35, 247
Coconut Grove, The, 68, 219
Cohen, David, 273–4
Columbia Records, 14, 49, 52, 61, 65, 91–4, 111–12, 215–16, 223, 235, 246, 250, 258
'Come And Get It From Me,' 91
Command Performance, 125
'Como,' 294
Connors, Carol, 48, 53, 65, 185, 229
Continental Hotel, 112, 115, 133, 275
Continentals, The, 49
Cooke, Sam, 40, 47, 69, 80
Cookies, The, 298
Cossette, Pierre, 54, 77–8
Country Joe & The Fish, 118, 197
'Country Woman (Can You Dig It All Night?),' 217
Coyote, Peter, 193
Crayton, Pee Wee, 49
Crazy Horse, 140
Cream, 213

Crescent Heights, 33, 36–8, 40, 139, 257
Critters, The, 259
Cropper, Steve, 217, 304–5
Crosby, David, 113–16, 194, 287
'Cry Baby,' 302
Crystals, The, 55, 61
Cuban Missile Crisis, 26

Dali, Salvador, 213
Damone, Vic, 80
Daniello, Gino, 135
Darin, Bobby, 20, 52, 68–9, 108, 270
Darren, James, 62
Davis Jr., Sammy, 32
Davis, Clive, 235–6, 240, 246–7, 267–7, 282
Day, Doris, 50–1, 65, 93–4
Dean, James, 21, 37
Deasy, Mike, 47
Dee, Sandra, 62, 68
'Delia's Gone,' 49
Diamond Jim's, 133
'Diana,' 91
Dick Dale & The Del-Tones, 241
Dickinson, Jim, 92
Diggers, The, 193
Diken, Dennis, 259
Dimension Records, 52
Dion & The Belmonts, 42
'Dock Of The Bay,' 217
Dr. Z, 274–5, 277–8
'Does Your Chewing Gum Lose Its Flavor On The Bed Post Over Night,' 56
Dolton Records, 143
'Dolphin, The,' 219
Domain Records, 58, 60–1, 125
Domino, Fats, 40, 42, 64
Don & Dewey, 114
Donahue, Tom, 198
Donegan, Lonnie, 56
Donovan, 134, 291, 301
'Don't Come Running To Me,' 91
Don't Look Back, 104
'Don't Make A Beggar Out Of Me,' 238
'Don't Worry Baby,' 128
Doors, The, 149, 168, 197–8
Dore Records, 59
Dougherty, Denny, 121
Douglas, Steve, 51
Dowd, Tom, 216, 218
'Drag City,' 63, 124
'Dragon Lady,' 295
Drifters, The, 54, 182–3
'Dry Bones,' 79
Dunhill Records, 55, 77, 78–80, 91, 96, 99, 118, 120, 152, 156–8, 160–1, 180, 185, 187, 204, 207, 214, 220, 223, 227, 229, 262, 271, 283

Dunn, Duck, 217
Dylan, Bob, 20, 23, 49, 65, 87, 89, 92,
    101, 104, 111–13, 115–17, 119,
    130, 133, 144–5, 152, 189, 210,
    212, 220, 252, 272–5

E Street band, The, 282
Ed Sullivan Show, The (TV show), 35,
    99, 159–60, 204, 226, 240
El Monte Legion Hall, 113–14
Elliot, Cass, 28, 121–2, 128, 141, 154,
    194, 203–4, 240
'Eddie My Love,' 48
EMI, 57, 80, 105
Entner, Warren, 162, 183
Epics, The, 303
Epstein, Brian, 57–8, 80, 101–2, 105,
    109, 161, 163, 165, 194, 202–3
Eric Anderson, 144, 260
Ertegun, Ahmet, 137
'Eve Of Destruction,' 19, 10, 20, 25,
    81, 88–9, 95–6, 98–9, 101, 104–5,
    109, 126,113, 121, 124–5, 129–30,
    132–3, 139, 148, 233, 268–71,
    280, 283, 285
Eve Of Destruction, 109
Everett, Betty, 55–6, 148
Everly Brothers, The, 38, 57
'Everybody's Talkin',' 219
'Everyone Can Tell,' 80

Fabares, Shelley, 68, 132, 175
Fairfax Avenue, 34, 37–8, 42, 45–9,
    53, 58, 255
Fairfax High School, 47, 49, 58
Fantastic Baggys, The, 9, 64–6, 69,
    70, 125
Fantasticks, The, 110
Fantasy Fair, the, 12–13, 197
Far West Folk Alliance, The, 130
Fast Man-Raider Man, 76
Faulkner, William, 94
Feinberg, S.E., 19–24
Ferlinghetti, Lawrence, 119
Fidelioi (opera), 272
Fifth Dimension, The, 74, 180–1, 197
Fillmore West, The, 199, 203
Fitzgerald, Ella, 73, 172
Flying Dunhills, The, 78
Folk & Roll, 124–5
'Folk City,' 124
Frazier, Al, 66, 67
'Friendly Persuasion,' 250
'From A Distance,' 227, 260, 273,
    279
From A Distance, 278
'From Me To You,' 57
Fulton, Bill, 119, 160, 312
Funk Brothers, The, 51
Furay, Richie, 136

Gable, Clark, 36
Garcia, Jerry, 118–19, 192
Garden Of Allah, the (club), 36
Garfunkel, Art, 194–5
Gari, Brian, 259
Gates, David, 50
Gay, Noel, 50
Gaye, Marvin, 71
Gazzarri's (club), 133
Geraldo Live, 281
Gerry & The Pacemakers, 71
Gidget (book), 62
Ginsburg, Arnie, 50
'Girl Never Knows, A,' 54
'Go Where You Wanna Go,' 129, 180
Goat's Head Soup, 244
Goffin & King, 52, 56, 58, 177
Gold Star Studios, 73
Goldberg, Paul, 276
Good Luck,' 217
'Goodnight Irene,' 127
Gore, Leslie, 71
Gospel (bible), 24
Grand Funk Railroad, 186
Grass Roots, The, 9, 74, 116–18, 120,
    133, 157, 160–3, 182–5, 197, 229,
    233, 284, 289
Grateful Dead, The, 118, 198
Gray, Dobie, 49
Great Society, The, 118
Green & Stone, 137
'Green Back Dollar,' 95, 130
Greenblatt's, 34, 36, 77, 128, 233
Greenfield, Harold, 52
'Green, Green,' 95, 126, 130
Griffen, Jimmy, 66
Griffin, James, 50
Grill, Rob, 162, 183
Gruber, Barry, 270–1, 275
Guthrie, Woody, 49, 86–7, 130-1, 144

Hair (musical), 10
'Halloween Mary,' 283
Hammond, Albert, 249
'Hard Day's Night, A,' 128
Harmony Recorders, 51
Harris, Emmylou, 140
Harris, Thurston, 45
Harrison, George, 102, 166–7, 198
Hendricks, Jim, 121
Hendrix, Jimmy, 194, 201, 213, 286
Henry, Clarence 'Frogman,' 49
Herald Examiner Eight Star Edition, 37
Here's Where You Belong, 273, 285
Herman's Hermits, 134–5, 233, 288
'He's My Man,' 55, 297
'Help Me Remember To Remember,'
    272–3
'Here They Come From All Over The
    World,' 71

Hesse, Herman, 262
'Hey Little Cobra,' 53
Heywoods, The, 229
Hightone Records, 16, 283, 285
Highway 61 Revisited, 111–12, 275,
    280
Hillman, Chris, 114
Hiroshima, 25
Hold On!, 135
Holden, William, 36
Holly, Buddy, 35, 76
Honeys, The, 16
'Honolulu Lulu,' 63
Hooker, John Lee, 213
Hootie & The Blowfish, 281
Hopwood, Keith, 135
Horn, Jim, 249
'Hot Dusty Roads,' 136
Hot Tuna, 296
Howe, Bones, 73–4, 78, 96, 109,
    120–1, 132–3, 148–9
'How Can I Be Sure,' 217–18
Hullabaloo (TV show), 19
Huss, John, 24

'I Can't Hear You No More,' 56
'I Can't Help But Wonder Elizabeth,'
    198, 285
'I Count The Tears,' 182–3
'I Don't Care If The Sun Don't Shine,'
    29, 46
'I Found A Girl,' 125, 133, 152, 276
'I Get Out Of Breath,' 132
'I Just Don't Understand,' 55
'I Know You'll Be There,' 132
'I Wanna Be Your Man,' 58
'I Want To Hold Your Hand,' 80
'I Wonder Who The Lucky Guy Will
    Be,' 158
Ian & Sylvia, 144, 213, 215
ICM, 237
'If You Believe In Me' 51
'If You Knew,' 283
Iguanas, The, 90–1
'I'm Having A Nervous Breakdown,' 247
'I'm Into Something's Good,' 135
India, 22, 85, 141, 150, 255, 261–2,
    265, 278–9, 284
'Is It Any Wonder,' 289
'It Ain't Me Babe,' 131–2, 289
It Ain't Me Babe, 132, 147, 299
It Happened To Jane (film), 50
'It Never Rains In Southern California,'
    249–50
'It's All Over Now, Baby Blue,' 110

Jackson, Al, 217
Jagger, Mick, 64, 71, 102–3, 164–5,
    242, 244
James, Dick, 101–2, 158, 161, 181–3

James, Etta, 140
Jan & Arnie, 50
Jan & Dean, **16**, 50, 59, 62–5, 69, 71–3, 75, 77–8, 92, 100–1, 113, 124–5, 133, 150, 248, 276
Japan Times (newspaper), 280
Jefferson Airplane, 118, 197
Jim Morrison, 141, 170–2, 198
Jim, Big, 40–1
Joe Frank & Reynolds, 229
John Burroughs Middle School, 7
John, Sir Elton, 75
Johnson, Lyndon, 192
Johnson, Plas, 47
Johnston, Bruce, 50, 63
Joplin, Janis, 19, 118, 194, 199, 286
Judaism, 28, 30, 34–5, 45, 48, 109, 194, 263
'Just Goofed,' 48
'Just Love Me,' 55

K., Evy, **7**
Kasem, Casey, 99
Kaye, Carol, 72, 76
Kaylan, Howard, 131–2, 148, 276, 289
Kennedy, John, 58, 126, 218
Kennedy, Robert, 126, 192
Kerouac, Jack, 62
'Kick That Little Foot Sally Ann,' 54, 60–1
King, Carole, 52
'King' Cole, Nat, 80
King, Martin Luther, 218
King, Ramona, 54, 313
Kingsley, Sir Ben, 102
Kingsmen, The, 23, 66, 289
Kingston Trio, The, 95
Kip, 141
Kirshner, Don, 52
'Kisses For My Baby,' 80

Knetchel, Larry, 76, 96, 142, 151, 248
Kohner, Kathy, 62
K-POI, 65
Krampf, Craig, 282
Krasnow, Bob, 58–61
Kristofferson, Kris, 199

LA Times (newspaper), 140, 276
Laine, Frankie, 305
Landy, Eugene, 269–70
Lansbury, Angela, 36
Lanz, David, 272
Larkham, David, 249
Lasker, Jay, **10**, 58, 77, 80, 90, 100, 110, 112, 116–18, 120, 136, 153, 155–7, 161, 181–84, 187, 189, 204–5, 207–8, 214, 223, 227, 229, 239, 250, 269–70, 287
Laughton, Charles, 35
Laurel Canyon, 126, 139–41, 144

Leadbelly, 49
Lee, Arthur, 116, 174
Lennon, John, 51, 58, 102, 104, 149, 162, 202, 248, 252
Les Crane Show, The, 99
Lesh, Phil, 198
'Let Me Be,' 22, 132–3, 140, 148, 159, 233, 276, 285, 289
'Let's Live For Today,' 181
Lettermen, The, 147
Levine, Larry, 72–3
Lewis, Jerry Lee, 19, 34–5, 159
Liberty/Imperial Records, 64, 72, 143, 180
Lieb, Marshall, 48
'Like A Rolling Stone,' 111
Lilljequist, Eric, 22
Linhart, Buzzy, 212
Linstrot, Lanky, 73
Little Feat, 140
'Little Girl In The Cabin,' 47
'Little Liar,' 80, 302
'Little Old Lady From Pasadena,' 72, 74, 133
Little Richard, 46–7, 50, 152, 179
Live For Today, 183, 204
Living Daylights, The, 181
'Living In A Bombay Alley,' 255
Loma Records, 61
London, Julie, 47
Loog Oldham, Andrew, 58, 165
Loren, Donna, 70
Louie, Henry, 73–4
Louis! Louis! (musical) 21, 23
Love (band), 116, 118, 173
Love, Darlene, 55
'Love Go Easy On Me,' 276
'Love Is 4-Giving,' 239
'Love Letters In The Sand,' 250
'Love Me Do,' 57–8
Lubin, Joe, 50

MacLean, Bryan, 20, 116, 173–4, 282, 285
Mahal, Taj, 140
Malibu Colony, 240
Mamas & The Papas, The, **16**, 121, 126–7, 133, 141, 153, 155–6, 165, 180, 182–3, 194, 201, 204, 229, 233, 240, 284, 286
'Man Behind The Red Balloon, The,' 152, 276
Mann & Weil, 58, 177
Mann, Barry, 52, 128
Mann, Erika, 213
Mart/Arwin Records, 50–1, 65, 121, 124
Martin, Dean, 73, 159, 172
Martin, Dewey, 136, 287
Masekela, Hugh, 197

Mason, Dave, 61, 240
Matadors, The, 63
'Maybelline,' 55
McCartney, Michael (aka Mike McGear), 106–8
McCartney, Paul, 49, 58, 91, 103, 107
McGuinn, Roger (aka Jim McGuinn), 94, 95, 127, 287
McGuire Sings Your Favorite Hits, 110
McGuire, Barry, **10**, 19, 74, 95, 99, 101, 103, 109, 110, 121–3, 126–7, 130–1, 133–4, 154–6, 268, 270, 287
McKenzie, Scott, 192
McPhatter, Clyde, 40
McQueen, Steve, 79
Measure Of Pleasure, **12**, 218
'Meet Me Tonight Little Girl,' 91
Melcher, Marty, 50, 65
Melcher, Terry, 50, 63, 65–6, 68–9, 91–2, 94, 113–15
Melfi, Leonard, 260
Merv Griffin Show, The 231
Mesner, Eddie 45–6
Mesner, Leo, 45–6
'Michelle,' 91
'Midnight Confessions,' 229
Milburn, Amos, 45
Miller, Jimmy, 242, 244
Miller, Jody, 66
Miller, Mitch, 65
Million Dollar Party, the, **9**, 65
Mills Brothers, The, 241
Milton, Little, 45
'Miss Charlotte,' 217
'Mr. Jones,' 117, 120, 289
'Mr. Man On The Street Act One,' 110
'Mr. Tambourine Man,' 92, 113, 115, 117, 120
Moby Grape, 118, 197, 213
Moffitt, Tom, 67
Monkees, The, 74
Monroe, Marilyn, 36, 186
Monterey Pop Festival, **15**, 192, 194, 197, 203
Moody Blues, The, 102, 247
Morissette, Alanis, 281
Morrison, Van, 211, 247, 320
Most, Mickie, 134
Moulin Rouge, 108
Mozart, 23
Mugwumps, The, 121–2
Mulligan, Gerry, 92
Mums Records, 238, 249
Murray, Don, 131, 149–150
Murray, Jan, 34
'Must To Avoid, A,' 134–5, 289
Must To Avoid, A, 134–5
My Fair Lady, 276
Myman, Bob, 49, 64–5, 70

Nagasaki, 25
National Academy of Songwriters, **15**
Neil, Fred, 130, 144, 212, 215, 219, 286
Nelson, Ricky, 25, 51, 53, 64, 75–6, 112
Nelson, Sandy, 51
Nevins, Al, 52–3, 58, 137
New Christie Minstrels, The, 95, 110
'New Design,' 217
New York Times (newspaper), 62
Nico, 213
Night Of The Living Dead (film), 198
Nitzsche, Jack, 60, 71
Nixon, President, 17, 245
Noone, Peter, 257–8
Norty's Record Store, 53, 160
'Not Fade Away,' 58
'Nowadays Clancy Can't Even Sing,' 136–7

Ochs, Phil, 20, 75, 140–1, 144–6, 212, 286
Odetta, 49, 294
Olympia, The, 108
Omartian, Michael, 248
'On Top Of A Fence,' 152
'One Of A Kind,' 217
'One Piece Topless Bathing Suit,' 65
'Only Sixteen,' 80
'Only When You're Lonely,' 161
Orton, Joe, 108
Osborne, Joe, 72, 75, 79, 143, 182, 248
'Out Of Touch,' 183
Owsley, Stan, 197

Palmer, Bruce, 136
Palmer, Earl, 47
Parker, Colonel Tom, 44
Parlophone, 105
Paskow, Bruce, 270–2, 276, 278
Paul Revere & The Raiders, 91, 289
Perkins, Wayne, 248
Peter & Gordon, 66
Peter Paul & Mary, 95, 153, 223–4
Peters, Jon, 240, 244–6, 282
Peterson, Ray, 66
Peterson, Tom, 282
Pets, The, 50
Petty, Tom, 248
Philip's Folly, 272
Phillies Records, 53
Phillips, John, **15**, **16**, 121–2, 127, 129, 141, 151, 153, 155, 180, 192, 194–6, 202–4, 284, 287
Phillips, Michelle, 121–2, 127, 129, 153, 155
Phillips, Sam, 217
'Pied Piper Man,' 61
Pilafian, Peter, 121

Pillow Talk (film), 50
Pioneer Records, 273
Pitman, Bill, 72, 77
Pixies, The, 76, 283
Platters, The, 29
Please Don't Eat The Daisies (film), 50
'Please, Please Me,' 57, 80
'Poetry In Motion,' 294
Pohlman, Ray, 54, 72, 77
Presley, Elvis, 25, 29–31, 35, 43–5, 47, 57, 76, 79–80, 103, 112, 139, 145, 216–17, 233, 248, 251, 260
'Poor Little Fool,' 80
'Poor Side Of Town,' 180
'Postcards from Fantasy Land,' 106
Prince of Protest, 101–2
Procol Harem, 283

Quicksilver Messenger Service, 118, 199
Quincy Adams, John, 38

Radio Caroline, 99
Raised On Records, **14**, 248–9, 252
Rally-Packs, 125
Randi, Don, 77
Rankin, Kenny, 214
Rascals, The, 282
RCA, 47, 49, 99, 134, 161, 165, 278, 288; RCA Studios, 47, 288
Ready Steady Go (TV show), 102
Record World, 121
Reed, Lou, 213, 260
Report To The Nation, 58
Richards, Keith, 55, 71, 167, 242
Rincon Surf Band, The, 63
Rip Chords, The, 50, 53, 65, 91
Ritter, John, 70
'River Is Wide, The,' 229
Rivers, Johnny, 25, 64, 75, 75, 77, 142-3, 158, 180–1, 240, 252, 276, 284
Rivingtons, The, 66
Robbs, The, 282
Roberts, Bobby, **10**, 54, 77–8, 90, 133, 138, 155, 214, 236–7, 240, 246–7, 249, 287
Robertson, Cliff, 62
Robin, Round, 60, 61
Rock and Roll Hall of Fame, The, 47
Rogers, Kenny, 217
Rolling Stone (magazine), 272, 280–1
Rolling Stones, The, 58, 64, 71, 162, 169, 233, 242
Romney, Hugh, 193
Rooftop Gang, The, 28
Rose Café, 22
Rosengarten, Neil, 276
Rosie & The Originals, 114
Rubin, Rick, 71
Rumer, 16, 17

Russell, Leon, 54, 72, 75, 77
Rydell, Bobby, 54

Saenz, Mary, 66
Sai Baba, 32, 85, 150, 261–4, 266
Sailover, **16**, 239, 275, 283, 285
St. Clair, Miki, 212, 214, 216–18, 220, 227
St. James Club, The, 102, 165
Sam & Dave, 217
Sands, Tommy, 74
'San Francisco (Be Sure To Wear Some Flowers In Your Hair),' 192–3
Sanhedrin, 109
Sargent, William, 71
'Satisfaction,' 55
'Say It Again,' 80, 276
Scaffold, The, 107
Schlein, Claritsa, **6**
Schlein, Harry George, **6**
Scott Fitzgerald, F., 36
Screen Gems, 52, 54, 56, 58–9, 61, 64, 77, 128, 137, 185, 229
Searchers, The, 133, 158
Sebastian, John, 127, 212, 286–7
Secret Agent, (TV show), 142
'Secret Agent Man,' 143, 180, 221, 233, 276
Sedaka, Neil, 52
Sedgwick, Edie, 213
Seeger, Pete, 104, 144, 281
Sepe, Tony, 58, 60–1
Serenade Of The Seven Sisters, 272, 275–6
Seven Sisters Redux, 273
Shane, Hylton, 50
Shank, Bud, 92, 154
Shankar, Ravi, 92, 167, 194, 200–1
'She Belongs To Me,' 110
'She's My Girl,' 51
Shelter Records, 75
Shirley & Lee, 45
'Shoop Shoop Song (It's In His Kiss), The,' 55
Simon, Paul, 194–6
Sinatra, Frank, 54, 68, 73, 76, 80, 164
Sinatra, Nancy, 159
'Sing A Simple Song Of Freedom,' 270
'Sins Of A Family, The,' **10**, 20, 81, 83, 95, 99, 100, 105, 111, 132, 211, 223, 280, 282
Skaff, Phil, 64, 78
Skylark Records, 51
Slauson Avenue, 60–1
'Sloop John B,' 110
Smashing Pumpkins, The, 283
Smithereens, The, 259
Smokey Robinson, 134, 197
Solomon, Howard, 212–13, 218, 226, 260

Some Like It Hot (film), 186
Songs Of Our Times, **12**, 89, 133
Songwriters On Songwriting (book), 17
Sonny & Cher, 137
Sons Of Champlain, 118, 198
Soul City Records, 180
'Soul Of A Woman,' 283
Soundgarden, 283
Spanky & Our Gang, 197
Specialty Records, 45
Spector, Phil, 48, 51, 53, 61, 72,
   76–7, 189
'Spiritual Eyes,' 272–3
Springfield Buffalo, The, 136–7, 149,
   182, 286
'Star Gazin',' 217
Star, Ringo, 102, 194
Steele, Tommy, 56
Steppenwolf, 229
Steve Miller Band, The, 197, 213
Stevens, Connie, 54, 172
Sticky Fingers, 243
'Still On The Eve Of Destruction,' 271
Stills, Stephen, 136–7, 173, 194
Stookey, Noel Paul, 223–6
Storytellers, The, 53
Strollers, The, 47
Studio A, 63
Studio Three, 63, 96
'Summer Means Fun,' 65, 94
Summer of Love, 194
Sun Studios, 216–17
Sunflower, 63
'Sunflower, Sunflower,' 15
Sunset Boulevard, 33, 36–7, 49, 56,
   60, 63, 95, 108, 111, 126, 132–3,
   140, 168, 170, 172–3, 180, 235,
   242, 244
Supremes, The, 71, 134, 177
Surf City Allstars, The, **16**
'Surf City,' 62–3, 124

'Take Me For What I'm Worth,' 132–3,
   158, 223
Tallent, Garry, 282
TAMI Show, The 71, 142
Taylor, Derek, 194, 202
Taylor, Elizabeth, 39, 215
Teddy Bears, The, 48, 53
Tedesco, Tommy, 54, 60, 72, 76
'Teen Beat,' 51
Teen Queens, The, 48
Tell 'Em I'm Surfin',' 64, 66, 283
Temptation Eyes,' 229
Temptations, The, 134
Terry Knight & The Pack, 186
'Thank You Girl,' 57
'That's Cool, That's Trash,' 255, 289
Thaxton, Lloyd, 61
'Things I Should Have Said,' 204

Third Street School, 6, 34
'This Little Woody,' 65
'This Mornin,' 80, 85, 96, 133, 223, 226
'This Precious Time,' 152, 156, 186
Thomas Group, The, 293
'Three Window Coupe,' 65
Three Dog Night, 74, 229
'Tijuana Jail,' 127
Tin Angel, The, 222–3
'Tip Of My Tongue,' 310
Titelman, Russ, 48
TM Music, 69
'To Know Him Is To Love Him,' 48, 53
Todd, Mark, 39, 215–16, 295
Tollie, 79, 80, 157
'Tom Dooley,' 127
Top Of The Pops, 102
Topanga, 126, 132, 140
'Topsy 65,' 143
Torrence, Dean, 50, 125
Tracy, Dick, 135
Traffic, 242
Trip, The (club) 133–4
Trocadero Club, 132
Trousdale Publishing, 78, 132, 154, 177
'Try To Remember,' 110
Tucker, Jim, 131
Turner, Lana, 36
Turtles, The, 22, 74, 131–3, 147–9,
   248, 276, 289
'Tutti-Frutti,' 50
Twelve More Times, **13**, 151, 215
Twiggy, 102
Twilight Zone (TV show), 231
Tyndale, William, 24

UCLA, 46
United Artists Records, 52
'Universal Coward, The,' 124
'Unless You Care,' 54, 79, 276
'Up, Up And Away,' 181
'Upon A Painted Ocean,' 129–30, 156
Usher, Gary, 63

Valens, Richie, 51, 114
Valenti, Dino, 188
Van Ronk, Dave, 213
Van Stratton, Ray, 259
Vangoughberg, Vince, 255
Variety (newspaper), 240, 250
Vee-Jay Records, 55–6, 58, 77,
   79–80, 182
Vega, Táta, 249
Venet, Steve, 52–3
Ventures, The, 127, 143, 284
Vesuvio Café, 119
Vietnam War, 192, 216, 304
Vincent, Gene, 35
'Violence,' 311
Vogues, The, 100, 147–8

Volman, Mark, 131–2

'Wah Wahini,' 65
Waits, Tom, 74
Wallach's Music City, 38, 42, 48, 103
Wally Heider Studios, 248
'Walk Don't Run' 127
Warhol, Andy, 213
Warner Bros, 278, 283, 285
Warner-Elektra-Atlantic, 61
Warren, Lesley Ann, 240–1, 244
Washington Squares, The, 271
Washington, Dinah, 40
'Wax Up Your Board,' 311
'Way You Want It To Be, The,' 311
Webb, Jimmy, 17, 18, 22, 176, 180,
   194, 196, 231, 248–9, 260
Webster, Guy, 64, 110
Weil, Cynthia, 52
Western Recorders, 8, 63, 66, 96,
   109, 127, 182, 241
'(What Did She Mean) When She Said
   Good Luck?,' 217
'What's Exactly The Matter With Me?,'
   81, 86, 96, 98
'Where Were You When I Needed
   You,' 120–1, 125
Whisky A Go-Go, 75, 133, 136, 180
White, Barry, 61
'Whiter Shade Of Pale, A,' 115
Whitman, Slim, 32
Who, The, 194, 200, 203
'Why Not Stop And Dig It While You
   Can?,' 110
Williams, Hank, 44
Williams, Lucinda, 282
Williams, Tennessee, 213
Wilson Pickett, 118, 197, 217
Wilson, Brian, 62–4, 69, 76, 78, 120,
   128, 157, 165, 269–70, 283
Wilson, Carl, 66
Wilson, Dennis, 63, 120
Wilson, Jackie, 206
Wisconsin, 98, 161
Wiseman, Ben and Leonard, 51–2
'Wonderful, Wonderful,' 52
World Pacific Records, 92, 154
Wrecking Crew, The, 51, 73, 76–7,
   118, 120, 127, 129

Yanofsky, Zal, 127
'You And Me And The Devil Makes
   Three,' 77
'You Baby (Nobody But You),' 147,
   149, 154, 260, 276, 289
'You Say Pretty Words,' 54
'You're A Lonely Girl,' 120

Zanuck, Darrilyn, 62
Zollo, Paul, 17

Also available in print and ebook editions from Jawbone Press: